WARRIORS WITHOUT WEAPONS

INDEX MAP

SOUTH DAKOTA

RAPID CITY · INTERIOR · ROSEBUD I.R. · WASHINGTON · WASHABAUGH · SHANNON · BENNETT · PINE RIDGE · DAKOTA JUNC. · RUSHVILLE

NEBRASKA

LEGEND

Hospital	+
Dance Hall	■
Church	✝
School	⚑
Village	●
Road	═
County line	—·—·—
District line	- - - - -

TO RAPID CITY

CHEYENNE R.

Red Shirt

WASHINGTON COUNTY

Rocky Ford

MEDICINE ROOT COMMUNITY

WOUNDED KNEE

PORCUPINE

Little Wounded Cons Day Schl

Kyle

Day Schl No 12

WHITE CLAY DIST

WHITE DIST

DIST

Day Schl No 11

Day Schl No 6

Day Schl No 5

Manderson Day Schl No 9

Day Schl No 16

Porcupine

Oglala

Day Schl No 25

Porcupine Butte Look

SHANNON COUNTY

Wounded Knee

Day Schl No 7

Batesland

WAKPAMNI DIST.

Holy Rosary Mission & Schl

Denby

Lake Wa

Oglala Community High Schl

PINE RIDGE

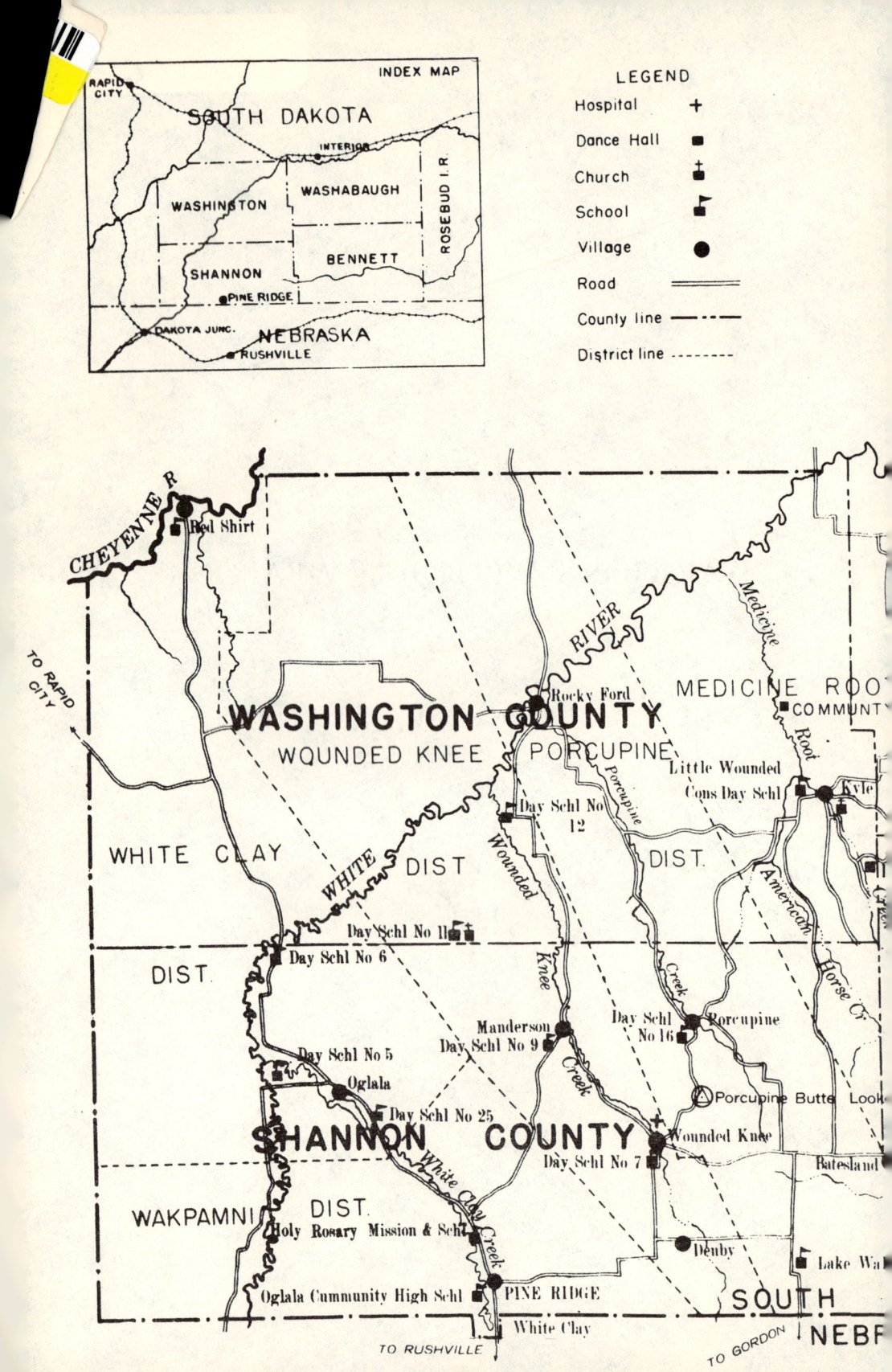

White Clay

SOUTH

TO RUSHVILLE

TO GORDON

NEBR

PINE RIDGE INDIAN RESERVATION
SOUTH DAKOTA.

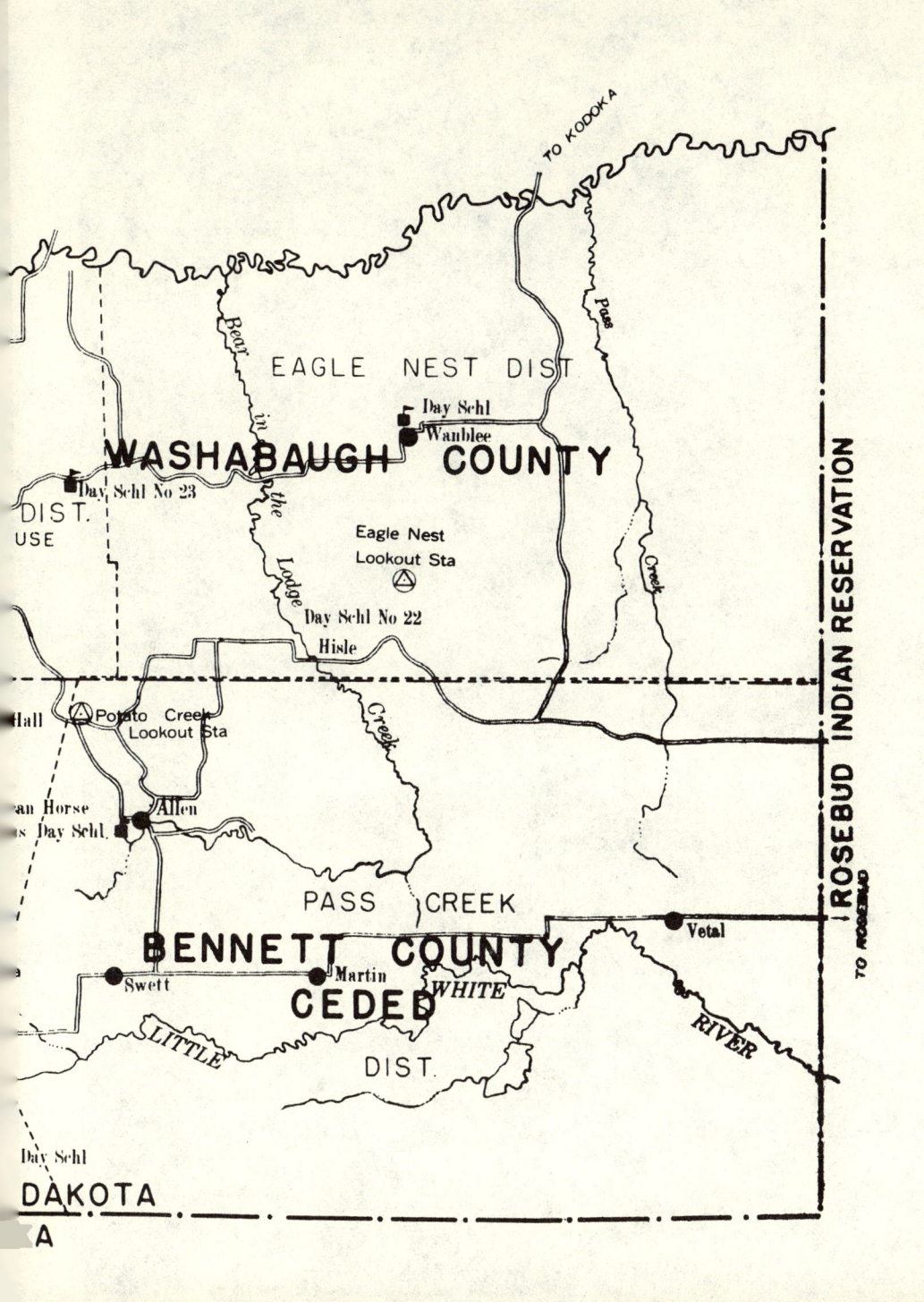

CHILDREN OF THE WARRIORS

WARRIORS WITHOUT WEAPONS

*A Study of the Society and Personality
Development of the Pine Ridge Sioux*

By
GORDON MACGREGOR

With the collaboration of
ROYAL B. HASSRICK
and
WILLIAM E. HENRY

THE UNIVERSITY OF CHICAGO PRESS
Chicago and London

The University of Chicago Press, Chicago 60637
The University of Chicago Press, Ltd., London

Published 1946. Midway Reprint 1975
Printed in the United States of America

International Standard Book Number: 0-226-50034-9

To
THE SCHOOL CHILDREN OF
PINE RIDGE RESERVATION

INDIAN EDUCATION RESEARCH STAFF

COMMITTEE ON INDIAN EDUCATION RESEARCH

University of Chicago
W. LLOYD WARNER, *Chairman*
ROBERT J. HAVIGHURST
RALPH TYLER

Office of Indian Affairs
JOHN COLLIER, *Chairman*
WILLARD W. BEATTY
RENÉ D'HARNONCOURT
JOSEPH MCCASKILL

LAURA THOMPSON, *Co-ordinator*

SIOUX PROJECT STAFF

GORDON MACGREGOR, *Supervisor*
ROYAL HASSRICK, *Field Assistant*

Field Workers
DOW CARNAL
PEARL CARNAL
JOSEPH CARRANO, M.D.
FRANCES DAVIDSON, R.N.
GERALDINE D. DIAZ
IMOGENE B. DOGEAGLE
AUDREY GUTHRIE
FRED HAMMERNIK
ADRIENNE HERSHEY
JUNE LYMAN
MARTIN MCNEIL, M.D.
LIZZIE B. MESTETH
IRA NICHOLS
FERN ROUILLARD
THEODORE SADOCK, M.D.
MARY SCHANANDORE
PAULINE WASHINGTON
RICHARD WASHINGTON
EVELYN WHIRLWIND HORSE

Test Analysts
Rorschach
   ROYAL HASSRICK
Thematic Apperception (adapted)
   WILLIAM E. HENRY
Grace Arthur Performance
   ROBERT J. HAVIGHURST
   RHEA R. HILKEVITCH
   WAYNE PRATT
Goodenough Draw-a-Man
   ROBERT J. HAVIGHURST
   MINNA KOROL
   INEZ PRATT
Emotional Response
   ROBERT J. HAVIGHURST
   IVA SCHMIDT
   JEAN HALL
Moral Ideology
   ROBERT J. HAVIGHURST
   JEANETTE MURSTINE

ROMA K. MCNICKLE, *Editor*

ADVISORY COMMITTEE

GRACE ARTHUR
RUTH BENEDICT
ALLISON DAVIS
JOHN DOLLARD
FRED EGGAN
ERIK HOMBURGER ERIKSON
LAWRENCE FRANK
A. IRVING HALLOWELL
BRUNO KLOPFER

CLYDE KLUCKHOHN
EUGENE LERNER[*]
KURT LEWIN
JEAN WALKER MACFARLANE
D'ARCY MCNICKLE
MARGARET MEAD
SCUDDER MEKEEL
MORRIS OPLER
ROBERT S. PLATT
STANISLAUS SZUREK

[*] Deceased September 21, 1944.

FOREWORD

THE conviction of racial and religious superiority which has characterized the white man in his contact with races of other colors is not uniquely a white man's characteristic. Each Indian group as well as every other racial unit around the world has thought of itself as the chosen people and frequently has so designated itself in the tribal name with which it refers to the "in-group." Therefore, in almost every conflict the successful warriors considered that they were dispossessing a less able, a less cultivated, a less worthy rival; and sometimes as a result of this attitude they destroyed their adversaries or enslaved them, forcing an acceptance of the dominant customs. Yet it is certain that never before white dominance in the United States began were the many Indian groups subject to a continuous suppression by a technologically superior alien race—suppression working, by intention, in one direction through centuries. The results of such suppression in one group of Indians are described in this volume.

One of the major contributions of democratic philosophy has been increased concern with the well-being of the individual. The declaration of human rights which characterized the democratic revolution both in Europe and in America carried implications with regard to personal values such as rarely before had entered into human planning. It is probably natural that the extension of this concern about the effect on human beings of gross and ruthless modifications of individual and group life should be extended to a "subject people" considerably later than to the members of the dominant society. To those of us whose professions presuppose the importance of the individual and the need for continuing knowledge of individual reactions to the interplay of social forces, it is difficult to justify the operation of an agency like the Indian Service, whose major concern is people, without the basic information about these people that psychological and anthropological research alone can make available.

The basic research of which this report on the Sioux is but one part, while long delayed, nevertheless marks a new and important departure in our dealing with the Indians of the United States. No single document reporting on a small segment of the Indian people can of itself be of great significance. As indication, however, of a new kind of thinking about a group of people which may be preliminary to new and constructive planning regarding federal service for these people, this volume and the other reports of this project may be of far greater importance than they first appear. In the cataclysm of this second World War it may seem incongruous that agencies of the American government should be greatly concerned as to the impact of our white culture upon a minority group (the Sioux) numbering less than thirty thousand souls. We have just witnessed millions of people in Europe and Asia whose lives have been disrupted and whose economic and cultural patterns have been ruthlessly destroyed. In the face of forces whose origins we are at a loss to understand and whose energies we are unable to control, why at this time should we be concerned with an analysis of what has happened and is happening in the lives of a few thousand Sioux Indians? The major answer is that, in addition to being important to the Indians themselves, this study may also aid in pointing the way to a wiser and better pattern of relationship between all people and may teach us how to conserve human values rather than destroy them.

The author of this volume, Dr. Gordon Macgregor, also supervised the field work and analysis of the results of the Sioux study of the Indian Education Research Project. He is an experienced anthropologist who has been in the Indian Service for eight years, formerly as assistant anthropologist in the Applied Anthropology Unit and as supervisor of education in the Division of Education and now as superintendent of the Tongue River Indian Agency, Montana.

Dr. Macgregor was assisted by two collaborators: Royal B. Hassrick, an anthropologist, formerly research secretary and executive director of the American Association on Indian Affairs and now with the Foreign Morale Analysis Division, Office of War Information; and Dr. William E. Henry, a psychologist on the staff of the Committee on Human Development and the Department of Anthropology of the University of Chicago.

WILLARD W. BEATTY
Director of Education
Office of Indian Affairs

CHICAGO, ILLINOIS
January 15, 1945

INTRODUCTION

THIS volume is the second of five integrative studies of Indian personality produced as part of the Indian Education Research Project, which was undertaken jointly by the Committee on Human Development of the University of Chicago and the United States Office of Indian Affairs.[1]

The objective of this project was to investigate, analyze, and compare the development of personality in the Sioux, Hopi, Navaho, Papago, and Zuni tribes in the context of the total environmental setting—sociocultural, geographical, and historical—for implications in regard to Indian Service administration. The project is the first step in a long-range plan of research, the ultimate aim of which is to attempt a systematic evaluation of the whole Indian administrative program with special reference to the effect of the new Indian Service policy on the Indians as individuals, to indicate the direction toward which these policies are leading, and to suggest how the effectiveness of Indian administration may be increased.

Since its inception in 1941, the research has progressed experimentally, under the supervision of the research committee of the University of Chicago, through the co-operative efforts of a large staff drawn from several disciplines—chiefly anthropology, sociology, psychology, psychiatry, medicine, linguistics, education, and administration. The specialists have brought their techniques to bear integratively on the manifold aspects of the task, namely, the development of methodology, the training of field workers, the field work, the analysis of field data, and the interpretation of results. Out of these efforts there has emerged a method of sociopsychological analysis which has been applied, within the limits of the available data, funds, and time, to the five selected Indian tribes.

The first field problem was to investigate the development of the personalities of a sample of about a thousand children, six to eighteen years old, selected by age groups so as to represent two or more communities in each of the tribes, in the context of the total environmental setting. The systematic study of individual personalities was limited to children of school age because of their greater accessibility in regard to the testing program. The personalities and life-histories of these children were studied by means of a battery of psychological tests of both the projective and the performance types, supplemented by interviews with parents, teachers, and other community members and by medical examinations. Most of the testing and interviewing was done by Indian Service teachers, and it was supervised by members of the research staff. Tests requiring highly trained technicians for their administration, such as the Rorschach, Thematic Apperception (adapted), and medical examinations, were given by staff specialists.

The data concerning the present Sioux culture were obtained chiefly through field work initiated and carried out by the project personnel, but information on the physical environment and history have been drawn mainly from the literature, both published and unpublished. All the psychological data were analyzed at the University of Chicago by members of the research staff. The statements and conclusions are those of the author and are not necessarily indorsed by the University of Chicago or the Office of Indian Affairs.

THE SIOUX STUDY

In the development of Indian Service programs since 1933, especially in economic rehabilitation, there have arisen several baffling and superficially inexplicable problems of acceptance and adjustment by the Indians. The Pine Ridge Agency has been particularly interested in having some analysis of Sioux behavior in order to advance the rehabilitation program with greater ease to the Indians. At this agency's request one study of the Indian Education Research Project was made on Pine Ridge Reservation.

This research was carried on in three areas selected on the basis of their relationship to white life: Kyle, Wanblee, and Pine Ridge town. Kyle, in which the major part of the work was conducted, is actually a district of several native communities which have a common center and school in Kyle village. Families from six of these communities were included in the study. They live in completely rural areas and, although a few white farmers live among them, are not under great pressure from, or in intimate relationship with, whites. These communities are fairly representative of the reservation in their life, economic status, and extent of admixture with white people.

Wanblee is a farmer's market town which boomed with the great wheat market of World War I. Most of its white population left during the depression of the 1930's, and in 1942 the majority of the population were Indians, many of whom had moved into town from near-by rural areas because they were not working their farms or because they wished to send their children to the local Indian school. The racial composition of this Indian community is very similar to that of the Kyle group: a few families with very little Indian blood are townspeople, and many of predominantly Indian blood belong to the rural, rather than the town, population. The only significant difference between the Indians living in the country and those living in the Indian camp at Wanblee is the latter group's greater dependency upon direct relief as a means of living.

Different in composition is the third community, Pine Ridge town, in which the Indian Agency is located. Here the majority of the Indians are mixed-bloods.

INTRODUCTION

These families, most of whom live by wage work, follow in their homes and society the local white way of life to a considerable extent. Their relationships, and probably their intermarriage, with whites are more frequent than for any other group of Indians on the reservation.

In order to determine the nature of Sioux personality, 200 children, aged six to eighteen years, were selected at random from the three Indian day schools and one public school in the three areas of study and psychological testing. The only limitations placed upon the selection of names from the school census were that there should be obtained the same representation of white blood admixture as in the total resident reservation population, an equal division between boys and girls, and an equal distribution among four age groups. It was impossible to obtain sufficient life-history information or tests on a number of these 200 children, so that the actual sample on which the personality section of this book is based was

TABLE 1

Degree of Blood	Children's Sample (Per Cent)	Reservation Population (Per Cent)
All degrees	100	100
Full-blood	40	40
Three-fourths Indian blood	21	20
One-half Indian blood	17	15
One-fourth Indian blood	13	16
Less than one-fourth Indian blood	9	9

reduced to 166. Of this total, the representation by blood group is shown in Table 1. The boys and girls were distributed by selected age groups, as listed in Table 2.

Information about these children was obtained through tests and interviews with the children, their parents, their teachers, and other persons in their communities. The tests used are described in Part III and in Appendix I. The results were analyzed to present a picture of the group personality of the children; differences between children in the four age groups and between boys and girls were also noted. Interviews were used to obtain voluntary information about each child's health, his early training, his relations with the members of his household and his community, and his behavior and interests. By setting all the information gathered through tests and interviews against the background of the community and the reservation, the influence of the children's social and economic situation upon their personalities and their reactions to the situation could be seen.

The special interest of this study of personality has been in the effect of cultural change and present social conditions upon the Sioux. The nature of this change and the resultant disorganization of the society have profoundly affected the

Sioux people and may fairly be assumed to be major determinants in their present personality adjustments.

However, the fact that this study was not concerned with biological endowment and physiological changes should not be construed to mean that these factors do not have far-reaching effects upon personality. On the contrary, this research was operated on the thesis that personality and individual development are the resultants of the interaction of a number of complex processes. Organic processes of the body (physical inheritance, present and past physical conditions and characteristics); psychological processes (the need for affection and emotional security, for some degree of status and recognition as persons, for a feeling of unity with something larger and more secure than the individual); social processes operating in the environment (the attitudes and modes of behavior of those who train the child and the demands and prohibitions of the social group to which the individual

TABLE 2

Age	Total	Boys	Girls	Per Cent of Sample
All ages	166	78	88	100
5– 7 years	23	12	11	14
8–10 years	41	20	21	25
11–13 years	44	20	24	26
14–18 years	58	26	32	35

belongs)—all these operate to influence and shape personality and behavior. Irregularities and experiences arising from any of these areas of influence may produce injuries and distortions in the entire personality structure. But long-enduring and intense cultural disruptions may be reflected in disturbances of behavior and personality organization as clearly as long-enduring or intense physical deprivations or irregular physical conditions.

One further major concept is assumed in the theory of personality development presented in this study. Any given overt behavior is a function of the entire personality organization rather than a simple reaction to a given objective stimulus. Thus only when the entire personality demands and experiences are considered, and only when the reaction is conceived as an expression of some "need," objective, or purpose of the individual, can the significance of any behavior reaction or any set of reactions be given genuine meaning.

In presenting the environment and the cultural changes and their effects upon the personalities of Pine Ridge children, the material has been organized on the following basis. Part I describes Sioux society in the past and at present, giving the historical and economic bases of reservation society today, the values and attitudes which characterized the pre-reservation culture, and those which it has retained or acquired in the last seventy-five years. Part II describes briefly how the Sioux child grows up. Against this background of the society as it has been and is today are set, in Part III, the personalities of the children who will be the adult Sioux of tomorrow. Conclusions follow in Part IV.

ACKNOWLEDGMENTS

The field work of this study was conducted during the period from August 1, 1942, to June 1, 1943. Deep appreciation should be expressed to all the members of the field staff for their conscientious and enthusiastic work, all of which was done in addition to their regular duties. To Dow Carnal, principal of Little Wound Day School, special appreciation is expressed both for industry and enthusiasm in making field studies in addition to his heavy responsibilities and for the information he gave from his eleven years' experience on Pine Ridge.

The months of work for the field staff would have doubled except for the active co-operation of many other Pine Ridge school and Agency employees who expedited the work of testing and made reports on the sample group of children. Grateful acknowledgment is made of the co-operation of the teaching staffs of Oglala Community High School and the Pine Ridge and Wanblee public schools. Appreciation is also expressed to the members of the Agency Health Division for their time and effort in making physical examinations of the children.

To W. O. Roberts, superintendent of the Pine Ridge Agency; William Nicholson, superintendent of education; Albert Pyles, principal of Oglala Community High School; Mrs. Ruth Heinemann, social worker; Rex Kildow, Everett Jordan, and their assistants on the Pine Ridge staff, thanks are due for their time and co-operation in assisting the progress of the survey and in contributing information and records. Mr. Roberts followed the survey with great interest, shared his wide information about the history and the behavior of the Dakota, learned from twenty years of work among them, and constructively criticized the manuscript.

Royal B. Hassrick, anthropologist from the Graduate School of the University of Pennsylvania, joined the staff to conduct the Rorschach Psychodiagnostic tests and to assist in the field work. For his assistance and analysis of the Rorschach data, I am greatly indebted. His knowledge of the Sioux culture, drawn from earlier studies among the Dakota, his manuscripts on the Dakota kinship system and native religion, which he generously offered for use in the study, his observations and discussions, and particularly his companionship during the field work are gifts and associations whose meaning is very incompletely described as collaboration.

Dr. William E. Henry of the University of Chicago, who acted as consultant in the analysis and preparation of the psychological material, clarified the basic psychological problems of the Dakota children in his interpretation of the Thematic

Apperception tests of the group and individual case studies. His particular contribution and insights and his assistance to me in getting my bearings in the field of psychology are gratefully acknowledged.

For suggestions, criticism, and insight into the social problems of the Dakota and for reading and helpful guidance in the preparation of the manuscript, I am deeply indebted and grateful to Professor W. Lloyd Warner, chairman of the University of Chicago's committee of the project, and to Professor Ralph Tyler, member of the committee. To Professor Robert Havighurst, also of the University's committee, I wish to express my gratitude for guidance and planning in setting up the psychological tests, for analysis of the psychological battery, and for critical reading of the manuscript. For their contribution in the analyses of tests, acknowledgment is made to his assistants and other members of the research staff.

Appreciation for consultation and advice is extended to Dr. Bruno Klopfer, director of the Rorschach Institute; to the late Dr. Eugene Lerner, formerly professor of psychology, Sarah Lawrence College; and to Dr. Grace Arthur, who gave instruction in the administration of her test at Pine Ridge.

To John Collier, Commissioner of Indian Affairs, who, from his deep insight into Indian problems and Indian needs, initiated this research; to Willard W. Beatty, Director of Education, for helpfully criticizing the manuscript and for writing the Foreword; to Dorothea Leighton, M.D., special physician in the Indian Service, for her analysis of the physical examination data and for her advice in the psychological analysis; to Dr. Laura Thompson, co-ordinator of the project, for criticisms and suggestions; and to the other members of the research staff, I wish to express my thanks.

For careful and understanding editing of this study, I wish to express my especial gratitude to Roma K. McNickle. I should also like to thank E. H. Coulson, of the Forestry Division, Office of Indian Affairs, for preparing the two maps used in the book.

To earlier studies of the Pine Ridge Dakota by Dr. Scudder Mekeel and Erik Homburger Erikson, I am obligated far more than acknowledgments or references can express. I have borrowed heavily from their ideas and insights and, if credit and references have not always been made in the text, acknowledgment of their great contribution is made here. Constant study of their writings, association with them at Pine Ridge in 1937, and especially the long discussions with Dr. Mekeel during the writing and editing of the manuscript have made much of their thinking mine. If this work has carried forward their earlier researches, I hope that they will consider themselves still active participants in the anthropology and psychology of the Sioux.

Acknowledgment of their many courtesies and aids and their co-operation in giving information and in taking the many and tedious tests is made to the

Indians of Kyle, Pine Ridge, and Wanblee. It was their friendship and interest that made this study possible. It is sincerely hoped they will find the analysis herein presented useful as a guide, and not a criticism, for themselves and for the people who are working with them toward greater understanding in their common endeavor in developing their life on the reservation.

GORDON MACGREGOR

WASHINGTON, D.C.
January 15, 1945

NOTES

1. The other studies resulting from this project are: Hopi—*The Hopi Way*, by Laura Thompson and Alice Joseph (Chicago: University of Chicago Press, 1944); Navaho—*The People and Their Children*, by Dorothea C. Leighton and Clyde Kluckhohn (Chicago: University of Chicago Press, forthcoming); Papago—*The Desert People*, by Alice Joseph, Rosamond Spicer, and Jane Chesky (in preparation, 1945); Zuni—(title to be determined), by Clyde Kluckhohn and Dorothea C. Leighton (in preparation, 1945).

TABLE OF CONTENTS

List of Illustrations 19

PART I. DAKOTA LIFE—THEN AND NOW

I. The Warriors on the Reservation 21
II. The Road to Civilization 29
III. Making a Living on the Reservation 43
IV. The Dakota Family 52
V. Reservation Communities 66
VI. Indians and Whites 78
VII. Power, Ceremony, and Church 85
VIII. Fathers and Grandfathers 105

PART II. GROWING UP ON THE RESERVATION

IX. Infancy 123
X. Childhood 131
XI. Adolescence 139

PART III. THE PERSONALITY OF THE DAKOTA CHILD

XII. Ten Dakota Children 153
XIII. Intelligence, Emotions, and Behavior 184
XIV. Looking beneath the Surface 204

PART IV. OUTLOOK FOR THE FUTURE

XV. New Weapons for Security 210

APPENDIXES

I. Techniques Used in the Study 215
II. Aggression in Personality 220

BIBLIOGRAPHY

Bibliography 222

INDEX

Index 225

LIST OF ILLUSTRATIONS

Children of the Warriors . . . . *Frontispiece*
Cabin, Tent, and Corral of a Typical Reservation Home 24
Survivor of the Battle of Wounded Knee 34
District Committee Distributes Rations 47
Seasonal Wage Work Important in the $458 Average Annual Income . . 47
A Home on the Range 61
Watching the World Go By 71
Transacting Government Business 80
Give-away 95
Four Generations 111
Warriors for a Day 129
Four Sioux Boys 136
Four Sioux Girls 141
Schoolboys Roping a Wild Horse 168
Adolescent Boy 196
Driving Home the New Herd 213

LIST OF MAPS

Pine Ridge Indian Reservation . . . . ii, iii
Medicine Root District 76

PART I. DAKOTA LIFE—THEN AND NOW

CHAPTER I

THE WARRIORS ON THE RESERVATION

To most white Americans the Dakota, or Sioux, are the typical Indians, who dressed in eagle-feather war bonnets, hunted the buffalo, and fought savagely against the wagon trains of emigrants and the cavalry of the United States Army. The Western or Teton-Dakota, with whom this book deals, are descendants of several of the bands and their chiefs who led the resistance of the Northern Plains Indians. The fathers and grandfathers of the oldest generation living today were men who for years fought off the United States Army and, in one battle against Custer, severely defeated it. Until 1855 these Dakota were free and independent, living as nomadic warriors and hunters and following the way of life which they had developed in two hundred years on the plains. In that year General Harney began a campaign against them which lasted for twenty years. By treaty in 1868 the Teton-Dakota agreed to accept a single large reservation, where their hunting rights were to be undisturbed. An uprising in 1876 was followed by defeat and final acceptance of reservation life. They had no choice but to accept, because the buffalo, their basic food supply, had almost vanished from the plains.

The Pine Ridge Reservation, on which 8,500 Teton-Dakota of the Oglala and Brulé subtribes are living today, is only a small part of the Great Sioux Reservation originally set aside for all the tribe. Pine Ridge itself originally included four counties along the southern boundary of South Dakota, covering nearly 4,400 square miles. This area, almost the size of the state of Connecticut, was later reduced by the opening of one county for homesteading by white settlers. To the east of Pine Ridge lies the Rosebud Reservation, where live most of the Brulé and other subtribes of the Teton-Dakota. Pine Ridge is bounded in part on the north by the White River, a large stream which flows in a northeasterly direction across the western part of the reservation and then eastward to join the Missouri. Many small streams, which flow throughout the summer in years of heavy snow and good rainfall, cross the reservation and empty into the White River. The Pine

Ridge country is rolling high-plains land covered with short grass and broken by long pine-covered ridges running out of the Black Hills at the northwest.

The Dakota came onto the reservation not as a vanquished people but rather as eagles driven by a winter storm to accept captivity and food until they could fly away again.[1] Yet, even before the last of the bands came to the Pine Ridge Agency to obtain their rations, there were some leaders and their followers who saw the inevitability of dominance by the white man. With the freedom for much individual choice which was characteristic of their society, some of these Indians began to adopt white ways and to extend their friendship to white men, both military and civilians. Some came very early into possession of a few cattle, probably by stealing them from whites as they had formerly stolen horses from other enemies. Some became scouts for the Army, although this was infrequent in the early days of the Sioux-white conflict. They wore white men's clothing, took jobs as they could get them, and later joined mission churches. These "friendly" Indians were few at first, but they paved the way for many others who, sometimes in entire bands, accepted settlement and peaceful life on the reservation.

The Dakota on the reservation today give the impression that they have now accepted white life and are far removed from the hunting, raiding, and tepee-dwelling life of a few generations ago. This is indeed the case; but, as in every change to another culture, the process has not been one of simple substitution. Indian faces are still to be seen, of course, and a few old men and little boys with long braids. Most of the women wear blankets, and a number of the people also wear moccasins. Among themselves many families speak Siouan. These are among the few remaining outward signs of a continuing Indian life.

The white visitor is more forcefully impressed by the frame and log homes, the schools and churches, and the country stores. Although the storekeepers are known as "traders" by tradition, the Indian customers buy with cash or charge and do very little trading as such. There are also beauty shops, movie shows, drug stores, and cafés and, in them all, Indian as well as white customers.

Except for their darker faces and large brown eyes, the children look like children of any rural town on the plains. They play basketball in the schoolyard and travel to school in orange-colored busses. Around their homes, little boys rope fence posts or puppies, while their sisters play with dolls or jackstones.

Traveling across the reservation, one finds whites living among the Indians both in the rural areas and in the towns. Around the white farms, barns, and sheds, equipment and livestock show greater prosperity. There are also signs of greater activity among the white men at work with their tractors or trucks. Property seems to be better maintained.

If a visitor goes inside both white and Indian homes, he will find the differences between whites and Indians not quite so clear cut. The outward symbols by which he has learned to distinguish the homes of one group from the other do not always hold true. The owner of an apparently prosperous ranch, when met at his door, may reveal physical characteristics that show part-Indian inheritance. The wife of a white farmer may be a distinctly Indian woman in appearance.

Visiting at Indian cabins, one may find an old, unquestionably full-blood couple living in a single room that is immaculately scrubbed. Each piece of household furniture is placed against the wall, and every article either hung up or packed away in trunks. The arrangement of the house may seem reminiscent of the old tepee, but the order and care show that the wife has thoroughly kept the habits of a good white housekeeper learned at Indian school forty or fifty years ago.

On the other hand, some Indian homes have litter and trash around them, and inside there are dirt, garbage, ragged blankets, and clothes strewn about the floor. The occupants may appear to be full-bloods or mixed-bloods. Among them there may be no sign of farming operations or a cattle herd or any economic activity. Many more Indians have their own cattle, chickens, and vegetable gardens. But the visitor will find as he goes from home to home that the majority of the Indians have little as compared to the white people of the countryside. The cattle herds are small, the gardens are small, the cornfields are small. Wheat and other grain crops are rare in Indian fields. Poverty characterizes most of the Indian homes.

Not only economic activity is lacking in Indian homes; there is little social interaction in the community. The tempo is slow and quiet, and life is marked by an idleness that reflects apathy as well as the lack of full-time occupation.

As one remains in the reservation communities, he becomes aware of a great variety in Indian habits and ways of living and also in Indian personalities. He will see that between the light mixed-blood rancher on his profitable cattle ranch and the full-blood in his cabin, living by government rations and a little work, there are extremes of behavior and outlook that makes them appear to belong to two different worlds.

The light mixed-blood talks of the difficulties of wartime restrictions and the price of cattle. He looks and lives more like his white neighbor than like his darker Indian cousin. In fact, he belongs socially to the group of whites who ranch and farm or keep stores in the area. He eats in their homes and attends their parties, and his children marry their children.

From the full-blood, a visitor will hear stories of the great days of the Sioux, told with many sign-language gestures. Perhaps a buckskin garment or a beautifully beaded pipe bag will be brought out for his inspection. Talk may turn to complaints about the Indian Service, the hard times, the failure of the garden, or the fact that the school bus comes too early or too far from his grandchildren's

CABIN, TENT, AND CORRAL OF A TYPICAL RESERVATION HOME

door. If the visitor goes to an evening dance at the school, he will find his full-blood friends dancing the Omaha Dance, performed as in the old days only by men and women in Indian dress, or the Rabbit Dance, which, as a concession to white ways, is danced with Indian reserve by couples. Upstairs the young mixed-bloods and the Agency employees will be dancing the waltz and foxtrot to fiddle and concertina. The older full-bloods are the nucleus of a large group which tries to maintain what it can of Indian life. Their dancing symbolizes their cultural position and attitudes—preserving the old and making slight concessions to change. Their chief satisfactions come from doing things the Indian way.

The cultural position of the majority of the Pine Ridge Indians lies between the two extremes of the white-assimilated mixed-bloods and the unassimilated full-bloods who live in the shadow of their former Indian culture. But running through the whole reservation society is a strong split, which basically is one of attitudes. There are political divisions over following the current administrative policy set forth in the Indian Reorganization Act and over past administrative measures. There are divisions based on being "full-blood" or "mixed-blood," which, it is important to remember, are actually *sociological* rather than *biological* groups, standing primarily for the way of living according to Indian or white patterns rather than the actual degree of Indian blood.[2] There are those who make a living by farming or wage work. There are the others who prefer to be dependent on the government and exert their efforts toward getting more help and financial restitution from Congress for wrongs they believe the United States committed in the past. This division of outlook within the tribe has brought an increasing amount of conflict of one group against another. It appears in every new issue the Sioux face and tends to retard their economic and social development.

This difference in attitudes began almost with the arrival of whites in the Teton-Dakota country. To the original group favoring white influence were added in a few years the full-blood young people who were taken away to Hampton and Carlisle schools for training in white vocations and habits. Then the half-bloods began to appear. They were the children of white fathers who sternly insisted that their sons and daughters follow the American, and often European, pattern in which they themselves had been reared. From the increase of this group by continued white intermarriages and intermixture of mixed-blood and full-blood, the biological mixed-blood group now ranges from fifteen-sixteenths to one-sixteenth of Dakota blood. It forms 60 per cent of the resident reservation population.

In spite of the predominance of intermixture with white, more than half of the Pine Ridge Indian population belong to the sociological full-blood group. They maintain a similar level of living on a very low average income, adhere to a number of Dakota customs, have a common set of attitudes (at least by generation), and usually talk among themselves in their Teton-Dakota dialect. They form the social group which comes to mind when whites, mixed-bloods, and even local full-blood employees of other tribes speak of the "Indians." Descriptions and life-patterns of the present-day Dakota in this study refer to the sociological full-blood group. Sharp differences in the habits of the sociological mixed-bloods are specifically noted.

The Dakota who have chosen to follow the "white man's road," as they term it, are looked upon by white people as progressive. Actually they are the more realistic. The Indians who first became cattlemen, settled in permanent homes, and sent their children to school were accepting the inevitable. The sons and daughters of the early white men and Indian women followed the customs and attitudes of their fathers because of early childhood training. They learned the white ways of life before they were old enough to choose or understand their cultural position. However, changing from an Indian to a white cultural pattern, or merely following a father's teaching, was not a simple process. For those adult full-bloods who changed, there were the old sentiments and attachments to a life that had been stamped in them in childhood. There were also the constant pressures of the conservative Indian group. Children trained by white fathers were attached to the Indian people and to Indian ways of living by the training of their Indian mothers and the associations with Indian playmates. Thus it is not surprising that within individuals themselves there were divisions of loyalties and affections and in their behavior much ambivalence and uncertainty.

The Indians who in the first years of reservation life tried to cling to Indian ways and cherished the values and attitudes which supported them have their modern counterpart in the conservative and more nearly full-blood element of the reservation. At first the conservative group would not accept the circumstances into which they had been thrust. They fought, negotiated, and even employed supernatural means to overcome the whites, to restore the buffalo, and to regain freedom upon the plains. As Erikson has well pointed out, they could not accept the fact that the "old days" were gone forever, that the buffalo hunts, the war parties, the long processions across the plains to tribal meetings, and their religious worship in the Sun Dance were no more.[3] This belief that the present situation is not here to stay still lingers in the minds of many. At least its conscious acceptance is avoided by thinking, dreaming, and believing that the old life can still be regained. To them the old life is reality, and the necessity for Indians to live much as whites do is still unreal, or at least to be avoided.

No one Indian, of course, is so completely out of touch with reality as this unqualified statement would imply. Indeed, only a people of such stamina and fibre as the Dakota could have stood without cracking under the terrific strain of events they have encountered in the last eighty years. Yet, despite their surface acquiescence, unwillingness to accept modern life and cultural change and the fantasy of an eventual return of the former Indian life are still common to the thinking of many Dakota.

This refusal or inability to accept the apparent fate of becoming socially and culturally white men has not prevented them from accepting many of the material aspects of white life: skin tepees have been exchanged for log cabins, open fires for iron stoves. The conservative group has moved toward assimilation, embracing many elements of white life into their own. This trend has not, however, taken place without great personal and social disorganization. Thus the conservative or less assimilated group, living in much of the spirit and the vestiges of their old culture, are on the fringes of both Indian and white cultures. In these respects the majority of the Pine Ridge Dakota are marginal people both as whites and as Indians.

It would be an error to assume, however, that the Dakota show social differences and disorganization because of sheer slowness and stubbornness. This process of cultural change takes place in all groups, although not always with such disastrous effects or sharp contrasts. Even European groups coming to America with the desire to change have not escaped difficulties and conflicts of adjustment that only time can iron out. The Dakota in their change have had to move from a simple to a complex culture—and to a complex culture that was changing from a frontier society to more stable, settled order within a growing young nation. Events moved with great rapidity; the physical environment changed under exploitation, abuse, and erosion; and one economy after another was swept from beneath them. The pressure to become "civilized" was intense. All the Indians changed to some extent with the course of events.

The wide range of Sioux behavior, the seeming sets of patterns within patterns, and the confusion of cultural values resulting in strong personal anxiety will appear in later chapters of this book. In their recent economic and social change the Dakota have had neither much opportunity to contribute to their new life nor freedom of choice or education or understanding before acceptance of white life. Frequently the direction and final decision rested in the hands of the whites. Forbidden by circumstance to remain warriors and hunters, they have had to find new roles within the new economic and social order. They found in cattle, as they did in the gun and the horse, a means of making a living and adjusting in their new cultural milieu. But they lost their cattle during World War I, and, as a result, they became even more disorganized from this second loss of the foundation of their economy. Under the present administration the Pine Ridge Indians have been able to purchase new cattle and take over much direction of their political affairs through a tribally elected council. Present signs give promise of a successful redevelopment of their economic and social life.

NOTES

1. Julia B. McGillycuddy, *McGillycuddy—Agent* (Stanford University, Calif.: Stanford University Press, 1941), p. 153.
2. Throughout the text the use of "full-blood" and "mixed-blood" will refer to the sociological, not the biological, groups.
3. Erik Homburger Erikson, *"Observations on Sioux Education," Journal of Psychology*, VII (1939), 105.

CHAPTER II

THE ROAD TO CIVILIZATION

THE known history of the Teton-Dakota has been a series of adjustments to new environments and ways of life. About two hundred and fifty years ago these Indians came from the woodlands and prairies onto the plains and adapted themselves to hunting the buffalo in this treeless country. A century and a half elapsed before the white man's encroachments on their territory and their food supply began the struggle which ended in acceptance of settlement on reservations. In 1869, when they began moving into reservation agencies, the Teton-Dakota started to travel in earnest the long road toward the white man's civilization.

THE WESTWARD MIGRATION AND CONFLICT

The Teton-Dakota are the western division of the Dakota people who lived formerly around Mille Lacs, Minnesota. Their language, which belongs to the Siouan stock, links them with the Omaha, the Assiniboine, and other tribes living on the plains and prairies and with a few scattered tribes in eastern and southern United States. From scientific research it appears that the Siouan group once lived in the Ohio Valley.[1] Historical evidence indicates that whites first met the Teton-Dakota at the headwaters of the Mississippi in 1680.[2] They moved into the prairies before, and independently of, the Central and Eastern Dakota divisions, the Yankton and Santee. All these divisions may have come to the Mille Lac region from the east and then pushed westward in historic times under pressure from the Chippewa, armed with white men's guns.

According to tradition, the Teton-Dakota in their westward trek moved in two groups.[3] The Oglala and Brulé subtribes moved south to the Blue Earth River in Minnesota and then west to the James River and finally to the Missouri, which they reached about 1760.[4] The second group, including the Minneconjou, Sans Arcs, Two Kettles, Hunkpapa, and Blackfeet Teton-Dakota, moved first to Big Stone Lake, on the present Minnesota–South Dakota boundary, and then westward on a northern route parallel to that of the Oglala and Brulé.

In taking this first step of their westward migration, the Teton-Dakota moved to the fringe of the eastern woodland area and into the high-grass prairie country, which presented them with new problems of living. As they went farther westward and came into contact with other plains tribes, they continued to modify their culture, until it became one of the typical examples of Plains Indian life. This culture developed around the great herds of buffalo which roamed the high plains west of the Missouri River, from north of the Canadian border to Texas.

When whites first encountered Indians thought to have belonged to the Teton-Dakota group, they were traveling on foot and transporting their baggage by dog-drawn travois.[5] By 1760, after they migrated to the Missouri River,[6] some Teton-Dakota, probably Oglala and Brulé, had obtained a few horses. Before they reached the Black Hills (about 1780),[7] they are known to have had good herds of horses, but just when they began to travel as mounted tribes is not yet ascertained. They first had guns in any quantity about 1750.[8]

With the gun and the horse, introduced by Europeans but reaching the Teton-Dakota first through other Indians, this tribe could spread over the plains country that abounded with buffalo. The horse made possible hunting and traveling over the vast stretches of the plains, and the gun gave them means to fight similarly armed tribes and overcome those who were without them.[9]

Like the whites who later followed them, the Teton found the plains occupied. The Arikara held the region of the Missouri Valley where the Oglala and Brulé wished to cross the river. For years the invaders were held back by the Arikara, but after smallpox decimated the latter's villages they were forced to retreat up the river. The Cheyenne, who also lived along the river, gave way to the newcomers with little resistance. Later the Teton had to fight the Pawnee, the Kiowa, and the Crow for the Black Hills, and they defeated the Mandan to obtain the best buffalo grounds. Once having obtained control over the region of western Nebraska, South and North Dakota, and eastern Montana and Wyoming, the Teton pushed no farther. It should be kept in mind that, although the Teton later fought with the whites and with alien Indian tribes to keep them from encroaching on their hunting grounds, they themselves had fought to conquer territory. This strongly qualifies the frequent assertion that their fighting was a kind of game, with only spoils or honor as the object.

The first coming of the whites brought great material prosperity to the Indians. The fur-traders—first the French and later the Americans—brought guns, knives, axes, and iron pots to trade for pelts. These articles came into the hands of the Sioux through trade with their eastern neighbors, the Chippewa, and later directly from the traders. These men were not interested in disrupting the life of the Indians; indeed, many white traders entered into Indian life by marrying Dakota women, as the prevalence of French names on the reservation today suggests. It was to the traders' interest that Indian economic activity should be encouraged in order that hunting and trapping might flourish. Later the first American pioneers into the west crossed the Teton country along the valley of the Platte but were not interested in settling.

By 1841, however, hundreds of people were emigrating by wagon train to the West Coast and raiding the buffalo herds for food. Then came the thousands over the Oregon Trail along the Platte River in the Gold Rush of 1849. Alarmed at the increasing number of whites and the threat to their food supply, the Sioux and neighboring tribes of Cheyenne and Arapaho began raiding the wagon trains. The government then attempted to protect the overland trails by making a treaty which set boundaries to the territory claimed by the Teton-Dakota and other tribes. This treaty, signed at Fort Laramie, Wyoming, in 1851, prohibited trespass by whites on Indian territory but guaranteed emigrants safe passage through it. Neither side lived up to the agreement. There followed thirty years of violent but sporadic fighting and raiding which reached its peak in the sixties and seventies. General Harney, who had begun a campaign against the Indians in 1855, finally secured a peace treaty with them in 1868. The government agreed to keep all whites from hunting or settling in Indian territory, to abandon the proposed trail from Fort Laramie to Bozeman, Montana, and the military posts along it, and to pay annuities for appropriated lands. In return, the Indians consented to settle on reservations.

The Teton accepted the Great Sioux Reservation and received hunting privileges to the west. This reservation was bounded by lines on north, west, and south which became the state boundaries of South Dakota, and by the Missouri River on the east. The Teton released all claims to territory east of the Missouri. In 1869 most of them moved into the Army-supervised agencies established within the reservation, where a few friendly Indians had already been living for four or five years.

In the following year war broke out again, occasioned by treaty violations by both Indians and whites. For several years hostile Indians came to and left the reservations.

In the fall of 1875 many of the Indians were permitted to leave their reservations for a buffalo hunt in the Powder River country of Wyoming. But in the dead of winter they were asked to return. When they did not do so, because of the heavy snows and lack of sufficient food stores, they were declared hostile, and the Army was sent to force their return. Allied with warriors of other tribes, the Sioux met a detachment of the Army under Custer and defeated him at the Little Big Horn in Wyoming. But shortly thereafter they suffered their final military defeat, and the majority, including Red Cloud, war leader of the allied tribes, returned to the reservation. Several bands fled to Canada, but in the following year, Crazy Horse, a chief of the Oglala, returned from Canada to surrender. Four years later Gall and Sitting Bull followed him.

In 1875, when reports of gold brought great pressure for white men to be let into the Black Hills, a government commission had drawn up a treaty for their cession, but the chiefs refused to sign. Nevertheless, the Army let thousands of impatient prospectors into the hills. In the peace settlement of the following year, some of the Teton-Dakota leaders relinquished their claim to the hills and the right to hunt west of the reservation line. The Teton have since claimed that the terms of this settlement were misrepresented to them and that not all the leaders of the bands knew of the action.[10] The loss of the hills has remained a controversy and a source of deep resentment among the Sioux to the present day. Suits against the United States government for compensation have been entered in the Court of Claims.

EARLY RESERVATION YEARS

For the Dakota the tragedies of 1876 and the few years that followed brought an end to armed resistance against the white man and the defense of their independence and territories. The buffalo were rapidly disappearing, and with them the chief source of food. The Dakota could not continue the fight against such overwhelming odds.

Events which have had a lasting effect on the attitudes of the Teton followed in so rapid a succession that they brought spiritual defeat soon after the segregation on the reservation and the loss of the provider and symbol of life, the buffalo. In 1881 the superintendent at Pine Ridge Agency forbade the continuance of the annual Sun Dance, the great tribal religious ceremony, after its performance during that summer. In 1882 the last great buffalo hunt was held; and in November of the next year the last buffalo was killed by the Teton-Dakota.

The Great Sioux Reservation was broken in 1889 into five separate Teton-Dakota reservations: Pine Ridge, Rosebud, Standing Rock, Cheyenne River, and Lower Brulé. The Oglala and part of the Brulé, who were finally settled on the Pine Ridge Reservation, had previously been placed at several agencies. At first they were located on the north fork of the Platte River not far from Laramie, then moved to the Whetstone Agency on the Missouri, then returned to the Red Cloud Agency on the Platte, not far from the place where the government had first quartered them. They were next moved to a place on the White River near Fort Robinson, Nebraska, and finally in 1878 to a site on Big White Clay Creek selected by the Indians and named "Pine Ridge."

The civilian superintendent appointed to take charge of the Pine Ridge Agency in 1879[11] immediately began a program of preparing the bands under his charge for the settled ways of white farmers. His suppression of the Sun Dance was only one step in directing the Indians away from their pagan and uncivilized ways.

Breakup of camp life and the family groups of tepees, the undermining of the authority of the chiefs, and the placement of children in school followed in quick succession. The disappearance of the buffalo, the loss of the old ways, and the anticipation of new ones culminated in a feeling of frustration and resentment which drove a large proportion of the Dakota to attempt to rid themselves of the white man by supernatural means. The center of this resistance was on Pine Ridge, where it ended in the last Teton-Dakota combat with the United States Army.

THE LAST BATTLE

In 1889 the Sioux heard of the Ghost Dance among the Indians in the western United States. It was prophesied that a messiah would appear, to destroy the white race and the evils which it had brought and to bring back the buffalo and the Indian dead, thus restoring the old life. A delegation from three Sioux reservations was sent to Nevada to visit Wovoka, the prophet of this cult.[12] They returned with glowing but distorted accounts, and soon Indians on all the Dakota reservations were dancing the Ghost Dance in a frenzy.

One great dance was held on White Clay Creek near the Pine Ridge Agency. As the bands gathered, the new successor to the first agent and the white settlers grew more and more uneasy. The ritual, which they mistook for a war dance, threw them into a panic, and they called for troops. Near Wounded Knee the cavalry, a part of Custer's former regiment, came upon the Big Foot band on their way from another reservation to the Ghost Dance camp to learn of the new messiah. As they were being disarmed, a shot was fired which fanned the smoldering fires of resentment among the Indians and the desire for revenge by the soldiers. In a savage attack the soldiers, armed with the Gatling gun, killed 128 warriors and massacred many women and children who were fleeing from the scene.

Commenting on the event forty years later, a Sioux remarked: "After the Battle of Wounded Knee all ambition was taken out of us. We have never since been able to regain a foothold."[13] The tragedy brought to a sudden end the hopes of the Ghost Dancers. Wounded Knee drove home the impossibility of escape from white subjugation.

The battle has remained in the minds of many Pine Ridge people as a symbol of injustice and abuse at the hands of the white man. Survivors are still living, but the event is discussed only by younger people. A trader's large billboard, "Site of the Massacre of Wounded Knee," helps to keep the memory fresh.

ACCULTURATION BEGINS

Mekeel in his history of the Teton-Dakota marks the Ghost Dance and the Battle of Wounded Knee as the end of one historical phase of Indian-white rela-

SURVIVOR OF THE BATTLE OF WOUNDED KNEE

tions, as seen from the Indian point of view.[14] From then to the present, he says, has been a period of "passive acceptance of white acculturation."

The period of acculturation actually began with the Indians' acceptance of white material goods, received by trade with Indians to the east and with whites in the seventeenth century. It has already been noted that as early as 1865 some Teton-Dakota were already accepting the peaceful life which the whites offered at the agencies. At least as early as 1870 the military were encouraging the Indians to take up livestock-raising.

The adoption of white life was also stimulated by missionary activities. In 1871 the Episcopal church established a school at the Whetstone Agency. By 1888 the Jesuits came to the reservation and established both a mission and a school.

In 1879, children of the Teton-Dakota had been sent east to the first nonreservation government school for Indians at Carlisle, Pennsylvania. The agent at Pine Ridge obtained government funds to start a local school, which he opened in 1881.

In all these activities there were some Indians who participated willingly. It appears, therefore, that the process of acculturation was functioning intensively among many of the Indians long before the Ghost Dance and Wounded Knee. These events brought to a close the last active tribal effort to combat white aggressors and also the decline of Indian resistance, but long before 1890 there had been a rising acceptance of white life.

Three aspects of the dramatic period of change from Indian to white culture which followed are important to note: first, the suppression of Indian custom and authority; second, the education of the children in the techniques of white life; and, third, Agency and other white pressures upon the adults to adopt white ways of making a livelihood.

The attempt to suppress native leadership and Indian social controls began under the agent who came to Pine Ridge in 1879. He had two particular powers by which he kept the Indians under his control: the ration issue of live beef and a police company of fifty Indians, which he organized with an Indian leader as chief of police responsible directly to him. These powers he utilized with no attempt at abuse to achieve the ends which he thought most desirable for the tribe. Only through the acceptance of stock-raising and settlement on farm tracts, he sincerely felt, could the Indian adjust to his new situation. However, like all people of his time, the agent also felt that this must be accompanied by a complete abandonment of Indian custom. Thus, when the Indians seemed to cling too tenaciously to camping by band groups, holding council by themselves, or being unco-operative, he withheld rations or utilized the police to force a change.

The agent, having control of the food supply and its distribution, as well as control over the Indians' personal freedom, held power with which the chiefs could not compete. All decisions had to be taken ultimately to him, and thus began a paternalistic system[15] which brought the virtual elimination of the position of chief. The last man to be made a chief of the Oglala Sioux on Pine Ridge tersely states in his autobiography: "If I tried to better the conditions of my people, while on the reservation, I found it another impossibility. So I had to do one of two things—keep my mouth shut or fight the agent all the time."[16] And so he left the reservation forever.

The undermining of native controls and native leadership was followed later by official regulations which forbade native dances, ceremonies, and pagan customs which were believed to impede the acceptance of white life.[17] These regulations were in force until 1934.[18]

The most effective means for cultural change lay in the education of the young people. Although the school established under the first agent at Pine Ridge got off to a bad start when the matron attempted to cut off the boys' long braids and thus threw the students into flight, the first classes soon had a large number of the children around the agency in attendance.[19] The formal school program was patterned after that of the schools in the East, but half the time was devoted to industrial training, agriculture, and housekeeping.

Excerpts from the statement of educational policy for all Indian children at this time are enlightening. The policy was "to civilize," "to humanize," and "to put the children in boarding school where they will learn English" and "not relapse into their former moral and mental stupor." In connection with this statement, the federal superintendent of Indian schools in 1885 makes one remark which is highly significant in light of this study. "The Indian is the strangest compound of individualism and socialism run to seed. It is this being that we endeavor to make a member of a new social order.... to do this we must recreate him, *make a new personality.*"[20]

Children were virtually kidnaped to force them into government schools, their hair was cut, and their Indian clothes thrown away. They were forbidden to speak in their own language. Life in the school was under military discipline, and rules were enforced by corporal punishment. Those who persisted in clinging to their old ways and those who ran away and were recaptured were thrown into jail. Parents who objected were also jailed. Where possible, children were kept in school year after year to avoid the influence of their families.

This policy began in the seventies and eighties and continued long after the Indians had made adjustments to reservation life. Physically enforced attendance at the schools and the use of corporal punishment, jails, and military drill continued into the late 1920's but are no longer sanctioned by the Office of Indian Affairs. The official belief in "civilizing the Indian," as such, has passed, yet the motivation to make him in the likeness of the social and economic ideal of whites has by no means totally vanished from the picture.

Accompanying the educational program for the children was a strong effort to have the adults establish permanent dwellings and undertake the running of cattle herds. This caused a radical innovation in the social organization of the Indians. When the Oglala and Brulé subtribes—the two main groups on Pine Ridge—came onto the reservation, they camped in a great circle about three miles from the Agency and then broke up into the smaller bands or large family camps. By establishing ration-issue stations and building homes for the band chiefs in different parts of the reservation, the Agency maneuvered most of the bands into settling in separate localities. After a short time the bands broke up, and the individual families spread along the creeks. Thus a great change was made from the old camp life, with families living at close quarters and under the direction of their chiefs, to a more isolated and independent type of family life. From 1900 to 1917 this pattern of Indian homes separate from each other became crystallized by allotting individual tracts to all Indians. As many as could do so chose for their allotment the quarter section of land on which their home was located.

In spreading along the creeks of the reservation, the Indian families built log cabins and established themselves on the land much like white rural families. Slowly each family also began to accumulate a small herd of cattle and horses. In the early years of settlement many families were content to live by government rations and to spend their time in idleness, gaming, community gatherings, or riding to other homes. In order to increase their efforts toward self-support, the Agency cut down the amount of rations. The Indians were also expected to earn their rations by working on a project to fence the reservation.[21] The reduction of rations and the requirement of work to stimulate industry on the part of the Indians came at the same time that the Great Sioux Reservation was broken up and large sections were set aside for white settlement. The chiefs opposed to co-operation with the government immediately took occasion to point out that all these actions were new proof of the government's lack of good faith and its intent to cheat the Indians.

However, the process of accepting the white man's life continued to gain impetus. Missionary work spread from Pine Ridge town into the new communities, but it was many years before a large part of the population joined the churches. The government established small country schools in which the Indian children learned the three R's. After the turn of the century, the reservation population entered a long period of comparative calm, during which it became fairly well adjusted to a settled rural life and cattle-raising.

THE STORY OF THE CATTLE AND THE LAND

The raising of cattle, which became the basic economy of the reservation, began in the 1870's, when, in keeping with the local economy, the military in charge of the Pine Ridge Agency began providing the Indians with cattle. They also prevailed upon the Indians to keep the cows from the cattle supplied for ration issues. Beginning in 1871, one animal on the hoof was included in each Indian's monthly ration. During the early part of this period, however, Indians were leaving the reservation to hunt buffalo, and a great number from Pine Ridge had become embroiled in the battles of 1876 with Custer and Crook. We cannot assume, therefore, that all the Indians had become livestock owners or that those who owned cattle were livestock operators in the modern sense. They ran their cattle much as they ran their herds of ponies. However, an interest in cattle had been stimulated among those Indians who had accepted reservation life and wished to remain at peace with the white man. The first civilian superintendent, following the program initiated by the Army, issued cattle directly for the purpose of building up Indian cattle herds. He was greatly impressed and satisfied that the Indians kept the original issue and allowed the calves to mature.[22] According to official reports, there were 10,000 head of Indian cattle on the open range by 1885, and by 1912 the Indian herds had increased to 40,000 head.[23]

The continued pursuit of stock-raising, however, was interrupted by plans for other enterprises. The Allotment Act of 1887 had been passed on the assumption that, by allotting every Indian a tract of land, all of them would rapidly become civilized and self-sufficient farmers. Individual allotments were to be held in trust by the United States government for twenty-five years, in order to protect Indian interests. At the end of this period their competency to handle their own affairs would be passed upon; if the judgment was affirmative, title would be vested in the allottee in fee simple. The allotment of lands to the Pine Ridge Indians did not commence until about 1904. By 1916 the major portion of the reservation had been divided into tracts of 160 acres for each Indian regardless of age.

Although allotments were not made on Pine Ridge during the nineteenth century, there was some pressure from private and government quarters in the East upon the Pine Ridge agents from 1890 to 1900 to promote dry farming. During this period the Pine Ridge Indians suffered from various ill-advised actions of the Agency and from political schemes and fraud.

In 1900 a new agent came to the reservation and remained for seventeen years. Under his direction Indian cattle operations gained fresh impetus which resulted in a good increase of the herds. The livestock practice of this era was that of the open range, of allowing the herds to move over the reservation ranges with little supervision. Each spring and fall great roundups were held, which were important events to all the Indians. During these years the Pine Ridge Dakota became steeped in the life of the cowboy, his existence in the open, his dress, his skill with horses—all of which would be extremely attractive to people who had been great horsemen and lived the life of the Plains Indians. Rations became so unnecessary by 1914, that they amounted only to token payments.

With the beginning of World War I, cattle prices soared and the Indians were encouraged to sell their herds, and in 1916 nearly all the herds were sold off. Besides the attraction of high prices, there was pressure from white stockmen to have the Indians dispose of their cattle so that white cattle interests could lease the reservation ranges in these years of tremendous profits. Only one small lease of reservation land had been made to a white man in 1914, but by 1917 the large cattle operators had secured leases on nearly all the reservation. The remaining Indian cattle merged with the herds of the whites and were sold in the fall round-up. A new agent, who believed in leasing Indian lands, took charge in 1917. In the following year all the reservation lands went under control of whites and remained in their hands until 1921.

The loss of their cattle herds was the greatest disaster that had befallen the Pine Ridge Indians since the vanishing of the buffalo. For a second time, the basis of their economy and the foundation on which their society rested were swept from beneath them. The full effect was not felt immediately. Although there was much fraud involved, the returns from the cattle sales created a sudden wealth in cash. The Indians indulged in an orgy of spending, for their cash income from high land rentals appeared to be endless. Feverishly they began buying the gadgets of civilization, especially automobiles. For these they traded their herds of horses, often twenty-five for a car. The Indians had always kept herds of horses on the reservation, and during the last years of their cattle sales, many had invested in fine-blooded horses to improve their stock. These horse herds now disappeared rapidly, and by 1930 there was left about one horse for each Indian.[24]

In 1921 began the postwar depression that forced many cattle operators to go out of business and default on their leases. Many Indians, now without cattle to sell, were hard hit by the sudden cessation of their income from leases. Then came the opportunity to sell the land. The Competency Commission arrived from Washington to arrange for handing over title to property formerly allotted to Indians. The sale of allotments thus became possible and was even encouraged by the Agency. In accordance with a policy established by the Bureau of Indian Affairs four years previously, only persons of one-half or less Indian blood were adjudged competent. Hence the holdings of many Dakota remained intact for some time, but pressure to sell increased.

By the end of 1922 the agricultural market had recovered, and there began a feverish buying of Indian lands by land speculators and crop farmers. The government, with little thought for the Indians' future, co-operated fully. The Agency placed notices of available lands in full-page newspaper advertisements. Again high prices encouraged the Indians to sell. Without cattle to run on their land, cashing in on their allotments appeared to be a profitable piece of business. Most of the Indians felt assured that they would always be able to live on the reservation and that there would always be lands of relatives to which they could move. There was much pressure from agents of land companies and land speculators, and not a little fraud in many of the dealings. An Indian might accept forty dollars and a new suit of clothes, believing it was a down payment, only to find later that he had signed his name or put his mark on a completed deed.

The purchasers of the land were in the main promoters who were reselling it to midwestern farmers for the cultivation of flax, wheat, and other grain crops in the first dry farming to be practiced on the reservation. Although the great drought of the plains area began in 1924, it did not reach serious proportions until the 1930's, and the white farmers on the reservation continued to be successful up to the financial crash of 1929.

It was during these years that the little towns of Wanblee, Batesland, and Martin flourished as marketing centers for the farming people. The white population continued to increase on the reservation, and their influence upon the habits of the Indians began to be discernible. Indians acquired a few milk cows, chickens, and small farm livestock. The success of the white farmers encouraged the government to promote dry farming among the Indians. Seed and farm equipment were issued through a system of reimbursable loans. Thus a new economy was started on Pine Ridge; it proved to be both short-lived and disastrous.

RECENT ECONOMIC TRANSITION

The drought and depression of the 1930's wiped out almost the last of the white leases and the Indians' own efforts at dry farming or raising cattle. In one community, in 1931, the average cash income for a *family of five* was $152.80.[25] From petty capitalists, which most of the population became after the sale of their cattle herds and the leasing or sale of their lands, they now became poverty-stricken dependents on charity.

After a year of Red Cross and federal direct relief, the Indians were given wage work on relief projects. With the establishment of the Civilian Conservation Corps in 1933, special projects were set up for the employment of Indians on reservations. Since married men were enrolled in the Indian C.C.C., nearly all the able-bodied men on the Sioux reservation were on the government pay roll. Thus, as in some other very low income groups, the period of the depression was undoubtedly one of hardship, but the average income of the population was greatly increased. In the year 1939 the average individual income was $213.11, of which 50 per cent was supplied as relief wages and payments and commodities distributed by the federal government.[26] The most lasting effect of this period has been the experience of nearly all the men in a wage-work economy.

In the last seven years the government has attempted to re-establish the Indians in the cattle industry. After bitter experience the lesson has been definitely learned that this is the only permanent economy possible on the reservation lands. Yet re-establishing this economy has proved difficult. The problems arising from the inheritance of land, past sales of land within natural cattle ranges, the limitation of credit, and the greater attraction of relief wage work and recent wartime industry have all hampered the development of cattle ownership. It has been necessary for Indians who start cattle operations to receive rations for a year or two to support their families until their herds begin yielding an income.

In 1942 all C.C.C. work ended with the liquidation of the program. Thus many Indian families faced for the first time in almost a decade the problem of supporting themselves without wages or other assistance from the government. From one point of view, this has been a fortunate event for the future adjustment of the people, for they will never accept full responsibility for their own welfare until they meet and solve their own problems of making a living, but many dislocations and frustrations have accompanied the sudden change. Opportunities for defense work off the reservation had already attracted many men, particularly the former C.C.C. enrollees who had learned marketable skills. Other young men have gone into the military services, a career still exciting and highly attractive to the Sioux. Many of the families remaining on the reservation have received cattle on a repayment basis in a rehabilitation program directed by the Agency. The adjustment to this economy is far from completed as yet, but there are traditions of the past and values in both the old culture and the adopted "cowboy culture" that give promise of successful transition from one economy to another.

NOTES

1. John R. Swanton, "Siouan Tribes and the Ohio Valley," *American Anthropologist*, XLV (1943), 49.
2. George Hyde, *Red Cloud's Folk* (Norman, Okla.: University of Oklahoma Press, 1937), p. 3.
3. *Ibid.*, p. 6.
4. *Ibid.*, p. 17. A band, possibly Teton, was living on the east bank of the Missouri near the present site of Fairbanks, S.D., in 1743 (John C. Ewers, *Teton Dakota Ethnology and History* [rev. ed.; Berkeley, Calif.; U.S. National Park Service, 1938], p. 87).
5. Ewers, *op. cit.*
6. Hyde, *op. cit.*, p. 17. Ewers gives this date as 1742 or earlier.
7. Ewers (*op. cit.*, p. 87) gives this date as 1765.
8. Hyde (*op. cit.*, p. 10) infers that they had guns before 1700. This is doubtful.
9. The Teton continued to use the bow and arrow to shoot buffalo after they acquired firearms, because the sound of the guns frightened the herds (Scudder Mekeel, personal correspondence).
10. By the treaty of 1868, two-thirds of the Teton-Dakota were required to ratify any new agreements with the United States government.
11. The first civilian agents to the Teton-Dakota were selected by the Episcopal church. This arrangement was in force from 1870 to 1876, when the Army took over the Great Sioux Reservation. In 1879 the Pine Ridge Agency was established and a civilian agent appointed without church sponsorship. This agent may therefore rightly be termed the first civilian agent to the Pine Ridge Indians.

12. Clark Wissler, *North American Indians of the Plains* (New York: American Museum of Natural History, 1934), p. 124.
13. Robert Gessner, *Massacre* (New York: Cape & Smith, 1931), p. 417.
14. Scudder Mekeel, "A Short History of the Teton-Dakota," *North Dakota Historical Quarterly*, X (1943), 139.
15. The agent is still called "father" today.
16. Luther Standing Bear, *My People the Sioux* (Boston: Houghton Mifflin Co., 1928), p. 277.
17. U.S. Bureau of Indian Affairs, *Report* ...., *1904*.
18. U.S. Office of Indian Affairs, "Circular Letter 2970" (Washington, 1934).
19. Julia B. McGillycuddy, *McGillycuddy—Agent* (Stanford University, Calif.: Stanford University Press, 1941), p. 205.
20. U.S. Bureau of Indian Affairs, *Annual Report of the Commissioner, 1885.* (Italics mine.)
21. Standing Bear, *op. cit.*, p. 242.
22. Allan Hulsizer, *Region and Culture in the Curriculum of the Navaho and the Dakota* (Federalsburg, Md.: J. W. Stowell Co., 1940), p. 48.
23. *Ibid.*
24. W. O. Roberts, personal correspondence.
25. Scudder Mekeel, *The Economy of a Modern Teton Dakota Community* (New Haven, Conn.: Yale University Press, 1936), p. 9.
26. U.S. Office of Indian Affairs, "Statement of Relief and Government Provided for Indians, ... 1939."

CHAPTER III

MAKING A LIVING ON THE RESERVATION

IN TRACING the history of the Dakota, their economic adaptation through the development of a livestock industry and the actions of the government which upset this adaptation have been described in terms of local events on the reservation. The economic history of the Pine Ridge Indians cannot be considered, however, as an isolated development. The local drama of economic changes and misfortunes was part of national movements and the settling of the West; it should be seen against the total setting of the history of the plains area. It should also be appreciated that the changes which occurred were due to more than the whims of government administration.

The history of the white man on the plains has been a story of exploitation of the land, for which he has paid dearly in money, in social chaos, and in personal insecurity. It was unavoidable that the Dakota in the midst of this area should also be affected. The exploitation and climatic changes which occurred in the plains area are still affecting the making of a living on the reservation.

EXPLOITATION OF THE PLAINS

Nature has been the primary determinant of how the resources of the plains must be used by man if he wishes to remain there permanently. The climate is characterized by heavy snows and extreme cold in winter and cloudless, burning skies and extreme heat in summer. High winds blow across this country at all seasons, bringing sudden changes in temperature and severe storms. Average rainfall is twenty inches, but the amount varies greatly from year to year. Accompanying this great variation are cycles of dry and wet years, which bring periods when wresting a livelihood from the land becomes highly precarious. Knowledge of the sequence of these cycles has come only in recent years with studies stimulated by the appearance of the Great Dust Bowl.[1]

The settlement of the plains began during a wet cycle, when cattlemen started operations in the southern plains. They soon began moving their herds north until they reached the Dakotas, which became the terminus of the cattle trails. This movement began the exploitation of the northern plains. By 1890 the ranges of all the plains were probably fully stocked; by 1934 they were 100 per cent overstocked.[2] Overgrazing left the soil exposed to erosion by the high winds.

Coverage was further depleted by the plows of the farmers who followed close after the cattlemen. The first farming, in the last quarter of the nineteenth century, met with great success, for in nearly every year the rainfall was plentiful. This was the period of great westward movement of population, induced by successful crop reports and the land advertisements of speculators and railroads. The introduction of farm machinery, which permitted the cultivation of far greater acreages, brought another expansion of dry farming on the plains about 1910.

Then came the inflation of wheat prices during World War I. Dry farms spread like prairie fires, and vast acreages of grassland were plowed. Although this reduced the cattle ranges, the herds were increased to meet wartime demands for food supplies rather than decreased.

Economic collapse in 1921 and 1922 broke both the farming and the cattle industries momentarily, but the exploitation of the soil continued. In 1924 began the great drought, which reached its climax in the thirties. The damage to the land from plowing and overgrazing had already been done. When the remaining coverage failed from the lack of rain, the high winds swept down the plains and blew the soil away.

As noted in chapter ii, after the first years of settling down to the new reservation life, the Pine Ridge Dakota made a good adjustment to a cattle economy. From the reports of individual Indians, it appears that on the whole the people were also making a good social and personal adjustment. The early development of farming among the whites outside the reservation does not appear to have affected the livelihood and economic practices of the Indians greatly, but the resurgence of dry farming about 1910 had a direct effect upon the reservation. Most of the Pine Ridge Indians had received allotments by this time, but the remaining large areas of unallotted land were now declared surplus by the government. In 1911 the southeast quarter of the reservation, where only a small part of the good farming land had been allotted, was opened up to homesteaders. This section is now Bennett County. The homesteaders were kept out of the remaining portion of the reservation, but the fact that lands were again being taken away for the white man stirred the anxieties of the Indians.

This anxiety was increased by the leasing of the reservation ranges by white cattlemen after 1916 and by the sale and leasing of allotments to wheat farmers in the heretofore restricted counties. The alienation of Indian lands continued through the onset of the depression and the great drought, when white farmers began to withdraw from the reservation. It ended with the enactment of the Indian Reorganization Act of 1934.

Fortunately, the reservation land which was leased to white farmers or broken up by Indians for dry farming was not exploited and plowed up beyond the point of recovery by natural processes.[3] In a few districts severe erosion did take place, but for the most part enough vegetative cover was left to retain the soil. Since the drought, the natural grass has returned, and the future of the land as cattle range seems assured.

THE USE OF THE LAND RESOURCES

The range land is the principal resource of the reservation. The economic program sponsored by the Agency and the Tribal Council since 1937 has utilized it by the raising of livestock. In 1943 the Indians owned and operated over 22,300 head of cattle.[4]

The herds of horses also grazing on the Dakota range—about 9,000 in 1942—form a very small economic asset. In the nomadic days horses were very important to the Sioux both for hunting and warfare and for the prestige which they brought to the owner. Today fewer horses are necessary for farm work and for travel; their chief value lies in the prestige and pleasure they give, for most of them are economically unnecessary and commercially valueless. Furthermore, they utilize good pasturage which could be more productively used by cattle. Good horses are, however, necessary for cattle herding, and in recent years stallions of Morgan and other strains have been introduced through the Agency to raise the quality of the horses for livestock work. This improvement among the horse herds should create a new market product for the Indians.

Various crops are produced on sections of the reservation not used for range. On some land wild hay is grown as supplemental forage for cattle and horses. Only 12 per cent of the Indian-owned reservation land is suitable for the raising of wheat, corn, and other grain crops.[5] Hence grain farming will always remain a small part of the Indians' agricultural enterprises. In the past few years the government has developed two large irrigation projects which will increase the amount of food raised for home use. All Indians are encouraged to raise small subsistence gardens, using the soil in the creek bottoms to which water can be pumped. Cultivation of gardens and the canning of food have increased tremendously in the past few years with the return of sufficient rainfall and favorable summer weather.

WAGE WORK AND OTHER INCOME

The majority of Pine Ridge families have not yet become self-sufficient through the utilization of their land resources. For many, in recent years, it has been necessary to receive rations until their cattle begin to yield an income. Others have had to undertake some form of wage work for part of the year in order to earn money for the bare essentials of living. Many families work on the ranches and in the potato and corn fields of the white farmers outside the reservation. This practice became extensive during the 1920's, when many of the Indians had no other work and received an insufficient income from the lease of their allotments.

With the current increased demand for farm labor, more Indians have become farm workers than at any other time in their history.[6] Sugar-beet growers of South Dakota, Nebraska, Wyoming, and Colorado are sending labor recruiters into the reservation and taking Indian workers and their families to the fields by busses. This new type of agricultural work gives Indian families employment from early summer through the late fall harvesting season. With the great increase of wage rates, they are finding farm work a profitable occupation, particularly since the whole family works in the fields. Even those who have gardens and large potato or corn fields at home go out to work and return for a short time in the fall to do their own harvesting.

The recent development of military air fields and ammunition depots at Rapid City and other towns near the reservation has provided another new opportunity for wage work. Many men who have not gone into the armed forces have found employment in these construction centers. Those who received training in handling machinery, laying cement, carpentry, and the like in the reservation C.C.C. projects before the war were well prepared to enter this work at high wages.[7] There has also been much demand for unskilled labor, which has offered employment for all Indians who needed it. Although most of the Indian war workers have gone to the areas near the reservation, many of the younger men have gone to the shipyards on the West Coast, to the factories in Chicago and Detroit, and to construction work in many parts of the country. Young girls have gone in groups as far as Washington and Oregon to work in the dining-halls of the shipyards.

One effect of entering these new fields of work has been to give the Dakota a feeling of being wanted and needed in white society and an experience of living in close association with whites, although this experience has not always been successful or happy.[8] Many Dakota worked off the reservation during the last war, but they did not leave in such large numbers or enter so many different and highly skilled types of labor. Most of the present war workers are receiving the highest incomes and enjoying the best food, clothes, and living conditions in their experience.

Another effect of this new employment has been the withdrawal from, or the postponement of, participation in the agricultural economy of the reservation on the part of many families. By its higher and immediate returns, war work has been more attractive than a small cattle herd. Since the wartime employment is not expected to be permanent, it can be anticipated that most of those now at work off the reservation will return in a few years to face a new economic readjustment. Probably few of them will have savings to invest in a small cattle herd or farm,

DISTRICT COMMITTEE DISTRIBUTES RATIONS

SEASONAL WAGE WORK IMPORTANT IN THE $458 AVERAGE ANNUAL INCOME

for reports and observations in 1942 and 1943 indicated that many were spending all they earned and were intermittently employed. There have been difficulties of adjustment to the requirements of war employment, the new living conditions, and the layoffs at the end of construction projects. Many workers have already returned to the reservation, exhausted their funds in travel or at home, and subsequently departed for another job.

For those who have remained on the reservation, there has been a small amount of wage work. The Agency offers some wage work to Indians for maintenance, building roads, and driving school busses, but this work has been at a minimum in 1942 and 1943, because of the sharp decrease in appropriations to the Indian Service.

Some Indians still receive an income from the leasing of their allotments and inherited lands to other Indians and white farmers. Their number is small, and the income is seldom sufficient to maintain a family.

The sale of native craft articles has always brought a small income to a few families. At the instigation of the Education Division of the Indian Service, the Dakota are reviving the manufacture of beaded buckskin articles and learning to make pottery and weave cloth, which should in time add to the income from craftwork.

GOVERNMENT ASSISTANCE

In accordance with treaty agreements by which the Indians ceded lands, each Dakota boy and girl of eighteen receives a gift from the Sioux Benefit Fund for assistance in establishing a farm enterprise or a home.[9] In recent years the individual payment has been about five hundred dollars. The recipient was required to make a budget of needs for starting out in life. The requests were usually for cattle, horses, saddles, clothing, household furniture, a stove, wagon, or farming equipment. Occasionally the benefit allotment was used for advanced or vocational education.

The issuance of rations, originally made to all Indians in accordance with treaty terms, is now limited to families in actual need.[10] All able-bodied family heads are expected to perform some work in return for this food. Thus ration issue has become a form of relief work. The Indians, however, do not regard rations as relief but as rights established by treaty.

The needy who are sixty-five years old or over are entitled to old age assistance payments from the state of South Dakota. Since most of the old people have no source of income except small returns from leased land, the old age payments are an important part of reservation income. Aid to the blind and aid to dependent children, also administered by the state, are other sources of income to the Pine Ridge Indians.

The Dakota receive other aids which relieve them of many expenses and make their low annual income not quite so inadequate as the figures by themselves imply. Younger children at school receive clothing in exchange for their parents' work. All day-school children receive a noon meal, and those at the boarding school receive full care, relieving their families of nearly all expense for them during eight months of the year. Hospitalization and the services of doctors, dentists, and field nurses are provided by the Health Division of the Indian Service. Living on federal trust land releases the Dakota from any land tax obligation, but the state taxes owners of fee-patented allotments.

AVERAGE INCOME

The pursuits and time devoted to various fields of labor vary so widely that statistics can be considered only general estimates in presenting the picture of family income. The mean family income on Pine Ridge for 1942 was $457.90.[11] As noted in chapter ii, this is a great increase over the early depression years, when average family income in one community (neither the poorest nor wealthiest on the reservation) was $152.80. The increase in income over the ten-year period is primarily due to wage work, but the cattle industry has also contributed substantially.

Despite this increase and allowing for the provision of various services by the government, incomes on the reservation are still very low. Total income of individuals in 1942, as reported by the Office of Indian Affairs, was $1,029,823, or about $120 per capita.[12] For the state of South Dakota in the same year, the per capita income was $725.[13] Even allowing for the fact that the state figure includes urban families and for the general difference in living costs, the Indian income is very low. In Mississippi, which ranked lowest of all states in 1942 and where income of the Negro group pulls down the average, per capita income was $407.[14] The mean family income of about $458 for Pine Ridge in 1940 may be compared with the average gross value of products produced on farms in the neighboring nonreservation counties in 1940, which ranged from $837 to $1,063.[15] Both types of comparison are, of course, very rough indeed, but in spite of probable errors the wide difference between Indian and white income is strikingly apparent.

Analysis of the total income for Pine Ridge in 1942 shows that, of the total reservation income, 60 per cent was earned and 40 per cent unearned.[16] The largest single item was for wages, 43 per cent of the total; second, relief payments in cash or expended relief commodities, 25 per cent; third, agricultural receipts (predominantly from livestock and livestock products), 16 per cent; fourth, receipts from leased lands and tribal payments, 14 per cent; and miscellaneous, 2 per cent.[17] The C.C.C. wages were stopped on July 1, 1942, and many of the relief wage-workers went off the reservation for employment. The amount earned and the number of workers in farm and industrial labor will undoubtedly increase as high wages and the demand for workers continue under war conditions. Labor then must be regarded as one of the great resources of the reservation. The importance of this fact to the adjustment of Indians to changing social conditions must not be underestimated.

The sources of income of Pine Ridge Dakota are highly significant. When the preceding figures are resolved into categories of income derived from government sources, reservation resources, and private or non-Indian sources, the present extent of dependency upon the government becomes apparent. From all government sources, including wages and federal and state relief, the Pine Ridge Indians received 52 per cent of their income in 1942. From the resources of the reservation, including livestock and farming enterprises, individual leasing of land, timber sales, and annuities, the Pine Ridge people received 29 per cent of their income. From wages paid by non-Indian employers, the great majority being outside the reservation, the Pine Ridge Indians received 19 per cent of their income.

These figures should change significantly for 1943 and 1944, with the liquidation of the C.C.C. and the increase of Indian employment in industrial centers. Nevertheless, the figures reveal the supporting cushion that government operations and aid create in the economic adjustment of the Indians. Furthermore, in the present Pine Ridge economy less than one-third of all income now comes from the land resources, and wage work has become the most available and desirable single form of making a living. For a population living in a strictly rural area, where opportunities for industrial and agricultural wage work are normally very limited or irregular, a satisfactory permanent economic adjustment based on wage work becomes problematical.

NOTES

1. Great Plains Committee, *The Future of the Great Plains* (Washington: Government Printing Office, 1936), p. 3.
2. *Ibid.*, p. 4.
3. U.S. Soil Conservation Service, "Reconnaissance Survey of the Pine Ridge Indian Reservation, South Dakota" (Denver, Colo.: Technical Cooperation, Bureau of Indian Affairs, 1938), p. 7.
4. U.S. Office of Indian Affairs, "Reservation Program, Pine Ridge Indian Reservation" (1944), p. 11. (Mimeographed.)
5. *Ibid.*, p. 7.
6. See John Useem, Gordon Macgregor, and Ruth Useem, "Wartime Employment and Cultural Adjustments of the Rosebud Sioux," *Applied Anthropology*, II (1943), 1.
7. The C.C.C. project employment was the first experience of wage work for most families on the reservation (see chap. ii).
8. The adjustment of Dakota in towns and cities is described in chap. xi.
9. Granted originally with an allotment of land by the Act of 1889, which stipulated two cows, two oxen or horses, harness, farm equipment, and the like for every head of a family or single person eighteen or more years old. These payments have been continued to all persons on reaching their eighteenth birthday, under the Indian Reorganization Act of 1934. When the remaining surplus land on which technical allotments are being made is exhausted, Sioux Benefit Fund payments will end.

MAKING A LIVING 51

These allotments are made to cover legal requirements and are an exception to the general policy of the Indian Reorganization Act of 1934.

10. Beginning in 1944, the year after this study was made, rations were no longer issued in kind but through purchase orders on local merchants.

11. U.S. Office of Indian Affairs, *Individual Income, Resident Population, 1942* (Washington, 1943), Table D.

12. *Ibid.*, Table A.

13. Daniel Creamer and Charles F. Schwartz, "State Income Payments in 1942," *Survey of Current Business*, XXII (1943), 11.

14. *Ibid.*

15. *U.S. Census, 1940, Agriculture*, Vol. II. Part I, pp. 727-33, and *Housing*, Vol. II, Part V, pp. 124-37. Neighboring nonreservation counties are Bennett, Jackson, Jones, and Mellette. Value of gross product was used rather than net farm income, since the former includes the value of products used on the farm, and food produced at home is important "income" to Indians. Number of farm dwellings was used as a base, rather than number of farms or number of farms reporting, since many farm dwellings are occupied by families of laborers whose status is comparable to that of many Indians. If number of farms reporting were used as a base, average product per farm for neighboring nonreservation counties would range from $1,181 to $1,367.

16. U.S. Office of Indian Affairs, *Individual Income, Resident Population, 1942*, Table D.

17. The income received from wages requires some qualifications, for it includes wages from regular and irregular Agency pay rolls, work-relief projects, and private or non-Indian employment. The last item was roughly estimated, as there was no way to check the amount earned from all farm, industrial, and war-project employment.

CHAPTER IV

THE DAKOTA FAMILY

To UNDERSTAND the social and cultural position and the behavior and attitudes of the Pine Ridge Indians, it is necessary to know in some detail the former family and tribal organization from which the present reservation society has developed. The social organization of the Teton-Dakota changed after they came onto the plains and never became thoroughly stabilized. Roaming bands and family groups changed their allegiances to the larger divisions at will; and, at the beginning of the reservation era, leaders sprang up to create new bands, adding confusion to the limited picture we have of the old social structure.

Historical records and information gained from old men on the reservation at the beginning of the twentieth century indicate that the Teton-Dakota society was probably organized somewhat as follows.[1] The fundamental social unit was the biological family, but the family always lived with from ten to twenty related families in a small band or *tiyospaye*. The band formed an extended bilateral family or group of people related by blood and reckoning descent through both the male and the female lines. The main biological family of the *tiyospaye* was that of the chief, and all other families were related to it. In the old bands the families were usually related through the male line, for men commonly brought their wives from other bands to their family group. Occasionally the band included other families who joined either to escape some unpleasant social pressure or to become the followers of a renowned warrior. There were also larger bands of related and unrelated extended families, which maintained social unity the year round.

The bands customarily camped separately during the wintertime, but late each spring groups of bands joined in a camp circle or encampment for their annual religious ceremonial, the Sun Dance, and for the co-operative buffalo hunts. War parties were made up from men of one or several summer encampments. Each band camped in its assigned section of the circle, the band with the leading chief of the encampment pitching their tepees in the section opposite the camp entrance. The encampments are not always defined in descriptions of Dakota social organization because they were not permanent the year round and were constantly shifting in band membership. This was particularly true of the period of Indian wars with the United States Army and the first settlement at the agencies. The encampments are also confused in historical literature with the smaller bands and sometimes with the larger subtribes.

The subtribe was one of the traditional divisions of the Teton-Dakota tribe. In their eastern homeland in Minnesota it is supposed that the seven subtribes of the Teton-Dakota (Oglala, Brulé, Sans Arcs, Minneconjou, Two Kettles, Hunkpapa, Blackfeet) once lived together, possibly as seven gentes of an original tribe. By the time the Teton-Dakota became dominant on the plains of South Dakota and Wyoming, the seven subtribes were independent of each other. This was particularly true of the Oglala and the Brulé, each of which was later split into two divisions.[2] The organization of the subtribes became more confused during the historical period when bands and encampments from one or another joined together in defense or to make war against the United States Army and later settled, regardless of their origin, at the first agencies.

Today there is no tribal organization of the Teton-Dakota, and the subtribes and odd bands settled on the reservations have become new tribes or social groups. For example, the Oglala and Brulé and families from other Dakota subtribes who came into the last Red Cloud Agency and were moved to Pine Ridge[3] have now become the Pine Ridge Indians. The *tiyospaye* is the only social unit particularly characteristic of the former Teton-Dakota social structure which has remained important in the reservation society.

The Teton had a governmental organization, which was developed only among the encampments. The political pattern of one Oglala group was organized in the following manner.[4] The main political body was the Chiefs' Society composed of the heads and leaders, forty years of age or older, who elected their own members. This society elected the Seven Chiefs of the Tribe, who held office for life. The position was partially hereditary, as it was the practice to elect a son or younger relative to fill the vacancy of a deceased chief. These seven chiefs appointed the Four Shirt Wearers, the real councilors of the division, who also held office for life but could resign their position.

Four executive officers of the encampment, the *wakicun*, were also appointed by the Seven Chiefs of the Tribe to hold office for a year. It was the particular function of this group to organize and control the camp.

The four *wakicun* selected two messengers, a herald, and two *akicita*, or head police, who in turn selected two others to serve with them. The *akicita* selected a body of police, or designated a group in one of the men's societies to serve as such, to keep order in the camp. These police had much authority and disciplined severely those who upset camp life, even to killing a murderer. On the buffalo hunt this group kept the hunters in order, so that no greedy or overexcited person would run in and stampede the herd.

In each encampment were men's societies, one group from which the police were selected, a second group to which headmen belonged, and a third group of warriors. New members were elected by each society in a secret meeting, and one man might belong to several. Membership in these societies was one means of rewarding the brave in battle and the co-operative in camp life. A second function of the societies was the distribution of property by which members honored others and helped the aged and unfortunate.

This social organization was democratic in that all heads of family groups participated in the council and in the annual election of camp officers. There is some evidence to show that the four *wakicun* were the original heads of the encampment and that the great war chiefs were a development that came after the first contacts with whites in the eighteenth century. Men like Red Cloud, who achieved a great reputation during the fighting with the whites in the middle of the nineteenth century, were classed as "chiefs," although originally within the encampment organization they were only warriors who became temporary leaders during raids.

THE SYSTEM OF RELATIONSHIPS AND SOCIAL BEHAVIOR

An understanding of the organization and functioning of the biological and extended families and the modern communities rests upon a full understanding of the kinship system, which dictates relationships and the mode of social behavior between individuals of the society and thus has an important part in developing the social character of the individual.[5] To the Teton-Dakota, social relationships were and are the most important thing in life, a value which is held by many people in white society but is frequently overshadowed by the importance of material things. Expressing proper social relationships, kindness, friendliness, and considerateness[6] is the chief source of happiness of the Dakota and the means of feeling that they belong and are accepted in their group. The individual learns his relationships to other people, and the behavior he is expected to show to them, in the home.

Relatives are classified according to their generation, regardless of whether they are related through the father's or the mother's line. Collateral and lineal relatives are also classed together; for example, the father's brother is called "father" and the mother's sister is called "mother." When the relative is of another sex than the person through whom he is related, the kinship term signifies this fact: the father's brother is called "father," but the mother's brother is spoken of by another term. Children of father's brothers and mother's sisters are called "brothers" and "sisters," but those of father's sisters and mother's brothers are given different terms, which may be freely translated as "cousins." Children of brothers and sisters (in the Dakota sense) are sons and daughters, and children of "cousins" are "nephews" and "nieces." All the grandparent generations on both sides are merged together, with only difference in sex designated in the kinship terminology.

The basis of relationships and social interaction within the kinship system was and is respect. The forms of showing respect have changed, but the essential principle is the same. In the old days the expression of respect varied according to the type of relationship one held to another individual. Thus toward one's blood brothers and those who became blood brothers through ceremonial adoption, respect was shown in affection and in complete loyalty on all occasions. Respect heightened by filial devotion marked the behavior extended to one's parents, their brothers and sisters, and one's grandparents. The respect shown between brother and sister was observed by complete avoidance of all face-to-face relations, a practice which was one Dakota method of preventing incest. Respect was positively shown by a brother in giving to his sister his best war trophies, and by a sister in making moccasins for her brother and the cradle-packs for his children.

Toward one's mate, sexual love and respect were natural and expected. Sexual love of a man for his sister-in-law and of a woman for her brother-in-law was acceptable because no blood relationship existed between them. In the old society it was therefore considered proper for a man to marry his wife's sisters or his brothers' widows even though he already had a wife, but love of and marriage to one individual were considered more virtuous. Known cases of a man's marrying several sisters were in the minority. Yet because an individual could consider brothers-in-law or sisters-in-law potential mates, there was always the possibility of sexual tension and sexual relationships. The kinship system offered some release for this by permitting a joking relationship which included jokes about sex between brothers- and sisters-in-law.

The relationship between brothers-in-law also brought potential conflict because of the differences in their attitudes toward the woman through whom they were related. One behaved with great respect and avoided anything suggestive of sex toward the woman, as a sister, whereas the other enjoyed intimate relations with her as his wife. This conflict was also released through camaraderie and joking in which brothers-in-law were expected to participate, especially in public.

A man's attitude toward his parents-in-law was one of extreme respect, which became complete avoidance in relation to his mother-in-law because the two individuals concerned were of different generation and sex and because the nature of their relationships to the wife differed. A woman observed corresponding forms of behavior toward her male and female in-laws.

The actual behavior of relatives today has been greatly modified by the changed economy and social life and the influences of the white social system. The modification seems to be toward the behavior pattern of the white family; but the Indian pattern has not been completely abandoned, and it gives insight into the contemporary social structure on Pine Ridge.

THE BIOLOGICAL FAMILY

The biological family of father, mother, and children merged with the extended family group with which it lived, hunted, and shared its food and social life. It was not the exclusively important group, as it is regarded usually by white people. Today, however, the individual family has risen in importance, largely because it has become the essential economic unit in the livestock, farming, and wage-work economies which the Pine Ridge Indians have successively followed on the reservation. The individual family was also forced into greater importance because of the white man's administration, which dealt directly with these units following the concept of white social organization. Although cattle and land were issued to individuals, it was expected that they would be operated and utilized by the biological family.

The family now lives with greater independence of related families in its own farm home. The father, as head of the family, is usually its chief support, but, as noted in previous chapters, his work is often irregular and not usually devoted to a single occupation. The circumstances which have made it impossible for the men to work steadily as cattlemen or farm laborers or to produce a regular income have affected their status and respect within their own families. Frequently it has been necessary for the mothers to earn wages to keep the family fed and clothed. This has increased the importance of the mother in the family, a change which has altered the children's relationships to both parents. The new relationships are particularly apparent in the present training of the children in the home and development of children's personalities which are to be described in detail in following parts of the study.

The ideal parent-child relationship among the Dakota is and always has been one of deep-seated affection; the small child is granted almost complete indulgence, which develops in him an affectionate loyalty to the parents. From an early age, the parents regard the child as an individual with responsibility for his own actions and in return they demand from him much co-operation. Most training is accomplished by rewarding the child for doing the desired thing.

As the child grows older, his parents' respect for his individuality and his responsibility to himself increases.[7] Mothers plead with fairly young children to give up school for a few days and go to a dance with them. The respect for the child's independence and decisions is most marked. Mothers say: "I ask her opinion." "You know she is eighteen years old and a woman of her own. If she don't go back to school, I can't help it." "I didn't because my boy didn't want me to."

Formerly the father assumed some of the training and disciplining of the boys, which was the basis of an intimate bond. This most important relationship between father and son—developing from the training of a boy for his economic and social role—has been badly dislocated by cultural changes. Compared to their position in the former nomadic life, the majority of fathers have no career and little social role to which they can introduce a son. A man may have a small herd of cattle or horses which a boy learns to care for early in his life, but there are now few special techniques which the father can pass on to his son. By the time a boy is fourteen or fifteen he can compete with his father as a common wage-earner. The father's role of teacher has been minimized not only by the disappearance of the men's former occupations and goals in life but also by the introduction of schools among the Dakota. Even the fathers who do not desire the white man's life for themselves appreciate the fact that it will be to their children's advantage to understand this way of living. They want the school to give their children such understanding and send them to school with this expectation.

The boy growing up in a Dakota family today does not appreciate the difference in the relationship that exists between his father and himself and that which existed between his great-grandfather and grandfather. He does, however, become aware of his father's lack of a continuous occupation and of the absence of a real career in which his father and the men of his community might offer him some participation. They have given him social drives, but modern Indian society offers little reward that produces a feeling of achievement. He has been pushed to early adulthood. Arriving at its threshold, he finds himself on an equal footing with the men of his community but, like them, without status or life-purpose.

The mother is the center of the present-day family, because she has assumed greater responsibility for its direction and support. The mother's role has also gained by the present isolation of the individual household. Formerly the family lived in a camp with several other related families, with whom the child associated freely. Now the child living in a farmhouse on an allotment is forced to spend much more time with his own family and especially with his mother. One small full-blood boy described very aptly the mother's position in the family by pointing to an ear of corn which had six small kernels sprouting from one end, "Mother, the ear of corn is like you, and the little things are the children."

The early attachment to the mother often becomes so strong that it is carried through adulthood. One man states, "My son gets lonesome when he is away from his mother." "My wife is that way, too," he adds complainingly; "she does not like to live away from her folks. I have a nice place, but she is like a sucking colt to stay so close to her mother." Mother-daughter relationship is commonly a very lasting one, and, after marriage, the daughter is constantly returning home to visit, to have her babies, or to help her mother in emergencies.

Although the observed mother-child relationships appear in general to be very pleasant and close to the ideal of affection and respect, there are mothers whose relationships to their children are bad according to Dakota standards and those of good mental hygiene as well. Observers in this study heard mothers call their children "dumb," "crazy," or a "crybaby." One mother had to be stopped by the school principal from beating her child with her fists, because she heard that a teacher called the child "Public Enemy No. 1." Enraged little boys were also seen striking their mothers.

There are other mothers who appear indifferent toward their childen. Two small childen were found who did not know their mother, although they lived at their grandmother's home less than five miles away from her. Some mothers have deserted their husbands and children to live with other men. On the other hand, children who find relationships with their mothers intolerable run away to live with other relatives. Children were permitted to leave their tepees in the old days, but such behavior in the old culture was considered a great affront to the parent's reputation.[8] The frequency with which children are now voluntarily living away from their parents' home without disapproval by the adults may be looked upon as symptomatic of cultural breakdown.

The stepmother has now entered the Teton-Dakota kinship system as an important factor. In the former society where it was the practice to marry one's wife's sisters, children whose mother had died found someone, whom they already called mother, ready to take the real mother's place. Plural marriage and the custom of marrying the deceased wife's sisters are no longer common practice. Today stepmothers are often strange and unrelated to the children, and the relationships between them are not always happy ones. The stereotyped attitude toward the stepmother in white society is being accepted by some Dakota. One woman said to an interviewer in this study, "Stepmothers are supposed to be mean." Although some stepmothers have proved to be very affectionate, it is quite common among older children to go to the home of an aunt or grandmother or leave the reservation when a stepmother enters the home. Very often, a family attempts to solve the friction by sending the children to a boarding school.

In cases of separation from their wives, fathers often seem particularly indifferent about their children, leaving them for the wife or grandparents to support, without regard for the wife's or grandmother's ability to do so. In leaving the children with the wife, the fathers are following customary practice, but in the past there were the wife's relatives and the families of her band circle to help feed a few more mouths.

The relationship between brothers has been described as the strongest in the Teton-Dakota kinship system.[9] This is still manifest, and brothers are close comrades and playmates.[10] In the former life the older brother undertook the training of the younger in many of the technical skills of men. Brothers today retain their close attachment throughout life, helping one another in the fields, sharing food, and bringing their children to one another's homes. In a crisis brothers join forces as they did in the past. One Indian stockman said, "If I have trouble with somebody, then all my brothers here would come to help me, and there would be big trouble."

The relationship between sisters has always been similar to that between brothers. If sisters live in the same community, they usually maintain an intimate friendship all their lives. The strongest devotion is expressed by accepting the care of the other's children, particularly at the death of one sister. Sisters, like brothers, are close playmates where the age differences are not great. The group of sisters also includes the girl cousins, some of whom are called "sister" in the Dakota kinship system.

The present behavior between brother and sister is one of the most marked changes from the kinship pattern of the former culture. The old avoidance has disappeared, but mutual respect is still observed. Little girls of six or seven, who were formerly taught to avoid their brothers, now may sleep in the same bed with them. They ride to school in the same busses, they play and fight together, and older brothers even accompany younger sisters to dances when their parents cannot act as chaperons. Loyalty to the sister is still strong. This was observed in the present study in the fights of young boys over insults to their sisters and in the behavior of an older man who attempted to avenge his sister's murder. The pattern is approaching that of white children in both the mixed-blood and the full-blood families, but the taboo against intimacy between brother and sister is not lost entirely among the latter. In the modern Rabbit Dance, performed by couples, neither full-blood brothers and sisters nor those classed as such in the Sioux kinship system will dance together.

The baby of the family is always privileged and deferred to by the older children and by the parents. In the interviews with parents, comments were constantly made about the youngest child in the family, and interviewers often observed the "babying" of the youngest child. Once a little girl was seen pulling a toilet pot from under her older brother, making him sit down hard. He immediately pulled her to the floor. Instead of rebuking the instigator, the mother's reaction was, "Shame on you. You pulled her down and she's just little." This petting of the youngest child continues beyond infancy for the one who is never superseded by later additions to the family. Older children share candy, food, and toys with the youngest child more than they do with each other. An older sister was seen to leave the room where she was reading rather than correct her youngest sister of eight who was pushing a toad at her. Of an eleven-year-old girl, her mother said, "The other children made a lot of her because she is the baby." Age differences also make some differences in parents' attitudes. Another mother said: "I guess she is spoiled. There was four years between her [the last] and the next older."

THE EXTENDED FAMILY

The Dakota still do not draw as distinct a line as do white people between the family of father, mother, and children and the group of relatives consisting of grandparents, uncles, aunts, cousins, nephews, nieces, grandchildren, and more distant blood relations who form the extended family. In the old extended family group or *tiyospaye* camp, a man's tepee usually stood next to that of his married brother, and in front might be the tepee of a married son. Family homes are geographically widely separated today in comparison with the band camp, and the associations within an extended group are less frequent and intensive; but the individual usually does have a few members of his extended family close by. Grandparents may be living in a tent beside the house, with brothers or sisters as the nearest neighbors. Frequently a relative not belonging to the biological family may be living in the home. All these relatives in the family circle for the most part continue to maintain the relationships of the kinship system.

The grandparents exemplify the ideal of kindliness and generosity of the old Sioux culture. The grandfather, formerly a counselor to the young, still attempts to continue this function, but his prestige has declined because he can no longer participate in activities formerly carried on by the older men and because he does not understand the changing ways.

The grandmother who was a "second mother" in the old society, taking over the hard work of the household for her daughters during their childbearing period and sharing the care of the new grandchildren,[11] continues this role today. Her major responsibility is looking after the smaller children when the parents are busy. This may last at times for several weeks while the parents are working in the harvest fields. The affection of the grandmother and her freedom from the permanent and complete responsibility for the children make for an exceedingly pleasant and lifelong relationship. Adult grandchildren reciprocate her devotion during their early childhood by sending home money and gifts to "the old people."

A HOME ON THE RANGE

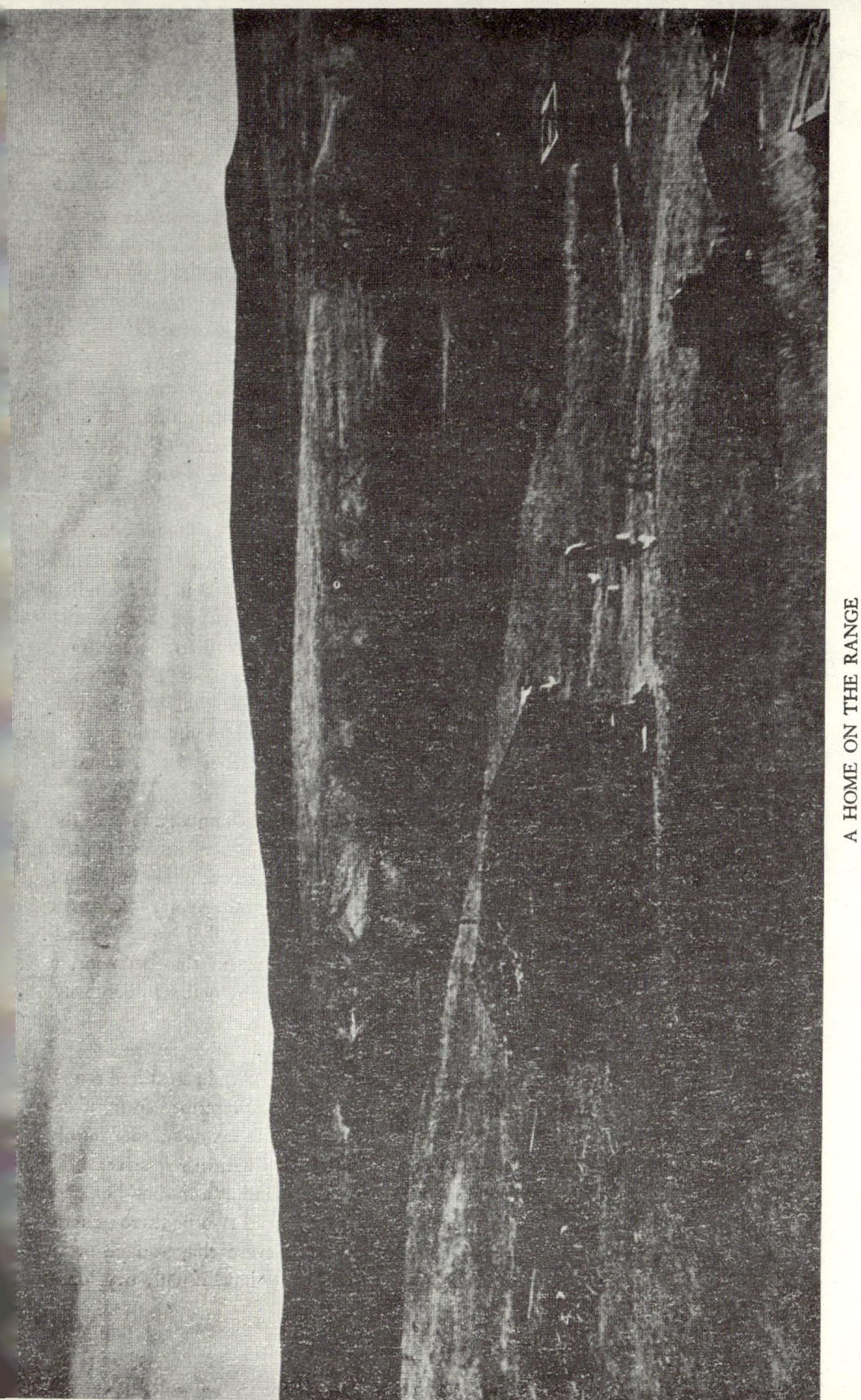

The grandmother who will give or do anything for her grandchild is a person to whom the child turns when in need and in times of crisis. When a divorced person finds his children difficult to care for, he usually regards the grandmother's home as a place where they may be left. The generosity and kindness of the grandmother are sometimes abused by young people, who, when they are old enough to support themselves, will visit grandparents for a long period of time without contributing to the household and expect to be supported by the old people's rations or old age assistance check.

It is difficult to ascertain how much of the kinship terminology that embraces the extended family is now used by the present youngest generation, for they have learned English terminology, which they use in the presence of white people. Some children draw a clear distinction by saying to a white person, "That is my father—of course, he is really only my uncle—but we call him 'father' in Indian." Another child will say, "My mother is here for me," if he believes this is the stronger argument for being excused from class, but in another circumstance he will mention the same individual as his aunt. Other children use the English kinship terms at home, calling the "fathers" and "mothers" of the extended family "uncles" and "aunts" and behaving toward them differently than toward their own fathers and mothers. This change is more marked among the mixed-blood people, because of their greater use of English and the classifications which white relatives make. The adoption of English kinship terminology appears to be a strong factor in breaking down the ties and behavior patterns of the extended family organization.

Among full-blood families which still speak Siouan, the language aids in the preservation of the old terminology and related behavior. When members of the extended family live as neighbors, they continue to act according to the role of their relationship position. Thus a child born into such a group receives treatment as a son, a grandson, or a brother from those he is taught to call "father," "grandfather," or "brother." If the younger people appear lax in this behavior, a grandparent will often reprimand them for not adhering to the Indian way.

THE CONJUGAL FAMILY

Under the old kinship system, when an individual married, he acquired a new set of relatives—the affinal—toward whom he observed a prescribed form of behavior based on his relationship to a person of the opposite sex of another family and on potential sex relationships and ensuing conflicts with his relatives. The behavior of a young man and woman before marriage and as a husband or wife is now markedly different from that which they observed two or three generations ago. Courtship is no longer conducted under severe chaperonage or in momentary escapes from it. Friendship and congeniality have usually developed between the couple at school or in the neighborhood, and the feeling of being strangers to each other that formerly existed is overcome.

Marriages are now made with little or no family sanction or symbolic expression of contract between the two families or the two persons involved. Formerly the man made gifts to the girl's parents, and his father's sisters and mother's brothers' wives equipped the new tepee of the couple with the necessary furnishings. Marriages of social importance were celebrated with an elaborate feast and religious performance. Today, the couple are married by a local missionary or a justice of the peace outside the reservation. The couple are more likely to announce that they are going to be married than to ask permission, and the man makes no gift payment.

It is usual for the couple to live at first with the parents of one or the other. The custom of the bride's gradually entering into the women's work of her husband's home or, if in her own home, of transferring the heavy household work to her mother and devoting her time to the lighter craftwork, has disappeared. Most couples soon establish a home of their own and often leave the reservation for work.

This change toward the independence of the young married couple is not being made, however, without some tension between the couple or with their own families. The co-operation of a strongly knit extended family is still an ideal. The desire of the man to set up an economcially independent home may conflict with his wife's desire to be near or with her relatives.[12] This may be overcome by constant visiting or returning to live among her people. Similarly, a man who has attempted to keep a job or operate a farm independently may feel compelled to return to the family homestead to help out.

The high respect and avoidance patterns between persons of different generations who are related through marriage have been described previously. This complete formality was not observed in any of the homes during the field work of this study, yet the feeling of distance, particularly by older women toward their sons-in-law, was occasionally apparent. Some women would address a son-in-law only on trivial matters or in an unavoidable emergency. One woman was seen shouting directions from a distance to her son-in-law who was building her a house, because there was no one to relay her wishes. The restriction upon in-laws of different generations and sex traveling or appearing in public together is in greater force, revealing that any suggestion of intimacy is still regarded as improper. The fact that the parents frequently live in a tent beside the home of one of their married children may be an effort to observe a certain amount of avoidance. The strength of this old avoidance taboo now varies from family to family. Sons- and daughters-in-law seen sitting in the homes conversing with the older people indicate that this pattern of avoidance among them is passing.

The relationship and pattern of public joking between brothers- and sisters-in-law is also varying with the changing marital relationships. Although the privilege of the joking relationship is utilized by some men as a sexual outlet toward sisters-in-law, the ideal relationship now rests upon the respect held for a sister and another man's wife. However, the old attitude that a sister-in-law was a potential mate and an individual with whom one might joke on sexual matters has led to illicit sex relations. Some women openly live with their husband's brothers while the husbands are absent and even boast that some of their children were born of such affairs.

The loyalty and co-operation that one gives and expects from blood relatives continues to function between relatives by marriage in the same generation. This extends beyond immediate brother- and sister-in-law. Remarks are commonly heard, such as, "My sister-in-law's brother took care of my cattle while I was away," or "My boy is helping So-and-so. He is my sister-in-law's sister's son; that is why he is helping him." These indicate that even the extended affinal relationships are still counted upon.

The most notable aspect of in-law relationships that comes to light from interviews is the expression of hostility. This is undoubtedly not new to the Teton-Dakota, for affinal relatives have always been outsiders to the extended family and have been received at least with reservations by some members. One function of the old avoidance pattern was to control such outbreaks. Some older women today pride themselves in never criticizing or even discussing with a daughter-in-law her affairs, even though a divorce may be imminent. However, these older women will freely gossip with others about their daughter-in-law's behavior. Misbehavior of children, accidents, and even death are openly traced to the daughter-in-law or son-in-law and other individuals in the affinal set of relatives. In this behavior there appears the solidarity felt toward one's own extended family and the potential jealousy and resentment felt toward other relatives with whom the only connection is through marriage.

NOTES

1. Dakota social organization has been treated more fully by Donald Collier, "Plains Camping Groups" (MS); Scudder Mekeel, *The Economy of a Modern Teton Dakota Community* (New Haven, Conn.: Yale University Press, 1936); Jeannette Mirsky, "The Dakota," in *Cooperation and Competition among Primitive Peoples*, ed. Margaret Mead (New York: McGraw-Hill Book Co., 1937); Clark Wissler, *Societies and Ceremonial Associations of the Oglala Division of the Teton-Dakota* (New York: American Museum of Natural History, 1912).
2. George Hyde, *Red Cloud's Folk* (Norman, Okla.: University of Oklahoma Press, 1937), p. 11.
3. See chap. ii.
4. Wissler, *op. cit.*, chap. i.
5. This section is based largely upon information from Fred Eggan, "The Cheyenne and Arapaho Kinship System," in *Social Anthropology of North American Tribes*, ed. Fred Eggan (Chicago: University of Chicago Press, 1937); Royal B. Hassrick, "The Teton-Dakota Kinship System" (MS); and Mirsky, *op. cit.*

6. Such behavior was given supernatural sanction by the White Buffalo Maiden in the mythical ceremony described in the section on Dakota ceremonies in chap. vii. See also the section on standards for women in chap. viii.

7. This respect for the child's accountability to himself for his own actions is difficult for white people to understand and is often interpreted by them as indifference on the part of Indian parents to their child's behavior. Parents do not force their children to conform because "mother knows best" or to avoid damaging the parents' reputation or self-esteem. A child who runs away from school is usually not asked why he came home. Likewise, the grown son who leaves the reservation and is not heard from for years is rarely questioned on his return about what he has been doing.

8. Cf. Mirsky, *op. cit.*, p. 425.

9. *Ibid.*, pp. 394-95.

10. This is also true today of "brothers" in the extended family.

11. Mirsky, *op. cit.*, p. 397.

12. See the previous section of this chapter on the bond between mother and children.

CHAPTER V

RESERVATION COMMUNITIES

Nowadays the old *tiyospaye* no longer exist as organized units, but they are the bases of most of the rural communities. There are also on the reservation communities of related mixed-blood people and villages which have not developed from the native social groups. The difference in origin of full-blood and mixed-blood communities can be found in the desire to cling to either Indian or white lines of descent and ways of living.

THE FULL-BLOOD RURAL COMMUNITIES

As people from the eastern woodland area, the Teton-Dakota were undoubtedly drawn to the wooded creek valleys for their camp sites when they first entered the plains. Fuel and water were plentiful, and the cottonwood and elder growth offered shelter from the high winds. When the Indians spread from their first camp at the Agency over the reservation in the 1880's, they settled by bands along creeks according to custom. The new band camps were not maintained for long, however, for individual families began building permanent homes up and down the creeks. The extended family group which formerly erected its lodges together now stretched in a line of separated homes. When a family increased, an older man might take his children and perhaps the families of his brothers and sisters to some distance below the original band site or to another creek and form another group, which ultimately developed into a separate community. This followed the process by which new bands were created in the former society. Most of the present-day reservation communities are thus derived from original bands.[1]

The first reservation camp sites chosen by a band may be marked now by the old chief's house, which was built by the government, or by a round dance hall. Such is the case in the Kyle area, where the major part of the present study was undertaken. A few houses have been built near the old sites, but there is no evidence of anything resembling a village or clustering of the homes of the descendants of the band. In one Kyle community, American Horse, a son of the old band chief lives in the two-story frame house built for his father. His brothers and sisters live in log cabins on their individual allotments a quarter to a full mile apart along the creek. Below them is the home of a white rancher who leases Indian land. Continuing down the creek for ten or twelve miles are the homes of Indian families, each now on its allotment. Every three or four homes belong to a group of brothers and sisters and their families, forming an extended family neighborhood.

This pattern of the extended family living on adjoining lands was created in part by the allotment system, when a man, his wife, and children received adjoining allotments of land. As the children grew up and married, they built their homes on their own allotments, thereby retaining the family grouping and establishing a family neighborhood. Other members of the original band also received allotments along the same creek, so that the descendants of the band have maintained a community grouping. All these families can trace their common relationship to the original large extended family group; but, with each new generation and the growing importance of the individual family, the common relationship becomes weaker and less meaningful. The new family neighborhoods are developing into independent extended family groups.

A second distinct community in the Kyle area was formed by Thunder Bull, a lesser chief of the American Horse band. He led his immediate relatives from the first camp site to another creek where they and their descendants received their allotments.

A third community of the Kyle area is composed of the descendants of the band of Little Wound, one of the leading chiefs of the Oglala. This community is now spread over a long valley drained by two creeks. Along these creeks there are developing new extended family groups which are becoming independent of the larger community. One of these groups, whose members are nearly all full-bloods, has formed a cattle association and has pooled land for a joint range. All the men of this association are relatives either by blood or by marriage. This particular development, which has been duplicated several times on the reservation, reveals the continuing strength and importance of the extended family.

There is much social as well as economic participation within the modern extended family neighborhood. The women are frequently seen at work together or chatting in one home or under a bough-covered shade. The small children who form a group of brothers, sisters, and cousins play together around a single house. The men not only share their labor and form economic groups but also meet in one another's homes to discuss local events, programs proposed by the government, or problems of the community.

The cohesion among the members of each community has been maintained in part through the ties and mutual obligations of blood and marriage relationships. Social events, such as a Rabbit Dance or a party for a departing soldier, bring together the individuals of the total community to share in the feasting and to give presents in honor of the person being feted. Funerals also are occasions when all relatives come together, reuniting especially the community group. At Kyle each large community has its church and church community house for social affairs. There is an Episcopal church in American Horse and in Little Wound, and Thunder Bull has a Catholic chapel. Each church has a community house for social affairs. The government also built a neighborhood house in the Thunder Bull community during its recent rehabilitation program. The round dance hall built in the early days at the Little Wound camp site still serves as a community center for Indian dances. Most of the reservation communities also use the day school for community meetings and entertainments. All these institutions and religious and social gatherings function to preserve the unity of the community.

On the other hand, several factors, such as the geographic separation of families and the development of new extended family groups, have led to the disintegration of original band grouping. The individual and the individual family can, if they desire, support themselves on a farm or by wage work without the assistance of others and can find companionship and social life outside the community. Individuals are now frequently leaving the group to live and work elsewhere. Such separation of the individual from his or her relationship group rarely took place in the old days, except by moving away with one's entire family or joining another band by marriage.

The band integration has also been weakened by the decline of Indian leadership and the passing of the functions of government to the Agency. The newly formed Tribal Council, which exercises some measure of local self-government, has not restored integration or local control to the community, for representation is based on the government-formed district.[2] The loosening of Indian social and political organization and the absence of full recognition by the government of either the existing native communities or their traditional functions and continuing potentialities for economic social and political organization and development are producing community disintegration. This disintegration and the development of individualism are resulting in insecurity for the group and the individual which are major problems of Dakota adjustments to reservation and white life.

THE MIXED-BLOOD RURAL COMMUNITIES

The preceding description of community development and organization has been concerned with the Indian community which is typical of the rural areas of the reservation. There are also two other types on the reservation—the mixed-blood and the village communities—which have no roots in the old bands.

In the Kyle area there are two rural communities of predominantly mixed-blood people in addition to Kyle village itself. One community is descended from a group of Spanish and Mexican men who came to the reservation as traders from New Mexico, later marrying Sioux women and settling among the Indians. Their wives and their children received allotments along Three-Mile, or Spanish, Creek, and their descendants have remained there. The Indian pattern of extended family group co-operation is strong among them. There is exchange of labor in managing cattle, building homes, canning food, or breaking horses, visiting and working together at one another's homes, and taking care of one another when sick. The children move easily from one home to another for a meal or to spend the night.

On the other hand, many things about this community distinguish it from full-blood communities like Thunder Bull and American Horse. Some of the homes are made of logs, but they usually have more rooms than the average full-blood's cabin. There are more tables, chairs, beds, clocks, and decorations, which show a home life and interest in property that is closer to the rural white pattern than to the Indian. In the operation of their cattle and horse herds and their farms, these mixed-blood families are highly individualistic. They exchange labor, but they wish to operate on their own land, to buy and sell individually, and not to form associations. In this, too, they follow the pattern of the rural white people of the region. The community has a Catholic chapel which is attended mainly by the local mixed-blood people. They organize their own Sunday afternoon rodeos and baseball games and have their own little orchestra of fiddle, guitar, and concertina for community dances. The parent generation grew up speaking Siouan and Spanish and learned English in school. The children speak English, which is now the language of the community, and know little Siouan and less Spanish. It is characteristic of the children in this community to finish high school and take some vocational or college training. These people have married whites and other mixed-bloods, especially members of the second mixed-blood community in Kyle.

This community along the White River in the Badlands area near Kyle is descended from English, French, and Spanish traders, trappers, and pioneers who came on the reservation when it was first established; nearly all its members are now related through intermarriage. They raise cattle and horses and farm small gardens and live much like the poorer white ranchers on the reservation. Several of these mixed-blood families have frame and rammed-earth houses which are superior to any homes found in the full-blood communities.

These ranchers and their fathers before them have carried on independent cattle businesses. In the years before World War I they had big herds of cattle. When they sold their herds, they had large sums of cash for a short time. Some also sold their lands; others leased and then entered dry farming. In the financial crash of 1922 several of these families became bankrupt and lost most of the land which they had held in fee simple. Some were forced to leave the community; others were able to carry on with a small amount of farming and, later, wage work. Since about 1937 they have built up their herds and are advancing toward economic independence.

In 1942 the Army took over a strip of land along the northern border of the reservation that included the allotments of this mixed-blood community. Some of the families moved into Kyle village and others into the Three-Mile Creek community; still others leased land in the full-blood communities. The families in the rural areas have built new homes and moved their stock onto the new lands. In a few years they should be re-established as independent ranchers.

Kyle village is composed of several Indian families, a few resident whites who farm and run stores, and a group of government employees. The Indian residents have homes in the other communities but have moved into the village to work for the traders or the government. This Indian population is always in flux. During the years of relief work and the construction of the day school at Kyle, there were many more families, but most of them have returned to their homes to raise cattle and plant gardens or have left the reservation for war work. There is no integration of the Indian residents of the village because they do not share a common blood relationship, which is the basis of close social interaction among the Dakota. Each family of the village carries on its most intimate relationships with relatives in the outlying communities. If a family has no such relatives, it remains somewhat isolated and on only superficial social terms with its neighbors. There are also a few related mixed-blood families living on the outskirts of the village who farm and run a few dairy cows.

The village is situated at the confluence of three small streams which form Medicine Root Creek, the main stream in the area. The Indian communities extending along the small streams therefore also converge on the village, so that it is a geographical and integrating center. The offices of the Indian Service farm agent and doctor, the district school, the ration commissary, the post office, a store, and a small café are also located in the village, making it the political, commercial, and official center for the communities as well. The life of the village revolves around these several institutions.

The most important single establishment of the village is the trader's store, the only place in the area where groceries, clothing, and general merchandise can be purchased. The store serves as the local communication center. Here notices of community dances, of feasts for visiting soldiers, and of church bingo parties and government activities are posted. The store is also the post office, where letters are opened and the contents reported to relatives or other interested listeners. The place is usually full of Indians, who have come to make a purchase or get the mail and stay on to gossip with friends. It is also a vantage point to watch the coming and going of government employees, especially those driving in from the Agency.

WATCHING THE WORLD GO BY

Any bits of official news, reports on the war, or gossip about unusual activity of any individual or family are passed about and later carried into communities. As many of the Indians, particularly the men, have a great deal of idle time on their hands, they have ample opportunity to sit around for purely social purposes.

Across the street is a second communication center, a little restaurant which also sells candy and gasoline. Everything and everybody are discussed: the latest activities and treatment by officials at the Agency, the complaints and resentment reported by Indians, and the developments of the war.

A Catholic church in the town serves the local people and those close by in the rural communities. A priest from the central mission conducts services here on alternate Sundays. Occasionally a bingo party or cake sale is held in the church basement by the local Catholic guild. The church also owns a building of five or six rooms which it rents to older homeless people and locally employed families.

The school–farm office–clinic–store–church nucleus is one which appears with all or some of its elements as a center for each district which the government has organized on the reservation. The village center at Kyle is one of the larger and more important of these centers because it serves a large district of several rural communities.

THE RESERVATION TOWNS

The town of Pine Ridge as the official center, with a large number of government employees and a local population of mixed-blood wage-workers and white and Indian tradesmen, has a composition and function unique on the reservation. In addition to its offices and employee quarters, the government maintains the reservation hospital and the Oglala Community High School, a primary and secondary school for boarding and local day pupils. The heads of the Protestant missions on the reservation also live at Pine Ridge. The Catholic church maintains a parish and parish priest in the town, but the center of its work is at the Holy Rosary Mission, about five miles north of Pine Ridge, where it maintains a large twelve-grade boarding school.

The town is situated a few miles north of the Nebraska line in the southwest quarter of the reservation. A state highway, running north from Rushville, Nebraska, to the Black Hills, divides Pine Ridge into two sections. The west half of town is the official area of the Agency, the school, and the residences of the government employees. The government hospital is also on this side of the highway on a hill overlooking the town. An American Legion hall and the local county public school are the only non-federal buildings in the official area.

On the east side of town are the churches and missionaries' home, the local hotel, the traders' or general country stores, a few cafés, a drug store, a hairdresser's shop, and two gasoline stations. The local Indian population, many of whom are employed as irregular laborers and assistants by the Agency, also live in this part of Pine Ridge. Their small houses, built close together on small assignments of government reserve land, range in style from small stucco cottages, with flag poles in the yards and pathways lined by whitewashed stones, to tar-papered shacks and disintegrating log cabins. The appearance of the house is a good index of the occupant's prosperity and his degree of assimilation into white ways.

A large majority of the local Indians have less than one-half Indian blood. As a group they prefer wage work to farming. They want homes of their own and education and training for their children, so that they may also get jobs and advance in the white social scale. These Indian residents are nearly all newcomers who moved in from the reservation and from the outside during the years of the depression to obtain relief wage work at the Agency. Since the cessation of this employment, many have left the town for war-work centers. The remaining group has become the most assimilated (in terms of behavior, attitudes, and desire to become like white people) of any group in the reservation proper. They follow in general the pattern of life of the white people of the lower-income group of any South Dakota town.

There is very little Indian custom to be observed in the life of Pine Ridge; such as there is, is followed by the oldest generation. Most of the Pine Ridge residents, however, are proud of their Indian blood, as may be observed in the satisfaction they take in the success of Indians in the war and the outside world.

The social life of the town is almost as sharply divided as its official and nonofficial areas. The Agency employees, with the exception of local people, are a group sent in by the government. They are frequently transferred to other parts of the reservation or to other reservations, so that they have few roots in Pine Ridge. They are placed on the reservation to teach the Indians or perform other functions for the Indians' welfare, and hence they feel somewhat apart. This gap is widened by their higher incomes and standard of living, for most of the employees come from a higher economic, educational, and social status than most of the Indians or resident whites and wish to maintain that status. Thus by both their official standing and their social status in terms of white society, the government officials, whether they wish to be or not, are placed in a superior relationship to the Indians.

The employees and residents of the town mix socially to some degree in the community affairs and entertainments which the boarding school sponsors. The two weekly moving pictures and the bowling matches, which are open to the public, and the meetings of the women's club and the parent-teacher association are the most important of these functions. The employees attend the churches and church social affairs and occasional meetings or dances sponsored by the people of the town. There are also some informal social relations between the schoolteachers and residents of the town. The small group of women teachers married to local men and living on the east side of the town are an important link between employees and the local population.

There is also a group of local white people who have many close friends among the more well-to-do and educated Indians, and marriages take place between these two groups. These white people have in many ways more influence than the official group upon the type of modern life which the Indian people are adopting. The Indians can mix upon more equal terms with them as neighbors, attend the same churches, and have similar homes and living standards.

There are a few other small towns in the reservation where Indians have settled. The town of Wanblee is in the center of the northeastern quarter of the reservation, about a hundred miles from Pine Ridge. Most of the Indians here belong to the sociological full-blood group. They have their Indian camp or quarter where many live during the winter, while their children attend the local Indian school. There are also a few families of white men with wives of a small degree of Indian blood. During the depression and recent war years, most of the white population departed. In 1943 the county was forced to close the Wanblee public high school and send the few remaining children to another town.

Martin, in ceded Bennett County, is a larger town, although it, too, has suffered from the movement of people to areas with more employment opportunities. Many mixed-blood people have settled here and in the surrounding country. People of Indian blood hold positions in the town as clerks in the store, post office, and bank and as clergymen. The assimilation of the mixed-blood people can be seen functioning under more natural conditions in Martin than in Pine Ridge because they can move fairly easily into business and social life, without the limitations of civil service and the social status that accompanies it.

THE DISTRICT

Pine Ridge Reservation is divided into six districts, which were established in the 1880's for issuing rations to the several groups of Indian bands. All the Indians of a district were required to go to their district ration station for beef and other supplies. The district lines followed the watersheds so that all the Indians within a single system of creek valleys were grouped in a natural geographic area.

In the development of the agricultural extension program by the Indian Service, these districts were employed as areas which each farm agent or assistant could supervise with a fair amount of ease traveling by horse or by car. The districts have been used by other Agency divisions as areas of service, but areas vary with the division. The doctor at Kyle, in the Medicine Root District, also serves a second district. The Little Wound Day School at Kyle, one of the two consolidated rural schools on the reservation, receives children from all the major communities of the Medicine Root District except Potato Creek, which has its own day school.

The districts have also been made the political divisions of the reservation under the Pine Ridge Tribal Constitution drawn up under the Indian Reorganization Act. The districts send representatives to the Tribal Council and have their own local councils. Although this brings self-government into the district, it has not been always satisfactory, for the district is artificially created and is not a native social grouping.

The field agent of the Indian Service Extension Division is the only official who serves Medicine Root District exclusively. His work is primarily concerned with the development of agricultural enterprises among the Indians, including the supervision of the livestock and property acquired through government loans and the issuing of permits to slaughter or sell animals on which the government has any lien. In actual function, the farm agent acts as a local field representative for the Agency, distributing pay-roll and other government checks, investigating complaints of trespass on land, giving out information on government forms and procedures, settling family disputes, and making telephone calls and writing personal or business letters for the Indians. He is the information center in all matters which the Indians do not comprehend and their personal representative in relations with the Agency.

This work is shared by the school principal. As supervisor of community welfare and adult education and dispenser of the monthly rations, the principal has also become an individual to whom the Indians go for much assistance and advice.

The doctor holds a weekly clinic at Kyle. The remainder of his time is devoted to home calls and clients in the other Medicine Root communities and to the clinic in the second district which he serves, where he has a resident public health nurse to assist him.

Little Wound School is the most important institution of the district, for it brings together all the children and many adults of the neighboring communities of Kyle. School busses carry the 150-odd children from their homes to school, where they spend the day and receive a noon meal. The Kyle children are day pupils through the ninth grade and then go to the boarding school at Pine Ridge to finish their high-school work. During the nine years in the day school, the children become acquainted with nearly all of their age mates in the district. Working together in class and playing together in games and on school teams, the children make intimate friends with others outside their own neighborhoods and communities and overcome much of the segregation and clannishness which

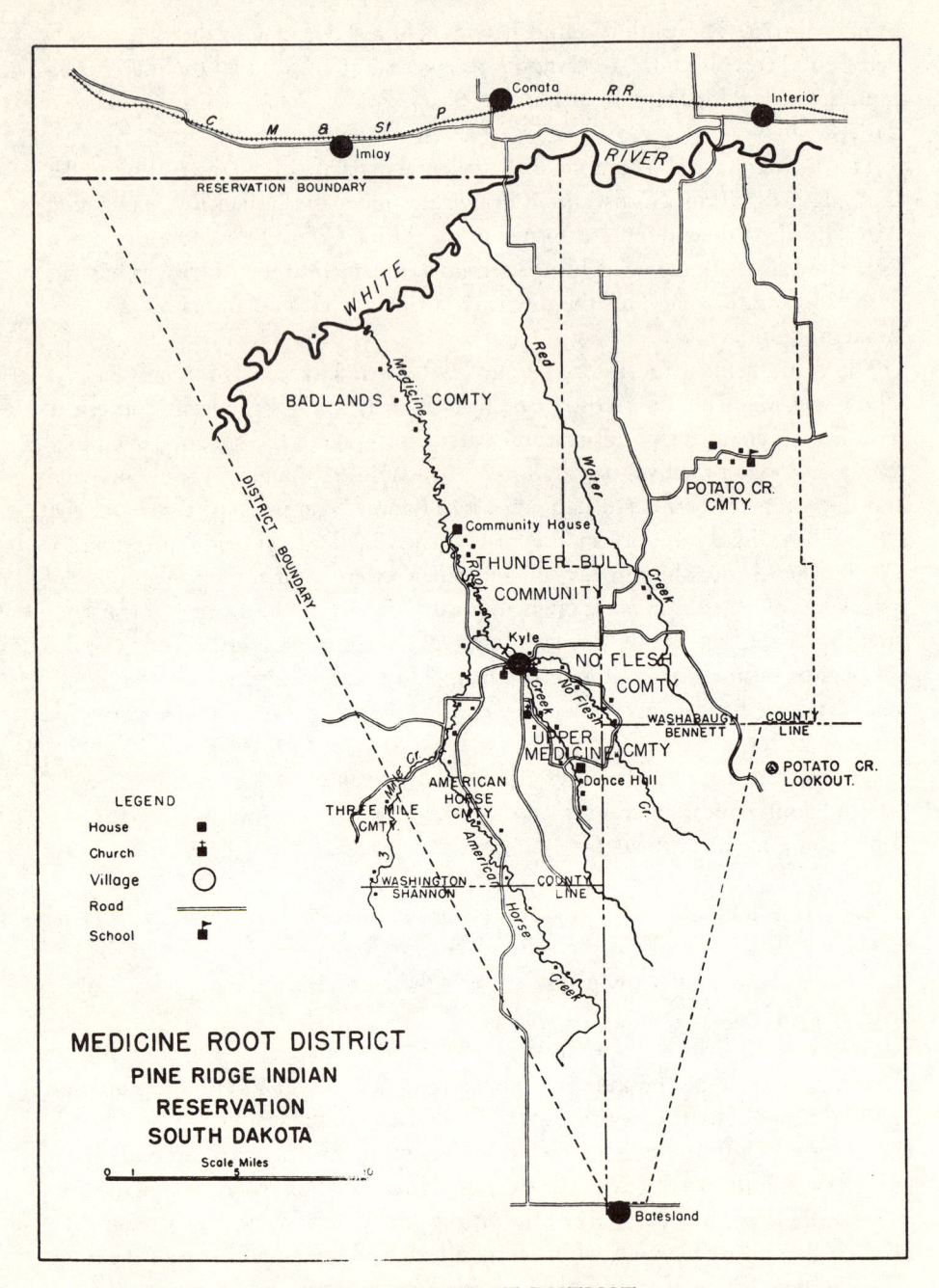

MEDICINE ROOT DISTRICT

life in the neighborhood of an extended family group tends to produce. This influence of the day school becomes very apparent in the cliques that the children of each district form when they enter boarding school.

The auditorium, gymnasium, and large kitchen and dining-room make the school a center for the adults of the district as well as the children. The women's club meets during school hours every Friday to sew and learn improved home and child care methods and to discuss school and district problems. It also sponsors dances, suppers, and other entertainment. The school is the meeting place of the district council, the exhibit hall for the district agricultural fair, the dance hall for both Indian and modern dances, and the local motion-picture theater. These activities in the consolidated school are developing the integration of the district into a more functional unit. The schools in district centers such as the villages of Wanblee and Allen are accomplishing a similar result.

NOTES

1. In a study of Pine Ridge social organization in 1935, forty-one such band-derived communities were located (Scudder Mekeel, personal correspondence).
2. See the final section of this chapter.

CHAPTER VI

INDIANS AND WHITES

It was stated in chapter iv that the Dakota on Pine Ridge Reservation have come to look upon themselves as the Pine Ridge Indians rather than Oglala or Brulé. Their segregation on a single reservation and supervision by an Indian Service agency, to which they have looked for care and assistance for over sixty years, have been the major influences in developing the members of the two subtribes into this new social group. This is but one of many profound changes in the Dakota society which have resulted from the relationship of Indians to the government, and hence the relationship needs to be discussed briefly.

INDIANS AND GOVERNMENT

The relationship of the Indians on federal reservations to the United States government has never been satisfactorily defined. For a long time the Indians have been regarded as wards of the nation. This concept has its constitutional basis in the power of the President (with the consent of the Senate) to make treaties, and the power of Congress to regulate commerce with the Indian tribes.

Blauch has succinctly described the wardship status, as it has been defined in modern times, and the jurisdiction which the government holds over the Indians.

"The Comptroller General has rendered several decisions on the matter [wardship], which in substance hold that a ward Indian is (1) one who lives on a Federal Indian reservation and maintains tribal relations, or (2) one who has restricted property (in his own right, not inherited) held in trust under Governmental control and supervision, whether or not he lives on a reservation or maintains tribal relations.....

"Guardianship over the Indians was assumed by the Government at a time when, as a group, they were unquestionably incapable of managing their property in the face of the white man's civilization and economy. Guardianship relates primarily to restrictions on property. These restrictions apply only to property secured to an Indian by Governmental action; they do not apply to property secured by him through his own efforts. Ordinarily he has complete control of his own earnings and of property purchased with such earnings, as well as of property obtained as a beneficiary. The words 'restricted,' 'incompetent,' and 'non-competent' are used interchangeably to denote the status of the Indian with respect to his property; they have no bearing on, or relation to, the actual ability of the individual Indian to order the affairs of his own life."[1]

Indians born in this country are citizens of the United States. Citizenship was granted to some Indians by the General Allotment Act of 1887 and was promised to those who were established as competent by receiving their allotments in fee simple at the end of the twenty-five-year trust period. However, citizenship was not conferred upon all Indians until 1924.

Since citizenship does not automatically confer the right of suffrage, not all Indians are eligible to vote. Today, however, in all but three states (Arizona, New Mexico, and Idaho) Indians may vote, and the proportion who do so depends upon personal or local attitudes. Many of the Pine Ridge Indians are active in politics. Indians are also entitled to the benefits of federal-state social security programs, although some states have questioned the validity of expending state funds for federal wards. Like citizens of other races, Indians are subject to the Selective Service Act, and many Pine Ridge young men have entered the armed forces through the draft as well as through enlistment.

The peculiar status of Indians as wards has led to many seeming contradictions in their relations to both federal and state governments. Indian lands held in trust are not subject to property taxation, but all other forms of taxation apply to Indians as well as to whites. Generally speaking, Indians are subject to the criminal laws of the state off the reservation, but Indians on restricted lands within the reservation are answerable only to the federal courts or to the Tribal Court.[2]

The federal government fulfils its responsibility to Indians largely through the Office of Indian Affairs and its field service. These duties and responsibilities fall roughly into two categories: the guardianship of the property of Indians and the promotion of their social and economic self-sufficiency. The present policy is to qualify Indians for assuming full management of their affairs, eventually without federal supervision, by building Indian societies based upon still-funtioning tribal life and integrated aspects of white civilization.

On the reservation this policy is executed through the Agency, under the direction of the superintendent and the heads of divisions responsible to him. Each division has its special function in the total program to develop the Indians' land, cattle, and farm assets, to minister to their personal well-being, or to advance their education. The Soil and Moisture Conservation Division protects and rebuilds the land by proper control. The Agricultural Extension Division promotes the expansion of ownership of cattle through government credit facilities and the production of food in family gardens; it instructs Indians in livestock and farm

TRANSACTING GOVERNMENT BUSINESS

management. The Irrigation Division develops dams and water-distribution systems for sections of the reservation adaptable to irrigated farming. The Forestry Division manages the timber supply, controlling the cutting of trees in order that the tribal forests may provide a perpetual supply of lumber and fuel; it also maintains a forest-fire protection service.

The Health Division operates the hospitals and cares for the sick. It attempts to help Indians to improve their own health through the work of visiting nurses and the holding of clinics on tuberculosis, trachoma, and other diseases which are prevalent among Indians. The Education Division provides school facilities and promotes a program to prepare young people for the economy and society envisioned for the reservation. The Welfare Division is represented on the reservation by a social worker who administers the Indian Service Relief Fund (until 1944 usually distributed as food rations), conducts child and family welfare services, co-operates with the state department of social security in its aid to the aged, the blind, and independent children, and acts locally for the United States Employment Service. The Law and Order Section of the Welfare Division maintains a chief of police and his deputies and the reservation jail.

The Indians of the reservation have a large measure of self-government through their tribal constitution, formed under the Indian Reorganization Act of 1934. The constitution provides for a tribal council which has as its chief functions the recommendation and approval of programs and administrative measures for the reservation, the management of tribal funds and resources in co-operation with the superintendent and his staff, and the promulgation of laws for the people. The regulations proposed by the Tribal Council must be approved by the superintendent and the Secretary of the Interior. This council and constitution have given the people a greater voice in reservation affairs and more participation in administration than they had previously had.

The Tribal Council appoints the judges of the Tribal Court, all of whom are Indians. This court has jurisdiction over misdemeanors, divorce, and petty crimes not involving the ten major offenses tried in federal courts.

WHITE RESIDENTS ON THE RESERVATION

In addition to government employees, there are white men in all parts of Pine Ridge Reservation. Most of them live on leased or purchased allotments within the Indian communities. In some parts of the reservation, whites have acquired most of the land and have formed predominantly white communities. These whites are stockmen, farmers, and storekeepers, often a combination of all three. Some are large landholders. White farmers employ a number of Indian families during harvest season and have a few Indian hired hands the year round.

Many of these white men were early settlers in South Dakota, and a few intermarried and lived with Indians before Pine Ridge was established as a separate reservation. Others are first- and second-generation Europeans, showing much of the industry and clannishness of the isolated European peasant in America. Their standards of living and education are those of the lower-class rural folk of South Dakota. A few have profited from a series of good crops and amassed small fortunes, but many were bankrupted by the drought and are now being aided by government agricultural agencies. Their successes and their failures, their homes, their clothes, their luxuries, and their recreations underlie many of the reasons why some Indians farm and take up white ways, while others do not. These are people who make their living from the land as the Indians are encouraged to do. They are functioning farmers, by whom many Indians prefer to be guided because they seem more realistic than the salaried officials who preach but do not practice farming.

These white residents are also neighbors and friends of Indian families and are especially friendly with a group of mixed-bloods of the lesser degrees of Indian admixture. Perhaps more than any other single group, these farmers transmit white customs and exemplify the habits and values of white life to the Indian population.

These whites are the people, too, who are envious and contemptuous of the Indian because of his free schools, hospitals, rations, and other government aids. According to them, the Indian with all his "privileges" cannot do so well as the white man in making a living. "Why should he be freed from taxes and paid for making a living? Why should he hold all this valuable land he does not use? Why should the Indian Service try to drive whites off their land to make room for these lazy men? The C.C.C. was the best thing that ever happened to the Indians. The government should employ all the Indians and leave the land for us who will use it." These typical remarks show much of their prejudices and deep conviction of the "inferiority" of the Indian population. However, intermarriage continues. Family after family of whites becomes identified with the Indian population, and the Indians become closer in blood and in manner to the local whites.

WHITE COMMUNITIES OUTSIDE THE RESERVATION

White men near the reservation have also influenced the Pine Ridge Indian. Parallel to the northern and southern reservation boundaries are a highway and a railroad line along which are located a series of small towns and market centers for the surrounding rural areas. These are also shopping centers for the reservation people who wish to buy from stores with more varied stock than the local traders carry.

The more important of these towns are south of the reservation in Nebraska. In Gordon is a new sales ring for livestock, which has made this town of considerable importance to the Indians. Rushville, twenty-six miles directly south of the Agency, is its chief freight station and shopping center. Chadron, just below the southwest corner of the reservation, is the largest of the three near-by Nebraska towns. From both Rushville and Chadron, highways run directly north across the reservation.

Just over the Nebraska line from Pine Ridge town is White Clay, a drab little village composed largely of stores along either side of the highway. This is the "Gay White Way" for the reservation employees, since they can buy beer here. Although sale of liquor to Indians is forbidden by federal law, the Indians get it through bootleggers. White Clay's beer parlors are its chief attraction, but its stores and garages offer competition to the few in Pine Ridge and draw the business of government employees and Indians alike.

Northwest of the reservation in South Dakota are the towns of the Black Hills. The little towns have Wild West shows and annual "old timers" celebrations to which the Indians come to have a holiday or to earn money or win prizes. Rapid City, a city of about 14,000 population in 1940, is the one truly urban center near the reservation and as such is highly impressive to the Indians. The city is a center of year-round Indian employment, and by 1942 over a hundred and fifty Pine Ridge families were living there. The town's summer fairs and other tourist attractions draw many Indians for temporary work as performers and craftsmen. Rapid City has grown fast, owing to war activities. In 1942 at least three hundred more Indian families went there for employment in military construction.

During the harvest season Pine Ridge families drive their wagons to the towns just outside the reservation to look for work. If they do not have former employers to go to, the men stand on the streets until a farmer in need of help picks them up. The families camp outside the towns on their week ends or when unemployed.

Job-hunting is not the only reason why Indians visit these towns. Shopping trips are great occasions. The whole family goes and stays all day. Parents purchase the food and other things they need on the farm, buy candy and presents for their children, attend a movie, and visit with friends from distant places whom they meet on the streets.

The attitudes of the whites of these towns toward Indians are conflicting. Employers want Indians to harvest corn and potatoes. They are invited to participate in the summer fairs and rodeos, to which they add a great deal of color. The stores enjoy their trade, particularly in the fall, when Indians buy winter supplies and clothing before returning home from the harvest.

On the other hand, the white people in the towns look down upon the Indians. Part of this feeling is a reaction to the fear in which the Indians were once held. It is also due to their present demoralized condition and occasional drunken brawls. On the occasions when an Indian drinking party breaks into a fight or wild carousing in the streets, police make immediate arrests, and the usual penalty is several days of imprisonment and cleaning the streets of the town. Such incidents revive for a time the talk against Indians and the latent prejudice against them as a group. This attitude is also derived from the fact that the Indians when working off the reservation are usually associated with transient harvest laborers, whom the townspeople and employers regard as a lower economic and social group.

To sum up, attitudes vary generally with the social status of the white man. The tradespeople, well-to-do farmers, and government employees,[3] who form the middle class of South Dakota and Nebraska, look upon most Indians as socially and economically inferior. The Indians who are acceptable to this white group are those whose education, employment, and social behavior are like their own.

There is, however, another group of whites in the area to whom the Indians, especially the mixed-bloods, are more acceptable and with whom there is some intermarriage. This group is largely composed of the poorer farmers and townspeople, often those who live on the "wrong side of the track." Because of the greater freedom of social relationships with these white people, the Indians are adopting their pattern of living and their social attitudes and values. In other words, the Indians are merging to a greater degree with the lower than with the middle class of South Dakota whites.

NOTES

1. Lloyd E. Blauch, *Educational Service for Indians* (Washington: Government Printing Office, 1939), pp. 9-10.
2. The federal district court has jurisdiction in the following classes of offenses: ten major crimes (murder, manslaughter, assault with intent to kill, assault with a dangerous weapon, rape, incest, arson, burglary, larceny, and robbery); offenses which are ordinarily under federal jurisdiction throughout the United States; offenses committed in violation of special laws enacted for the protection of Indians and their property; offenses between Indians and non-Indians or between non-Indians on territory within the exclusive jurisdiction of the United States (U.S. Office of Indian Affairs, *Manual of Instructions for Special and Deputy Special Officers and Indian Police* [Chilocco, Okla., 1943], pp. 36-37).
3. See the section on Pine Ridge town in the preceding chapter.

CHAPTER VII

POWER, CEREMONY, AND CHURCH

Dakota religion was based upon a belief in a great supernatural power which dwelt in the sky, the earth, and the four cardinal points or the four winds. Since life depended upon this power and from it came all good and necessary things, the Dakota believed that it must be invoked for the welfare of the tribe and for individual success in the daily tasks of life. It was also believed that the people must follow a moral life, express friendship for one another, and strive to perform their proper functions as men, women, and children. Otherwise the elements of this power would take revenge by sending sickness and other misfortunes. Hence a series of rituals was developed to show reverence to the great power, invoke its strength, and atone for misdeeds.

The ceremonies and beliefs which were elaborated around this central theme have disappeared, but the basic belief in the need for power remains. It functions in minor native cults, the work of medicine men, and the Peyote cult, which embraces the worship of the Christian Deity. It has been conveyed into the orthodox Christianity introduced by missionaries. Hence the contemporary religion among the Pine Ridge Indians must be looked at in terms of the old.

THE DAKOTA RELIGION

The Teton-Dakota regarded themselves as superior to all other people and were confident of their ability to vanquish all enemies, but before the supernatural they presented themselves as weak and humble suppliants for power. To be successful warriors and hunters, to win women, to be leaders, to have social status and join the tribal societies and cults, and to achieve the virtues of Dakota life, men had to have the power that came only from the supernatural.

To achieve power, a boy or man had to seek it by going alone into the plains, where the supernatural power of the universe might come to him in the form of some animal or bird to be his guardian spirit. Here the candidate, unarmed and naked or clad only in a breechcloth and moccasins, humbled himself by fasting and telling of his poverty and weakness and by enduring self-inflicted torture.

The guardian spirit which appeared in a vision, usually on the fourth day of the ordeal, became his protector for life, and its behavior, songs, and message, as interpreted by a priest, determined much of the man's later character and social role. If the vision revealed the spirit hunting animals successfully, the individual tested his new power by hunting in the same way. If he was successful, men believed in his visionary experience, and he was thought to have power. Similarly, a vision interpreted as that of a warrior successful in raiding sent an individual on the warpath with a few companions who were willing to follow him. These visions were believed also to predestine the roles of those who were to remain poor, become transvestites (individuals who dressed and lived like women), or be priests or doctors.

The visions and spiritual instructions conformed to a pattern and did not produce, as might be expected, a great variety and confusion of religious experiences and subsequent unapproved or strange behavior.[1] Any great deviation from accepted Dakota custom was averted by certain conditions in the society. It can be appreciated that on a psychological level an individual would be likely to see in a self-induced dream the actions and things he had learned to expect from folk belief and the preliminary instructions given by older men. In other words, the culture exerted a pressure upon the vision-seeker to conform to sanctioned experiences.

On the other hand, the vision might sanction peculiar and highly individualistic behavior by releasing the expression of unconscious drives or desires.[2] For example, in a culture like that of the Dakota, which demanded robust masculine qualities of its boys, a young man who had an effeminate nature and wished to follow the pursuits of women would have to suppress all such desires. These tendencies might appear in the vision or dream, when conscious controls were relaxed. Ethnological accounts show that young men occasionally did have visions recognized by the culture as indications of the supernatural sanction of the pursuit of a woman's career. Similarly women occasionally had dreams which permitted them to go on the warpath with men. With the exception of these unusual psychological cases, such purely individualistic differences as the vision-seekers reported were only slight deviations from accepted patterns of visions. A man might learn a new song, a change in costume, or a new dance step, with which he might organize a religious cult to carry out the instructions given him by his guardian spirit.

The Dakota had priests or shamans who gained their power through visions and visitations of the supernatural and through instruction by elders in songs and ritual. The priests interpreted omens, foretold future events, and served as ceremonial mediators between the people and the deities or recognized manifestations of supernatural power. They instructed the candidates who were to perform in the great tribal ceremony, the Sun Dance. They directed the rites of this dance and made the prayers and offered the ceremonial pipe to the sun; but in the climax of the dance, when the dancers gazed straight into the sun, the priests stepped aside, giving the dancers complete control of the ceremony and the right to appeal directly to the sun.

Wakan Tanka, whom the Dakota invoked for tribal and personal welfare and assistance, was not a deity or personified Great Spirit, as has been frequently assumed, but an all-pervasive, mysterious power.[3] It accounted for the appearance of the buffalo, the storms, exceptional bravery or wisdom in men, and peculiar and otherwise inexplicable behavior. Wakan Tanka encompassed all the Dakota deities, of whom the more important were Sun, the chief god; his comrade, Buffalo; Sky, the god of power; Earth, the creative god; and Rock, the executive god. Sky and Earth had the male and female powers. There were also many lesser gods and spirits: the benevolent and malevolent gods, the associate gods, and the kindred gods.

Although the Dakota had a greater systematization of their deities than did the other plains tribes, they did not conceive of a clear-cut divine hierarchy or organization, nor did any one priest appear to be acquainted with all these who have been reported.[4] This lack of development of a systematized authoritative power which ordered the universe or demanded obedience seems in keeping with the religious emphasis of the Plains Indian: to acquire power for himself.

DAKOTA CEREMONIES

The Dakota had many ceremonies invoking the supernatural power for the good of the tribe or of individuals. The pattern of the basic ritual and the arrangement of ceremonial objects appears to have been derived from a ceremony which, according to tradition, was performed by the White Buffalo Maiden, sent to the earth by the Buffalo Spirits.[5] This occurred, according to native calendrical count, at the time when the Teton-Dakota reached the high plains.

When the White Buffalo Maiden first appeared, she requested that a tepee be placed in the center of the camp circle. In it were to be a fire, buffalo chips, a square of cleared earth on which was marked a white cross (indicating the four cardinal points in later ceremonies), a pipe rack, a painted buffalo skull, and, behind all these, the place of honor strewn with sage.

When these preparations were made, she appeared from "where the sun rolls off the earth" and took the place of honor in the ceremonial ledge. She spoke first to the people as a group, then to the women, the children, the men, and the leaders, in turn, telling each their duties and admonishing them to lead exemplary lives and to show kindness, friendship, and consideration for others. Finally, the White Buffalo Maiden lit the ceremonial pipe she had brought, and after offering it to Sky, Earth, and Four Winds, gave it to the chief at her left. When she went out of the tepee, she turned into a white buffalo calf.

The ceremonial fire, the buffalo skull, the earth square and sage, the sacred pipe, and the white buffalo skin became the ritual objects of the major Teton ceremonies.

The great religious ceremony to obtain divine blessing and strength for the people was the annual Sun Dance. This was performed by a number of bands or an entire subtribe gathering into a single encampment. The ceremony was actually a series of religious rituals and social affairs with various purposes, which together presented a pageant of the essential functions and values of Dakota culture. The climax was the Sun-gazing Dance performed by a few men, from which the name of the whole ceremony has been taken. The details and sequence of the rituals have been described fully by Walker.[6] It is necessary in our interest in the religious background and changes among the Dakota to understand the meanings of these rituals and the implication of their loss rather than the manner of their performance. As will be apparent in the following brief discussion, the loss of the ceremony has meant the loss also of sanctions of behavior and of social institutions, and the weakening of tribal unity and security, as well as the loss of strength and confidence from supernatural or divine support.

The Sun Dance took place during two four-day periods in summer when the earth was fertile. The buffalo were fat, the wild berries ripe, the grass tall and green. There was much ritual feasting as acknowledgment that the people had had an abundance of food during the year. In several of the ceremonies the Buffalo Spirit was honored for food that he had sent and supplicated for continuance of his favors. Feasting was also an expression of the friendship and solidarity of the people.

Fertility was ritualized by a procession of the adults, in which the men sang in praise of Sky and the male element and the women praised Earth and the female element. This was followed by a day of sexual license and banter. Effigies of a man and a buffalo with exaggerated genitals representing two of the lesser deities were hung from the Sun Dance pole when it was erected, but at the end of the period of license these effigies were shot down and the normal regulations on sexual behavior reimposed. The whole ritual appears to have been an honoring of procreation and fecundity which perpetuated the tribe and then the symbolical driving of evil or licentiousness out of the camp.[7]

In the selecting, cutting-down, and erecting of the Sun Dance pole and in the choosing of its location, there were imitation rites of scouting, raiding, capturing, and celebrating victory, all of which were sanctions of making war. A similar performance was enacted in a mock capture of the dance candidates and ear-piercing ceremonialists. There were also races which stimulated competition among men to achieve personal war honors.

It was during the Sun Dance ceremony that the men's societies performed their rituals and elected new members who had achieved honors during the past year. Members also took part in rituals of the general ceremony. One of their special function was to hold feasts and "give-aways," the distribution of property to the poor and unfortunate in honor of the people. In these society meetings and on other occasions when men had to prove their right to perform ceremonial functions, they recounted before others their feats in war or the coups which they had counted to establish their claim to honors and prestige.

Women had societies for honoring adherence to the ideals of Dakota womanhood. During the Sun Dance period a feast was held at which faithful wives and chaste maidens might attend. Every participant was subject to challenge by men who could disprove her claim to honorable conduct; if they were successful, the challenged woman's eating utensils were thrown out of the circle of women.

A virgin of exceptional character was selected by the priests to fell the tree chosen for the Sun Dance pole. This was the greatest single honor which the tribe bestowed upon a woman. Three other maidens were selected to assist in cutting the tree.[8]

Recognition was also given to the women in other parts of the ceremony. Virtuous young girls were selected to bathe the wounds of the sun dancers, an act which was believed to insure these girls the love of some young man. Pregnant women and little children were thought to acquire special protection by gathering the small branches and twigs trimmed from the Sun Dance pole. On one evening all the people were enjoined to observe friendly and jovial relationships in their tepees, and the men were instructed to treat their wives with full equality and respect.

Children received attention, too, in a ritual known as the Ear-piercing Ceremony. Parents who wished to honor their child or fulfil a vow made when he was ill asked some medicine man or notable warrior to sponsor him and to pierce his ears. Before the actual ritual the director of the Sun Dance ceremony admonished the parents to train their children to be good Dakota. Children who had their ears pierced were regarded as having sacrificed themselves in much the same way as the dancers. In a sense, they were dedicated by their sponsors to loyalty to their kin and to the values of the people.

With the exception of the ear-piercing, the last four days of the whole Sun Dance ceremony were devoted to the performance of the four grades of dances by which the chosen candidates sought to come into communication with the power of Sun and of Buffalo Spirit. The camp had to be cleansed by hunting down evil spirits, and those persons whose behavior in the past or at the ceremony might displease the gods were removed. Sun was met at each dawn and evening and supplicated with the ceremonial pipe for his favors. Dancing was postponed if his face was clouded.

The dancers undertook various degrees of self-torture according to the grade of dance they chose. All fasted during the days and nights of the dance and were given only moist roots or leaves to quench their thirst. The most severe form of torture occurred on the last day, when the candidates of the fourth dance were suspended from the dance pole by thongs attached to wooden skewers thrust through their back and chest muscles. The bravest and most honored dancers were those who tore their flesh and freed themselves without assistance. Throughout this torture and the previous dances they gazed directly into the face of the Sun. This torture or sacrifice of one's body was the characteristic means of winning the favor of the gods and entering a direct relationship with them. The dancers sought not only to gain power from Sun—a power by which they might become medicine men—but also to fulfil a vow to dance made previously during the year, when they had called for supernatural aid during a war raid, a child's sickness, or similar crisis.

Although the experience of the Sun-gazing Dance was personal for each candidate, it was also an experience of all the spectators or the tribe, who identified themselves with the participants. They knew that the participants suffered for the group, so that all might receive the well-being that came directly from the supreme power that dwelt in Sun.

In this whole Sun Dance ceremony there appears a tremendous social force and value for the perpetuation of Dakota life as well as the invocation of supernatural blessing for the tribe and the several participants. The religious value can be summarized as the attainment by all the people of power and strength from Wakan Tanka, the great reservoir of supernatural power, and the winning of divine favor for the continuance of the life of the tribe, especially for the continuance of its food supply. The social value of the Sun Dance appears to have been the reaffirmation by each individual of membership in the tribe, the sense of security gained by camping and participating with the large number of people, and the re-establishment of solidarity among relatives from other bands.

The ceremony publicly rewarded also the types of social behavior which were sanctioned by Dakota culture. The rituals sanctioned the economic occupations and roles of men and women, the training of children to become hunters and warriors or wives and homemakers, the begetting of children, the men's institutions, and acknowledgment of the gods and seeking their power. But, above all, the rituals sanctioned the great Dakota virtues of bravery, fortitude, generosity, and wisdom by calling upon their practice during the ceremony and rewarded the highest virtues of women—industry, hospitality, kindness, and chastity among unmarried girls and fidelity and fecundity among wives. In the Sun Dance each member of the tribe saw in actual function or in ritualized imitation all the approved conduct and major social institutions and the rewarding of those who adhered to Dakota life. The Sun Dance was a drama of Dakota culture. In this highly emotional and intense atmosphere the adults rededicated themselves to the cultural precepts, and the young people received a vivid education in the meaning and objectives of the life they were to follow.

THE OLD RELIGION IS PROHIBITED

The Sun Dance was prohibited in 1881 and was under official ban until 1933.[9] It is not difficult to see the effect upon the Dakota of this action and of the pressures by the government and missionaries upon other parts of the old religion. With it were lost the feeling of having made contact with the supernatural, the gaining of a sense of power, and the winning of the help of the gods in providing food and protection to the people. That the Dakota felt helpless and overcome without supernatural help in meeting their unhappy situation is amply illustrated by the fervor with which many of them took up the Ghost Dance nine years later, to invoke divine assistance in overthrowing the whites and bringing back the old days.

The prohibition of the Sun Dance took away not only much of the security which religion gave to the people but also the public rewarding and sanctioning of social life and social institutions. The ending of this reinforcement of the Dakota custom and the instruction of the young people by observation and participation contributed greatly to the weakening of social controls and the crumbling of Dakota culture.

There is no evidence to show just how long after settlement on the reservation the young men continued to seek a guardian spirit, but we can safely assume the custom virtually disappeared among the first generation of reservation-born children. The young men had little need of obtaining power for hunting or warfare.[10] The fact that they went to school, which supplanted much of the parental and community training and gave the boys new interests, may also have accounted for the decline of the vision quest. At the same time as the younger generation were receiving new training experiences, the men's societies and cults, which reinforced the vision quest, were losing their function. The shamans were dying off without passing on their lore or training successors.[11] These changes seems to have been both causative of, and resultant from, the abandonment of the general practice of seeking power.

THE DAKOTA TURN TO CHRISTIANITY

It was a great many years, however, before the majority of Pine Ridge Indians became Christians, in spite of the suppression of most of their native religious ceremonies. Their acceptance of Christianity was at first, and continues to be to some extent today, an acceptance of the deity of their conquerors and a search for his power, without complete abandonment of the old beliefs. As one early convert stated: "I found that their [whites'] Wakan Tanka the superior .... and have served Wakan Tanka according to the white people's manner and with all my power. I still have my *wasicun* [ceremonial pouch or bundle of a shaman], and I am afraid to offend it because the spirit of an Oglala may go to the spirit land of the Dakota."[12] The Christian God was identified somewhat with the Dakota supernatural power through the missionaries' practice of calling God "Wakan Tanka." The belief in the Wakan Tanka of the past still continues, as the existing native cults, to be described later, reveal.

The Dakota also accepted Christianity because it was the one part of the white man's life in which the Indian was accepted as an equal. Christianity taught that all people were held to be the same before God. It taught that happiness could be attained in a life after death, a promise which may have given some hope to the Indians when most of their happiness was being taken away from them. Furthermore, this teaching had some resemblance to the native belief in a "happy hunting ground" of the Indian dead.

Some other beliefs and symbols of Christianity could be readily understood by the Indians from concepts of their own religion. Asceticism, the torture of the crucifixion for the good of others, giving to others (especially the poor), and the high honor accorded virginity were not unconnected Dakota beliefs and cultural values. The Dakota also interpreted some church practices in their own fashion to fit with the values of the old religion. For example, putting money into the collection plate on Sundays is still used as a means of giving honor to another person and gaining prestige for generosity in the native give-away pattern. An offering is made with as many small coins as possible, each given separately in order to increase the appearance of one's generosity.[13]

On the whole, the Dakota were slow to accept Christianity. The missionaries created resistance by trying to eradicate all the native religion instead of using it as a frame of reference in which to introduce Christianity. They attempted to impose Christian morality by suppressing Indian custom. One objective of their proselytizing was to "civilize" the Indian; and, to accomplish this, they tried to drive out indiscriminately Indian ways which had no relation to religion in the Indian mind. In this effort the missionaries influenced the Bureau of Indian Affairs to impose regulations against not only the Sun Dance but all ceremonies and Indian customs, which they believed impeded the progress of the Indians toward a civilized state.[14]

Such action naturally incurred the antagonism of many of the Indians. As a result, native religious practice was driven into hiding, and what remains of it today is kept from the eyes of all but a few friendly whites. Part of this secrecy is also due to the fact that native religion is often used for curing, and health authorities have strongly preached against these practices in favor of white medicine and sanitation. The extent of the belief and religious practice in so-called "pagan" cults is still more extensive than most missionaries and officials are willing to believe.

One of the chief sources of conflict, particularly to the missionaries, was the unwillingness of the Indians to accept marriage as a religious rite, to abandon polygamy, and to forgo the right of divorce in accordance with the tenets of the Catholic and Episcopal churches. Dakota marriages, except those of noted families, involved no religious ritual or sanction. To make confession before the marriage rite in matters about which the couple felt no wrongdoing, to publish banns bringing public attention to the couple—always a source of embarrassment to any Dakota—and to make the marriage a public ceremony rather than a family matter transformed the wedding ritual in the two leading churches into an ordeal. Old people cautioned the young not to be married by a priest, lest they later be forced to choose between remaining with a mate they might find undesirable and breaking the law of the church by separating and marrying again.

Although the moral code of Christianity concerning sex relations appears in harmony generally with that of the Dakota, they have not accepted fully the Christian strictness or demand for chastity by both sexes before marriage. The old society did not require continence of the young men; and, although virginity was desired among the young women, it appears to have been enforced principally among the daughters of prominent families. No great feeling of wrongdoing or sin appears to have developed over premarital sex relations or even pregnancy. Shame and loss of honor followed, and the family might move to another band to escape criticism. But if the unmarried mother married soon, the matter was forgotten. Christian standards and attitudes seemed to the Dakota harsh and overly upright in face of their own practices.

Since the coming of the first missionaries among the Teton-Dakota sixty years ago, the resistance or indifference to Christianity has passed, and all the Pine Ridge Indians profess belief in Christianity and nominal membership in some church. All but a few of the very oldest people have been born on this or some other reservation or in a white community and have attended school where religious education was conducted by local missionaries and by many of the schoolteachers. The Indians accept now most of the principles of Christianity, the ritual, and the sacred calendar and symbols. This has been part of their general acceptance of white life. The process of religious change has been the dying-out of the old native religion before the full acceptance of Christianity as the religion of the people. As long as there was a body of older people trained and experienced in the native rituals and led by the native priests or medicine men, the resistance to Christianity endured.

The acceptance of Christianity by the Dakota cannot be considered a real substitution of one religion for another. The younger generations learned less of the old religion and had fewer native religious leaders, while they learned more of Christianity from childhood. The absence of a real or direct substitution is emphasized here because there is now much in the churches and religious life which has the function of old religious form and ritual but became a part of the Dakota life only in recent years.

The church has ceremonies for the transition from one stage of life to another, known in social science as the rites of passage, for some of which the Dakota culture also had ceremonies. There was no direct substitution of one for the other but the passing of Dakota rites with one generation and the acceptance of Christian ceremonies by a second generation.

In the Dakota culture there was no special ceremony at birth. The naming of a child took place often at the Ear-piercing Ceremony. At puberty boys received no ceremonial attention, but a few years afterward they were sent on a vision quest. Some girls, after their first menstruation, received the Buffalo Ceremony, dedicated to the buffalo-god, the patron of womanly virtues. This ceremony was performed to aid the good influences which surrounded the girl at this time, to continue their effect upon her, to banish all evil influence, and to inculcate in her the virtues for which Dakota womanhood was respected, as well as to announce her physical maturity. The elaborate Buffalo Ceremony was abandoned in the nineteenth century, but a simple ritual was conducted by many families on the reservation until recent years.

The marriage ceremony has been described as a social and family affair. Elaborate weddings were held only by families of importance to honor their children and to give away much property. At these ceremonies a priest performed at a special altar a ritual in which a deity of the Dakota was called upon to bless the union.[15]

At the death of an individual, his relatives and friends gathered at his tepee to mourn. The women spent four days in intermittent wailing. Parents often gashed themselves or severed a finger to express their grief. A bereaved father might wander from camp, singing a death song, to shoot down the first person whom he met and then kill himself. A give-away of the family's property to the mourners was a part of the funeral ceremony, and another give-away ended the year of mourning. This rite might be elaborated into the Keeping of the Ghost Ceremony, whereby a lock of hair was kept as a symbol of the deceased for a year; at the end of this period, beautiful beadwork and other articles made by the mother were given away, as well as family possessions.

GIVE-AWAY

These life-crisis ceremonies, except those connected with death, have now been abandoned. The Ear-piercing and Buffalo Spirit ceremonies had not been performed among any of the children whose life-histories were gathered for this study. Mekeel attended a native wedding ceremony in the Oglala community in 1931 at which a shaman performed the religious rites, and dog meat, a traditional ceremonial food, was eaten to distinguish the ceremony from a Christian wedding, at which chicken is regarded as appropriate.[16] No native wedding ceremonies were reported in 1942.

The Christian rites are now accepted for the life-crises of the individuals. Baptism is usual for babies born today. Puberty rites as such are nonexistent, but confirmation or joining the church is made an important celebration among the young people. Graduation exercises from both the primary and the secondary school are also now important, though not sacred, ceremonies for Dakota young people and their families.

Christian marriage is still strongly encouraged by the churches, but the full ceremony with invited guests and feast or reception afterward is accepted mostly by the townsfolk or assimilated country people. The majority of Pine Ridge Indians prefer a quiet civil marriage.

The pattern of the old funeral ceremonies—the wailing, the four-day mourning, and the give-away after the burial and at the end of a year's mourning—is still practiced, but self-torture has long been abandoned or suppressed. As in the old days, widows and bereaved mothers and sisters usually cut their hair short as soon as a death has occurred, and those who do not are severely criticized. The minister of the local church is asked to conduct services, and the body is buried with the church ceremony. The give-away and final feast by the relatives of the deceased follows the burial and often takes place at the church community house or in the churchyard.

The Dakota formerly placed their dead upon a scaffold. When the government and missionaries wished them to inter corpses, they objected strongly, believing it would interfere with the passage of the spirit to the land of the dead.[17] Burial in a cemetery is now universally practiced. The Dakota celebrate Memorial Day as a time to refurbish the graveyard, clearing the graves of weeds and windblown debris and decorating them with new bouquets or wreaths of paper flowers. Such attention to the dead is entirely new, and it is highly significant that greater attention is paid to the death rites than to any other in the life-cycle.

Missionary work and churches have been established on the reservation for many years by the Roman Catholic, the Episcopal, and the Presbyterian churches. The principal Protestant churches and missionary headquarters are in the town of Pine Ridge. The Episcopal church has a large number of community churches and several Indian ministers and lay readers in the reservation districts. The Catholics operate from Holy Rosary Mission north of Pine Ridge town, sending priests to the community churches on week ends. One priest conducts services in the Pine Ridge town church and devotes all his services to this parish. The Catholic church is the only religious group which conducts a school on the reservation, but the Episcopalians maintain in the state a boarding school for Sioux children.

The Catholics conduct a summer Bible school for children at the mission, primarily for religious instruction and recreation but also as a means of interesting new students for the winter session of the boarding school. The other churches have Bible schools at some of their community churches. Both the Catholic and the Episcopal churches hold large summer conventions or convocations attended by delegates and a large number of church members. These gatherings are held annually, but, since they include all the Sioux reservations, Pine Ridge is the meeting place only once in every seven or eight years. Although, of course, no Indian ceremonial is a part of these meetings, the summer gathering of friends and relatives from different parts of the reservation and the camping in tents give the convocations some of the social function of the old Sun Dance.

The services and organization of the community churches, as observed in the Kyle area, follow closely the pattern of small rural churches of white communities. The visiting priest conducts Mass in the two Catholic chapels and administers the marriage, funeral, and other personal rites of the church. An Indian minister lives in a parish house beside the Episcopal church in one community and serves the church in a second community on alternate Sundays. Indian Episcopal lay readers conduct morning prayer and, in the manner of former Indian elders, occasionally indulge in unsanctioned sermons, discussing the behavior of church people, the Peyote cult, or community social situations.

The social organization of the membership of Episcopal and Catholic churches is similar, but the Episcopalian communities seem to be more active under local leadership. They have full Sunday services and a weekly evening meeting of prayer for the men in the armed services. There is also Sunday school and a young people's fellowship which meets on Saturday afternoons for religious instruction and group socials. The Sacred Heart Society of the Catholics has a similar league for young people. Both churches conduct women's guilds for stimulating home improvement and teaching home crafts. The Episcopal church also had at one time a men's brotherhood, but its activity seems to have ended with the death of its lay leader.

Individuals in the rural communities all tend to join one church, especially if there is any common bond of a band origin. It was noted that, in many families, a Catholic or a Protestant has joined the church of the other upon marriage. In one family a Catholic mother became an Episcopalian, but her Episcopalian daughter became a Catholic upon her marriage. Children in one family may be divided in church membership between Catholic and Protestants without conflict. However, in 1943, in school and community meetings led by a minister, the children who were not of the same religious following were observed to remain outside. This stimulation of competition and exclusiveness in church groups, developed under white leadership among a single and once strongly integrated people, has been injurious to social cohesion and has brought confusion and criticism among the Indians.

The evangelical type of church has not made much headway on the reservation. Occasionally, Seventh-Day Adventist and Church of God preachers come from Rapid City to seek followers or to establish a new church. In Kyle these visitors are well accepted, possibly out of curiosity and as sources of entertainment, for the people enjoy group singing and the emotional participation of these evangelists' meetings. They make a strong appeal through the prayers for the sick and their particular emphasis on divine cure. There is much discussion of such experiences as a cure resulting from a two-day community prayer and the healing of a woman taken to Rapid City in order that a white congregation might pray for her life. Consciously or unconsciously, these preachers follow the Indian pattern in making friends and establishing themselves in the good graces of the community by making many gifts, but they have established no permanent churches. These outside sects, especially the Pentacostal, have yet made little appeal to the full-bloods in spite of their interpretation of the deity as a power who cures the sick and controls the lives of individuals in a very personal way.

One church of this sort without affiliation to any organized sect is struggling for membership and recognition in Pine Ridge town. It seems to appeal to the mixed-blood and more assimilated group, however, as it does to the poorer and less stable whites, because of the definite security and authority of God which it offers. As an institution of lower-class membership and outside the long-established church group, it is subjected to informal ostracism by the other local churches and the government employees.

CONTEMPORARY NATIVE RELIGIOUS PRACTICES

Certain religious cults that do not stem from Christianity, at least in forms recognized by white society, are practiced on the reservation. There are also surviving some remnants of the practices of medicine men.

The only continuing cult of the old Dakota religion is the Yuwipi meeting, whose ceremonials and function in the old culture have scarcely been touched upon in the ethnological literature.[18] This cult worships manifestations of four chief Dakota gods and invokes supernatural power for curing the sick and occasionally for finding lost articles. In discussing the beliefs of the Yuwipi cult, an older member stated that they believed in "the Sun and the Daylight—that is Wakan, our god [the chief god]. Then, we worship Darkness [the creator god]; this is why we sit in darkness in the tepee at a Yuwipi ceremony. The women think of sexual things and later they go home with their men. That is creative; that is not bad; the Darkness is holy. Then, there is Rock [the executive god]. The leaders have a little bundle of sticks in their hand when they are tied up and a blanket is thrown over them. The Rock makes sparks and lightning shoots all over the tepee. The Rock is hard and steadfast and that is what our faith must be. It is like the earth. Then, there is Wakinyan or Heyoka [an associate god]. It flashes through the sky, and storms come, and strong winds, and floods that wash away the soil. The Yuwipi people say that is cleansing them and cleansing the earth. Wakan washes away everything and makes everything clean and new."

The objective of the Yuwipi ritual is the calling of the spirits, or "little people," who live about the countryside, to advise the medicine man in curing or finding lost articles.[19] The ceremony is held in a cabin completely darkened while the medicine man performs magical feats and calls in the spirits. Sounds of knocking stones, strange noises, and flashing lights appear in all parts of the room as the spirits respond. The medicine man talks to them, while four men drum and sing. Suddenly all the sounds stop and the medicine man recounts to the group, before the lamps are relit, the cures and information learned from the spirits.

Before the ceremony begins, the medicine man is bound very tightly by others and placed under a blanket. Those who have requested his services place offerings around the altar or platform where the medicine man is bound. When the lights go on, he is standing, free from his bindings, and the offerings have disappeared.

In Kyle, only one Yuwipi practitioner was reported during the period of this study. Because he feared that his supernatural power might bring some ill effects upon his family, he did not remain with them much of the time. His wife and daughters were good Catholics. The father traveled much to conduct ceremonies in other communities. The renown of his psychic power had spread over the countryside, attracting both Indians and whites, who had come to him for various reasons, from seeking a cure for appendicitis to finding a stolen horse.

Despite the fact that the practices of medicine men were long banned by Indian Service regulations and condemned by missionaries along with other native customs believed to impede the "civilization" of the Indian, some of the practices have survived, and medicine men and herbalists still prescribe for the sick. The work of these minor religious practitioners is mainly on an individual or family basis. The extent of their practice, like that of midwives, is hard to determine, because both performers and recipients are afraid of white censure.

THE PEYOTE CULT

The Native American church, or Peyote cult, has members in many of the reservation communities. This excellent example of an institution produced in acculturation developed in the United States years ago on the southern plains from an old Mexican religion which centered around the use of the mildly intoxicating peyote plant.[20] Native and Christian beliefs and rituals are combined into a religion closely related to Sioux religious attitudes. The cult is based on invocation of power from a supreme being—the Peyote Spirit, who appears to be identified with the Christian deity—symbolized by the peyote button or seed pod of the cactus plant. The eating of peyote induces a trance, an experience not unlike that induced in the old vision quests, in which the seeker of a guardian spirit attempted to get outside himself or into an abnormal state.[21] The eating of peyote and participation in the ceremony are believed to bring one in direct relation with the supernatural, but they are not believed to provide any personal power like that formerly obtained from a guardian spirit.

The ritual of the Peyote cult is conducted with members sitting in a circle in a large tepee erected for the ceremony. A fire burns before a small crescent-shaped altar. Tobacco is ritually smoked as a means of communicating prayers. A special drum is passed to each member to accompany his peyote songs. As in the Sun Dance, the sacred number is four.

This cult, like the old Dakota religion, delves into the realm of curing, one of its chief drawbacks from the point of view of outsiders and practitioners of modern medicine. The eating or drinking of peyote in a broth as a universal cure-all keeps many people in need of modern medicine or surgery away from the hospital. This is particularly serious for sick children, who have no choice in the matter; Indian Service doctors have stated to the writer that it is extremely difficult to treat pneumonia cases where the child has been previously fed peyote. It may also make employment of anesthetics before surgical operations dangerous.

The Peyote cult has been criticized for this practice, but the chief point of attack has been on the use of peyote itself, because of the state of lethargy and inactivity which constant use is said to induce. The Christian churches look upon the cult as a heretic and even pagan organization which they wish the government to aid in stamping out. Indian nonmembers of the cult on Pine Ridge Reservation generally regard it as a menace that causes laziness and depletes families' wealth. Many habitual users of peyote do become irresponsible and unable to care for themselves and their families. Members of the cult, as hosts to a number of ceremonies, purchase the peyote and the food that is eaten afterward, thereby demonstrating their hospitality and generosity. Because this giving is made to and approved by only a small group, the social prestige gained by a peyote host is slight, but such expenditure is often economically detrimental to his family as well as to himself.

The physical effects of peyote still remain a disputed point. Peyote of itself has probably worked little injury, but the behavior associated with the religion, stemming from cultural and psychological causes, can be harmful. The Pine Ridge people who partake of peyote appear to be individuals psychologically disposed to find some way of escape from their social environment. The cult appeals to those who, seeking to preserve the Indian way of life, find in the ceremonies the symbols and behavior which permit them, for a night at least, to return to the old life and escape the white man and all the pains of cultural change. The cult is also an escape from the poverty and depressing effects of reservation life. In this connection an interesting comment was made by a former peyote user, who said, "You feel very pleasant. You can sit and watch the government employees drive by, and it doesn't bother you at all."

The Peyote cult carries also influence for good, whether looked at from the Indian or white point of view. It teaches a strict sexual morality and abstinence from liquor. As an incorporated church, it places regulations upon marriage and divorce practices, bringing new strength to the lax social controls outside the church groups. The cult has been criticized for permitting sexual license during or after ceremonies. This is not a part of the belief of the cult nor practiced by its serious followers, as far as information on hand can tell us. It is possible that young men attend the meetings to seduce women who become pleasantly relaxed and lose some control of their emotions, but this cannot be blamed upon the religion. This is a point of which only long investigation can reveal the truth or falsity.

In Kyle the Peyote cult has only a small regular following, but at times it increases when a member becomes active in organizing meetings and provides the necessary peyote, which is purchased outside the state. During 1942 Peyote ceremonies were held in Kyle to cure the sick and to honor a returned soldier. In the latter case, the Dakota utilized the Peyote meeting for the completely Dakota social purpose of honoring.

In Pine Ridge town the Peyote cult was not reported as functioning. This may be due partly to the influence of the several churches and partly to the lack of appeal of Indian ritual and the escapist satisfactions of the Peyote cult to the assimilated townsfolk. Just outside Pine Ridge the cult is practiced by a group of rather incompetent and frustrated full-bloods.

The Peyote cult does not seem to be reaching many of the younger generation. In the first place, the ceremonies last all night, and the younger children are not taken. In Kyle the older children in our study who came from families reputed to be members of the cult expressed a strong condemnation for the practice. In the group outside Pine Ridge under the leadership of a former Catholic catechist, a special children's group has been organized after the pattern of the established churches. The leaders of the Peyote cult have also talked of giving instruction to the younger members in school during a religious period, but as yet they have taken no action.

CHANGING ATTITUDES TOWARD RELIGION

Belonging to a Christian church and attending Peyote or Yuwipi ceremonies bring no conflict to the Indian mind. Individuals pass from one group to another as the personalities of the leaders appeal to them or neighbors report unusual success in curing. The old sanctions of freedom of individual behavior within a certain prescribed area and the old informality of Dakota organization still allow individuals a great deal of choice in their religion.

The shifting from one religion to another of apparently conflicting concepts becomes more understandable when it is realized that there are certain elements fundamental in the native pre-Christian religion which are carried over into the contemporary religions. The first is the continuous seeking of divine power for strength and assistance in meeting the problems of earthly life. An adjunct is the specific use of this power for curing. The second is the seeking of social interaction and social participation which gives to the individual a sense of security and membership in a larger group not attained regularly in other institutions. The third is the sanctioning of a moral code.

The Yuwipi cult appears to be organized primarily for the purpose of curing. But the power of the old deities comes to the assembled group to give them strength, cleanse them of evil, and continue their fecundity.

The Peyote cult is also a curing religion. Its regular meetings, however, are not held expressly for the sick but to gain power or strength from the Christian God through native or imported Indian ritual devices. The Peyote cult sanctions the Dakota mode of social relationships but emphasizes also aspects of puritanical morality taken from white culture.

Without detracting from the work of early and contemporary Pine Ridge missionaries, it can be said in all fairness that much of the significance which Christianity holds has come from its interpretation by the Dakota in terms of their former religion. Similarly, the church organizations have become significant as they have supplied a center around which band organization and integration could continue. The first generations of converts translated Christianity into the Dakota way of life. Owing to conflicts between the Christian and Dakota moral code and the condemnation of all Dakota custom because it was related to paganism and uncivilized life, Christianity gained little authority at first over Dakota morality and social life. In the general process of assimiliation, it is the younger generations which have accepted Christianity as a sanctioning force of white moral behavior.

The so-called "pagan" cults today also offer a security which the usual Christian critic does not understand. Each oldest generation in the full-blood group seems to be the last which will carry on the native or seminative religious practice, but, as each generation grows older, it seems to accept and practice more of the old rituals and beliefs. On the whole, however, each succeeding generation has a little less interest, a little less acceptance, and a little less knowledge of the beliefs and rites that stem from the past. Under the pressure of the churches, the increasing knowledge of modern medicine, the fear of white criticism, and the general process of assimilation, the old religious practices seem bound for extinction.

The Peyote cult has a certain strength because it is fighting for survival. As an escapist cult and lacking prestige among the other churches, it may die eventually. But because it answers many of the psychological and religious needs of the people, it probably will continue as long as the basic Dakota religious values and traditional forms of spiritual experience are maintained.

Most of the Dakota ceremonies and the pantheon are gone, except for the vestige remaining in the Yuwipi cult and the practices of a few medicine men. Although it is doubtful that more than a small minority of the people today make a practice of attending Yuwipi meetings, this native cult will probably continue for a long time, for there is always an element of any population which believes in and enjoys magic. The hold which the past Indian life has on most of the people adds it effect also to the preservation of native religion. Even so, Yuwipi practices will doubtless decrease in influence as contacts with the world outside the reservation grow stronger.

The Christian churches, too, appear to be losing some of their former hold as the Dakota travel and associate more intimately and easily with white people. This is due in part to the fact that many Indians are now following the trend of the local white population away from control by the church.

NOTES

1. See Robert H. Lowie, *Primitive Religion* (New York: Boni & Liveright, 1924), chap. xi.
2. *Ibid.*
3. Royal B. Hassrick, "Teton-Dakota Religion" (MS).
4. J. R. Walker, *The Sun Dance and Other Ceremonies of the Oglala Division of the Teton Dakota* (New York: American Museum of Natural History, 1917), p. 56.
5. This ceremony is described fully in Frances Densmore, *Teton Sioux Music* (U.S. Bureau of American Ethnology Bull. 61 [Washington, 1918]), pp. 63-66.
6. *Op. cit.*, pp. 60-120.

7. Densmore learned from informants in 1911 that the effigies symbolized the enemy and the buffalo which had been captured by supernatural help. She reports none of the sexual symbols or ritual (*op. cit.*, p. 118).

8. *Ibid.*, p. 113.

9. U.S. Bureau of Indian Affairs, *Regulations.... Effective April 1, 1904* (Washington, 1904), sec. 584, and "Circular Letter 2970" (Washington, 1934).

10. It is interesting and significant to note that young Dakota purchased personal medicine bundles for power and protection before going into the armed forces in 1942 and 1943.

11. Medicine men have not, however, passed from the contemporary scene (see below).

12. Walker, *op. cit.*, p. 159.

13. Scudder Mekeel, personal correspondence.

14. U.S. Bureau of Indian Affairs, *Regulations...., 1884* and *Regulations...., 1904*.

15. Scudder Mekeel, "A Modern American Community in the Light of Its Past" (MS).

16. Scudder Mekeel, personal correspondence.

17. Clark Wissler, *North American Indians of the Plains* (New York: American Museum of Natural History, 1934), p. 96.

18. Densmore (*op. cit.*, pp. 204-18) describes the elements of the Yuwipi ritual (shooting stones, binding the practitioner) in the practices of the old medicine men.

19. The "little people" were reported by Lewis and Clark in the nineteenth century. No ethnological accounts known to the author describe them or the whole Yuwipi practice.

20. For a full discussion of peyotism see Omer C. Stewart, *Washo-Northern Paiute Peyotism* (Berkeley and Los Angeles, Calif.: University of California Press, 1944).

21. Ruth Benedict, *Patterns of Culture* (Boston: Houghton Mifflin Co., 1935), p. 81.

CHAPTER VIII

FATHERS AND GRANDFATHERS

IN REVIEWING the historical experiences of the Pine Ridge Dakota and the changes in their physical environment, basic economy, social organization, and religious beliefs, little reference has been made to the particular generation living at the time these changes occurred. Three generations have been born on the reservation since the Oglala and Brulé first came to Pine Ridge, and each has grown up in a different atmosphere. Only the oldest people living today have experienced directly the whole effect of the reservation era. The cumulative effect of reservation life, social disorganization, and assimilation has been transmitted in part by the older generations to the younger ones, but each generation has been oriented by the particular times of their childhood and early youth. As Mekeel was the first to demonstrate, people born in different eras of Pine Ridge history hold widely differing attitudes.[1] It is necessary to elaborate on these differences in attitudes in order to understand the kind of adjustments which the people are making and particularly to understand the orientation of the youngest generation, our especial interest.

THE OLD VALUES

The great majority of the oldest living generation were born on Pine Ridge or some other reservation. A few people who are nearing or have passed eighty—the great-grandparents of the present children—lived as children in the old camps and traveled freely over the plains. The boys hunted a few buffalo with their fathers, but they were not old enough to participate in the last of the Indian wars. A few of the grandparent generation hunted buffalo also, but for most of them the earliest memories are associated with the camp circles at the Agency or ration stations. There are also several survivors of the massacre at Wounded Knee and men and women who remember clearly the event and the feelings it aroused.

The key to the attitudes of the contemporary grandparent generation is the fact that they were trained by parents and grandparents who had participated in buffalo hunts and war parties and the great camp circles of the Sun Dance. These parents and grandparents experienced defeat, or at least subjugation, at the hands of the whites; but they could not appreciate that the Dakota way of life was doomed. Hence, the first adults on the reservation instilled in their children the belief that the customs, values, and glories of Dakota life were the best, and the best for all young Dakota. It is not surprising to find that today these young people, now become the grandparents and the old men and women of the reservation, still cling to Dakota tradition and custom.

The grandparents in their youth dispersed with their own parents from the band camps to settle on family farms, but they kept up the social integration of the band group and continued to conform to the Dakota mode of social behavior. These older people knew the last of the chiefs and the exercise of native authority and controls. They had some of the old childhood rites, such as the Ear-piercing and Buffalo ceremonies, performed over them. They married by the old customs and appear to have remained more frequently with one mate throughout life than have their sons and daughters. They respected the old sanctions and believe in many of them today. Even though they changed in their economic life, when the old economy had been swept from under them, they preserved many of the social aspects of the old culture through the momentum which had been started in their childhood training. They experienced receiving all their food from government rations for many years, but they were also able to give up rations and live almost completely by their own efforts in raising cattle.

The grandparents of today accepted Christianity as young people or have come to accept it in their old age. Probably only a few saw the last Sun Dance as children, but many attended the curing rites of the medicine men. Many were taught the beliefs of the old religion by their parents, and some were trained as medicine men and women, though not as priests for tribal ceremonies. With this religious background and the strong religious and moral education which many of them received at school, those who became Christians did so with more spiritual fervor than most of the Christian Indians of the younger Dakota generations.

The important training in moral code, however, came from the old virtues of Dakota life. As children they were taught to be brave, to fight against odds if need be, and not to run away without honor. Honor could be had by outwitting and by stealth as well as by dashing openly into combat. The inculcation of bravery in facing even the unknown is well described by Luther Standing Bear, who as a boy went off to school at Carlisle expecting that he would have to fight the white men and die far from his own people but that in doing so he would honor his father and himself as he had been taught.[2]

Fortitude, the second great virtue of the Dakota, was closely related to bravery. It was not only courage in battle but the enduring courage which enabled them to accept long hardships and to suffer pain and the self-inflicted tortures of their ceremonials. This quality of fortitude has sustained the people through much of the adversity and years of poverty on the reservation.

The third virtue, generosity, was one of the bases of behavior among one's own kindred. The "give-away," a dramatic ceremony of distributing all of one's own belongings, was a means of honoring others and gaining social prestige. By making gifts in the name of a child or deceased member of the family, a relative showed his love or his grief. He was also acclaimed and respected by his people, and especially by the recipients of the gifts, according to the amounts he gave and to the degree to which he impoverished himself. Such a system functioned without permanently ruining the givers, for everyone gave and in turn received gifts at subsequent ceremonies. One might also ask for articles of clothing or equipment from persons to whom gifts had been made.

The oldest generation retains the feeling of the necessity of making gifts to express the affection and ties they feel for others, and they have criticized those who have followed the white man's way of not giving. Generosity has continued to be an important virtue among the Dakota in spite of their poverty in the last twenty-five years and the great pressure of the government and missionaries to abandon the extremes of the give-away custom.

The fourth virtue of Dakota life is sometimes termed "wisdom" and sometimes "moral integrity."[3] Both were certainly ideals of manly behavior. Old men were expected to be wise and composed, and those who spoke well and showed good insight and judgment were elected to the councils. In the family the grandfathers were respected for their wisdom and were expected to pass it on to their grandsons. The present grandparents have tried to exercise this role; but, because their values come from the old culture and they do not understand many points of white behavior, they have not won the great respect accorded the old people in the former society.

Moral integrity based on the Dakota code has not been clearly defined. Certainly honesty and keeping one's word among one's people were qualities highly respected. A thief in his own group was highly disapproved and punished; in fact, reports of persons stealing from their own groups are rare. In a small camp where generosity was so prevalent, property had little personal value, and a man's own belongings were so well known by everyone that theft was unlikely to become common practice. However, stealing from the enemy was a virtue by which a warrior gained prestige.

These four virtues have always been described as those of the men. The same standards applied to women but in a slightly different way. In accepting hardship and suffering pain, even to the point of suppressing all outcries in childbirth, the women learned to show fortitude as well as the men. The ideals of womanly behavior are epitomized in the speech of the White Buffalo Maiden to the women in the ceremony described in chapter vii.

"Wakan Tanka intends that you shall bear much sorrow—comfort others in time of sorrow. By your hands the family moves. You have been given the knowledge of making clothing and of feeding the family. Wakan Tanka is with you in your sorrows and joins you in your griefs. He has given you the gift of kindness toward every living creature on earth. You he has chosen to have a feeling for the dead who are gone. He knows that you remember them longer than do the men. He knows that you love your children dearly."[4]

The sexual morality upheld by the churches coincides with the Dakota ideals of sexual behavior for women and has therefore been easily and willingly accepted by the older women. They also carry their former participation in religious ceremonies into regular church attendance.

THE ACQUIRING OF WHITE VALUES

The oldest generation, trained as they were by the last members of the functioning Dakota culture, have maintained most of the attitudes which this culture inculcated, but the influence of early training and contact with whites was also profound. Some of the grandparents of today attended Carlisle Institute, the all-Indian school established in 1879 in Pennsylvania, and lived with white families during summer vacations in an "outing" system set up to teach them white farming and household practices. The majority, however, had very little education, usually not beyond the sixth grade. They were introduced to white ways of making a living by government employees who were sent onto the reservation to instruct them in blacksmithing, carpentry, and stock-raising.

The cowboy who roamed with the great cattle herds in the territories of Dakota and Nebraska was one of the chief new culture-bearers. Of all the whites the Indians knew, the cowboy, who was their equal as a horseman and marksman, who lived in the out-of-doors, who moved independently and without fear of the Indian, made the greatest appeal. Into this type of life much in the activity of Dakota men could be transmitted. The cowboy made the cattle economy seem attractive, and this generation of Indians soon adopted it avidly. They prospered with their herds and made an excellent transition to the life of the white plainsman.

This experience is important in the redevelopment of the cattle industry at the present time, for it is the old people who encourage their sons to take up cattle-raising and especially encourage their grandsons to build up cattle herds while in school. In some communities the grandfathers, who know the advantages of raising cattle, have urged their grandsons to keep cattle given them or earned at school, in opposition to fathers, who advised their boys to sell and spend the cash return.

THE EFFECT OF ECONOMIC INSECURITY

The grandparents were able and willing to accept a new economy by which they were regaining security and a sense of self-reliance. They were approaching a satisfactory degree of acculturation when the cattle and land sales from 1916 to 1922 undermined most of the life they had built. The subsequent poverty and sickness and the return to complete economic dependency upon the government brought to them a sense of futility in following the white man's economy or accepting the white man's advice. To the so-called "New Deal" program of self-government and Indian management of economic enterprise, the old people are typically reactionary. Many of this generation, with some younger leaders opposed to the government, have organized a political group called the "Old Dealers." The hostility of the old people is not to changes from Indian to white life but to *any* change (especially threatened or anticipated changes) from the type of reservation life with allotments and direct government supervision, in which they had found some security. Even the revival of Indian handicrafts and art and the removal of restrictions upon Indian customs and religious ceremonies have not been received entirely as recognition of Indian culture or restoration of rights and liberties. Many of the old people have so thoroughly accepted the attitudes of teachers and missionaries of thirty and forty years ago that they feel a return to Indian custom is backsliding.

This attitude does not appear consistent with previous statements that the old people dream of a return to the old life. Individuals and groups of all races are never consistently logical or entirely rational, and the Dakota are no exception. Faced with specific acts or circumstances, the older Dakota appreciate the reality and the implications of the situation. But in their total situation in which they have experienced two almost overwhelming defeats, they have sought a psychological release in a very unrealistic dream of a life in which all the old freedoms and pleasures are regained and all the suffering and burdens are cast off along with the restrictions imposed by whites.

CONFLICT OF WHITE AND DAKOTA STANDARDS

The attitudes of the next generation differ to a considerable degree from those of their elders because the younger men had less training for Dakota life in childhood and as adults have not experienced the cowboy life or satisfactions of the cattle economy.

This generation went to school, usually to boarding schools. But since they usually started when they were ten or twelve, they had time to go through only some of the elementary grades. They learned the white man's work and housekeeping; but, as it was far removed from the actual needs or conditions of their homes and was usually based on necessary maintenance of the school plants, it proved to be inadequate training for making a living on the reservation. The schools forbade the use of Indian language and enforced strict discipline. When students returned to their homes, where control was not exerted by strict discipline, they often became behavior problems to their parents. The older present-day parents recall the former military rule and regulations somewhat unpleasantly, but many believe such school discipline desirable for children "to make them obey."

The outlook on life of the second generation has been greatly conditioned by the years of cattle and land sales and land-leasing, when their families were comparatively wealthy, and the subsequent years of poverty and hardship. The greater security of their childhood and the luxuries enjoyed just when they were starting out in life or had families of small children were lost, and for this they are now likely to blame the government, whose lack of foresight was one of the prime reasons for their plight. This antagonism toward the government has not decreased in the years since 1922 when they began returning to dependency upon government aid for their livelihood.

The loss of the cattle economy and the cowboy life for which the men of this generation were trained as children is closely related to an important need to have a role and function which gives the men importance in their own eyes and in the eyes of their people and of the whites. Hence, the opportunity to make a living, to have property, and to be independent of "charity" or government support attracts some of them now to become cattle operators.

Many Indians, however, have become discouraged over the possibilities of a satisfactory and permanent life derived from the land. The cumulative experience of the sale of the herds in the past, the continual loss of land resources by reduction on the reservation, the sales of allotments, the many failures of Indians who were encouraged to borrow money and enter dry farming during the 1920's, and the drought and successive failures of crops and cattle herds during the 1930's have created much doubt as to the wisdom of attempting to live by the land resources again.

Another attitude which is slowing the acceptance of a cattle economy is the inclination toward wage work. This type of work brings an immediate return and solves the present problem of living, whereas entering the stock business requires waiting for at least two or three years before receiving any adequate returns. For people who are as impoverished as most of the Pine Ridge Indians, the opportunity of obtaining an immediate income is very influential in their decision about how to make a living. Widespread experience in wage work began with farm labor in the twenties, was increased by relief work in the thirties, and

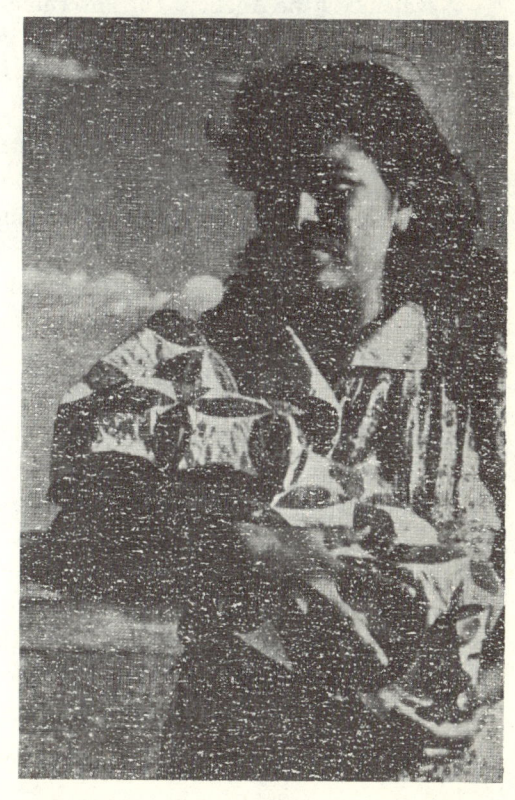

FOUR GENERATIONS

is now continuing in war and farm work at highly increased wage rates. The present employment is reinforcing the conviction that wage work is a highly satisfactory way of earning a livelihood.

One of the chief problems that have arisen over the development of the cattle economy is the attitude which the second generation in particular holds toward the land. In spite of the fact that land was not regarded as private property in the pre-reservation era, it has become property of intrinsic value to modern Dakota since the sale and rental of allotments began. The income from leasing or selling allotments gave them a new value in the eyes of the Indians. Here was a means of obtaining cash without effort. However, the real worth of the land was not realized: the desire to commute it to cash was uppermost. When the landless began to discover that they had no way of raising more money or any means of growing food, the value of their land struck home. Those who retained their land for rental also became aware of its value as other sources of revenue failed or disappeared.

Land is not conceived of as a source of food or income but as potential cash; the real value of the land to the Indian lies in its possible sale. This was demonstrated after the recent sale of allotments in the bombing area, when the cash became available at the Agency. The government made it mandatory that those who had sold their lands establish a budget for investment in new land in order that they might improve their earning capacity on the reservation. But all of them demanded cash, and not 10 per cent of the Indians wanted to invest money in new land. Most of the people therefore requested livestock and equipment in the hope that they could turn these into cash at a later date. One Indian with a record of good management voiced the prevailing attitude when he said he wanted cash—some to give his wife, some to buy things for his children, some for clothes, and the rest for travel and a little good time. Here again is the old premium on disposing of wealth. Behind this also lies the belief that land held in trust is something really belonging outright to the Indian to do with as he pleases. This same Indian, who would spend all his money from land sales, also proposed to ask the government for a loan to rehabilitate himself on rented land. Such apparent impracticality stems from attitudes derived from past experiences and the wardship status.

It must be remembered that the able-bodied men who can become the stockmen of the reservation today have had little experience in managing cattle and buying and selling on the market. Twenty or thirty years ago they were only boys whose fathers ran the cattle herds. They gained some experience with cattle in working with their fathers, but when they were old enough to take over the full operations, the cattle were gone. There is, then, for many of the men the problem of entering a business in which they are very inadequately trained.

Lack of confidence in the ability of other Indians deters many from leasing land to them or co-operating in group economic ventures. In every community there are some Indians who have been in the cattle business for several years and prefer to continue on an independent basis. Some of these are the sons of white men who trained them to keep away from other Indians and work individually like the white farmer. Others have been established on an independent basis by government assistance under programs which attempted to help the able-bodied and willing families in the community. These Indian farmers are frequently uninterested in pooling their land in a co-operative range and joining a cattle association of inexperienced men who are just commencing business.

Conflict has developed between individualistic and competitive ranching and the co-operative associations which the government is now promoting. Co-operative operations appeal strongly to the full-blood people. The Dakota man was individualistic only in making his tools and weapons and in the choice of time and nature of his daily work in support of his family. Most of his hunting, his warfare, his travel, and his camp were organized in co-operation with others. To act together and share together were highly important values. These are still important values which many of the people express in modern economic enterprises.

The individualism and competition of the white man have, however, been learned, and they have made inroads into the attitudes of many Indians, especially mixed-bloods. Those who are unwilling to co-operate in co-operative enterprises or wish to withdraw from them often impair the efficiency of these enterprises by withholding necessary lands and creating jealousies and bad feeling because of their adherence to non-Indian traits.

The conflict between the developing individualism of the white man and the co-operation and sharing of the Indian also crops up in the difference in attitudes toward the accumulation or sharing of wealth. The second generation, especially the mixed-blood members, have diverged greatly from the Indian customs surrounding generosity.

The Indian who amasses a large herd of cattle, builds a good home, and receives an income of a thousand dollars or more but does not distribute his wealth on ceremonial occasions, such as a wedding or funeral in his family, becomes the subject of severe criticism and ostracism by his relatives and friends. This is just what happened to many mixed-bloods who followed the white pattern of accumulating property and thus lost favor and status with the majority of the people in their communities.

Pressure to abandon the practice of the give-away has had some effect, and the recent poverty of the people has diminished the amounts given. The result of these influences was observed at a recent ceremony. A widow gave stacks of hay to her husband's relatives and said privately that she would give away all her household furnishings. Her stepfather advised her that this would be foolish, for she would need them later. The next day the widow gave away great lengths of calico purchased at the store but kept her house intact. This was not entirely outside former Sioux practice, when the husband's relatives would request a woman to keep some things for herself,[5] but such encouragement from her own relatives was formerly looked upon as selfish. Now, reinforced by Indian Service and white opinion, the Indians are becoming more cautious in the giving-away of goods.

The give-away as one expression of the Sioux ideal of generosity and strong social cohesion is not such a detrimental factor today as its less formal aspect, the custom of hospitality. To receive and feed all visitors, especially relatives, is still an obligation. It is this custom which undermines economic development of individual families and keeps them poor. When there were greater food resources to be obtained by the skill of the hunter and everyone was close to the same level of wealth, hospitality did not tax the individual family too heavily. Individuals who remained too long to continue to receive hospitality at the home of a well-to-do family usually repaid their obligations by assisting the family.

This is not now the case. Relatives come for a meal, or for a few days while the food resources last, and then depart. If a man is a farmer with a good garden or his wife has a large store of canned vegetables and there is a steer in the pasture which might be butchered, relatives will come often and stay long. This cannot be a two-way affair, as in the past, for only the few are comparatively well off and the majority are impoverished. Moreover, a good farmer cannot leave his cattle and crops to travel about obtaining reciprocity for his previous generosity. Thus hospitality has become a burden to the few and a strong deterrent to accumulating material wealth.

The conflict of the old hospitality with modern economic machinery is also shown in the situation, so unfair according to white standards, in which idle young people visit over long periods of time with their grandparents who are on old age assistance rolls. The young people expect to be supported indefinitely on meager assistance checks without reciprocating, as they would have been obligated to do in the old society.

The man with a regular salary today becomes a target for his poorer and ne'er-do-well relatives. "He has enough. Why should he not feed us? He is my relative," is the prevailing attitude. In the rural communities regularly employed men are few, usually employees of the trader or of the government school and farm station. They live in the community center where people are constantly coming for provisions and mail. What could be more natural than for relatives to stop by for dinner or supper or both? In one community, the practice drove the school bus-drivers to petition that they be transferred elsewhere and that no local men be employed, in order that they might not be impoverished by their relatives.

The rarity of the man or woman with a regular cash income in the rural areas makes his position almost untenable. Thus the wage-worker solves his problem by going to work at the Agency, where nearly all the men are wage-workers, or by leaving the reservation altogether. This possibility of moving helps to make wage work more popular than farming in one's own neighborhood.

The attitude toward money, moreover, makes the position of the wage-worker socially more comfortable than that of a farmer who is doing fairly well. In Indian terms, money is not strictly property and the attitudes toward property do not fully apply to it. Hence it is not subject to complete requisition in the form of hospitality. To be sure, an individual will ask for a small loan or gift of money; but, although he may encourage it, he will not expect another to spend all his money on him or give it away ceremonially. Only when money is transposed into food or objects which can be eaten or received as gifts does it become property which its owner is expected to share. Therefore the wage-worker is in a safer position than the prosperous farmer. The wage-worker may hide his money and appear poor, or leave it in the hands of the government, whence it is thought to be difficult to draw out. Better than this is the possibility of spending the money quickly on himself. Saving exposes one to visits from poor relatives and is against good Sioux behavior. Spending therefore is approved, and if a man spends money on a car, a radio, good meals for his family in a restaurant, and expensive Stetson hats, cowboy boots, and silk shawls, he has behaved in an approved manner and avoided much possible criticism. Nevertheless, the owner of personal luxuries is still subject to the expectation of gifts and loans.

SOCIAL CONTROLS

It is obvious from the conflicting attitudes just described that the Pine Ridge people are under the influence of two cultures but are not living completely in either. The existence of conflicting standards of behavior makes it inevitable that almost any action of the individual is out of line with the standards of some members of his community. Normally a society attempts to bring conformity to its standards by the imposition of sanctions against the nonconformer. The Dakota, in seeking to impose the sanctions of the old society upon nonconformity to approved ways, have often intensified, rather than reduced, the deviation. The imposing of sanctions has also failed because the Dakota do not have the right to impose some of the old controls and have lost to the government the imposition of others.

As noted in chapter iv, the Dakota had a law-enforcing agency in the *akicita*, or camp police, whose authority was absolute. Early travelers among the Sioux have noted the whippings inflicted on the unruly. Murderers might be clubbed or shot on the spot. The family of the wronged person might also seek vengeance on the offender or a member of his family.

The most potent forms of social control, however, were criticism, ridicule, and ostracism. Public ceremonies in which men claimed war honors or women were honored for their virtue included the right to ridicule false claimants. Childhood training implanted a fear of shame which made criticism and ridicule very potent deterrents to any deviations from the accepted code.

Both the physical punishment by the *akicita* and the control by ridicule in ceremony have gone with the old encampments, but criticism, ridicule, and ostracism are still important methods of keeping the individual in line. People gossip about the nonconformer, sing satirical songs about him at the Rabbit Dance, or ignore him in public.

The story of the Indian who purchased a new wagon and, in the manner of white farmers, covered it with tarpaulin for protection from sun and wind is a typical example of this type of control. This man left his carefully covered wagon beside his house in the center of the village. His neighbors on their way to and from the store called out, "Hi there, who do you think you are—a *wasicu* [white man] covering up your wagon?" The jeering at white custom and the white man's sense of the value of property drove the proud owner to take off the tarpaulin at the end of three days and leave his wagon to dry and crack in the hot sun.

At present, such controls are used largely to enforce co-operation, the basis of Dakota interaction. The main area where attempts are made to enforce co-operation is in the use of property; conflicts in this area have already been described. The second area is co-operation in work and in family relations, both of which are changing rapidly. Controls are also exerted in the field of sex relations, but less frequently than in other areas because standards are more in conflict.

The varying economic policies of the government have had the effect at one time of dispersing the old extended family groups and at another of bringing them together. Allotments broke up the old band camps and dispersed family homes over a much wider area. When families sold their allotments in the boom of the twenties, they were forced to move from their homes. The usual procedure was to settle with parents or other relatives who did not want to dispose of their land or who could not establish competency. The extended family groups were thus re-established as in the old *tiyospaye* camps. However, there was little work to be done, little opportunity for the men to work together as they had in managing their cattle herds, and few means of support. Many families left for the summer to work in the potato fields but returned in the winter to share and live together.

With the development of C.C.C. work projects, the younger families and unmarried men went to live in the work camps and to move with them as projects were undertaken in different parts of the reservation. Since then many of these families have left the reservation to live near the war-industry centers.[6]

This dispersion of families over and outside the reservation has weakened the co-operation of the extended family and community groups. Frequently the stay-at-homes, the older people and women and children, have been asked to look after the horses or a few cattle of the absentees. Such co-operation is willingly given, but very often there is no return of assistance by the people who have gone away. This is due to changing attitudes. Those who have gone away expect those at home to co-operate by caring for property left behind, according to Indian custom; but, like white men, they have come to regard money earned on the job as belonging exclusively to themselves and their immediate families. Those left behind are at a disadvantage under both customs.

The older generation, trained more intensely in the Dakota tradition of cooperation, feel the desire to give and receive it more than do the younger people. When young people who have left home return, frequently without money, they become subject to the criticism of relatives and neighbors.

The younger people often feel resentful and sometimes confused. Frequently they are trying to live by two social codes: one which seems to be keeping them poor and another which is allowing them to gratify many of their personal desires. Because they are not linked with relatives and responsibilities when they live away from the reservation, they have much freedom. This lack of immediate responsibility creates attitudes that would bring difficulties even in white society, were these individuals to remain there permanently.

This situation is by no means universal on Pine Ridge, but it is frequent enough to cause much family disorganization. The breakdown of the family results in serious difficulties for the individual and particularly for children.

Another realm of social control closely related to family co-operation and organization is sex behavior and the attitudes between men and women. Like family relations, sex relations and attitudes are changing, and social dislocation is produced by partial adherence to Dakota customs.

In the former society unmarried men were placed under little control in their advances toward women and given no punishment if they succeeded in having sex relations. The controls were placed rather upon the women, through strict chaperonage of all unmarried girls and young women. There can be no doubt that this involved a concept of wrongdoing in extramarital sex relations, but immorality and evil were not emphasized as in white society. Premarital sex relations did occur; but, if known by others, they were forgotten as soon as the girl was married.

With the isolation of homes on the reservation and the increasing amount of travel alone by young people, girls can no longer be under the constant chaperonage of older female relatives. When the girls go away to school, they learn the white standards of freer association with boys. The acceptance outside the school of white standards of free association has made the complete protection and control of girls and women impossible. Furthermore, the sex standards of the whites with whom most Indians associate easily outside the school are not those taught by the school and the missionaries. It is not surprising, therefore, that control of extramarital sex relations has broken down and that the attitudes toward them are much freer than those sanctioned either by the former Dakota society or by the middle class in white society.

Parents try to use the old control of criticism, since chaperonage has become impossible, but criticism seems to have lost its former weight with the young people. Parents therefore frequently turn to white controls and ask school principals or police to bring back runaway daughters or to punish young men who have seduced them.

The breakdown in family control and the failure of the child-training system are not the only causes for increasing sexual delinquency. From time immemorial this has been a symptom of and sequel to general social disorganization. On the reservation the sex delinquency is to be found among the most disorganized generation—the parents—as often as among the young people. Hence it is probable that the illicit sexual behavior of parents and the amount of gossip about it in the community cause as much delinquency among the younger people as lack of social control.

The general attitude of Dakota men toward women also calls for comment. Dakota culture was definitely oriented toward the life and pursuits of the men, and the women's life was almost completely supplementary to the men's activities. The position to which most of the men have now been reduced by economic and political changes has not given them prestige by which they can maintain their pre-eminent role. The men have felt, therefore, some resentment, some guilt, and much dissatisfaction, and they often become critical of and antagonistic toward women. On the other hand, the position of women in the family and in the community has risen, and their function in the family is often more important today than that of the men. They have become critical of men's behavior and have held it up to ridicule. These changes in roles and status have led to hostile attitudes and relationships on the part of both men and women, and even to the breakup of many families. Women have left their husbands for men who can give them better homes with more to eat. Resentful husbands have left home to live with more congenial women or to work and keep their earnings to themselves.

In the old days a runaway wife's nose was cut off. If a husband deserted his family, he was subject to severe criticism and the pressures of both his and his wife's families to return. At present little heed is paid to family criticism. Many wives dislike to ask the Tribal Court or the Agency social worker to enforce support or mete out punishment, and so social disintegration goes unchecked. The primary cause appears to lie in the economic conditions, but increased incomes alone will not remedy the situation. It seems unlikely that social disorganization can be overcome unless its effects upon families, especially the children, are fully realized by the people and until the communities can take greater responsibility for imposing controls upon their own members.

The right of appointed police to impose physical punishment or of families to exact justice independently of the general society passed with the nomadic life. But the substitutes—the powers of the Agency police and punishment by fines and imprisonment—have not accomplished the same control. The people still fear the police, by tradition or through the experience of being taken to school, but the chief reaction to the penalties imposed by the Tribal Court has been annoyance at inconvenience. Going to jail now causes less embarrassment than resentment. Indians resent this type of punishment because, even though the judges are Indians, the court is regarded as an institution imposed by whites. Arrest and punishment, therefore, bring little sense of shame. Friends and relatives will help an offender to avoid arrest and commonly will not act as witnesses or tell the full facts of the case. Family co-operation and loyalty are strong in these situations, relatives being both unwilling to betray and afraid to expose themselves to criticism and retaliation. Such refusal to testify has often been the case even when relatives are the injured parties.

On the other hand, people do resort to the Tribal Court and police where other means of control are ineffective. Frequently they ask police or court to make a man pay damages or support his children. Most people prefer, however, to arrive at an amicable settlement in these cases with the aid of a local government official.

The Tribal Court and the adoption of a tribal law code have reduced some of the antagonism toward the white system of law and order, but new problems have also arisen. Indian judges and police are subject to all the pressure of Indian society. Relatives expect them to side with family groups, and nonrelatives accuse them of prejudice and special favors. The personal lives of judges are well known, and any infringement of the moral code or the law in the past is brought up as a means of criticism. Jealousy and resentment are usually aroused when Indians are elevated above the social level of the group. It is to be remembered that formerly people attempted to pull down those who rose by unapproved means.

ATTITUDE TOWARD WHITES

Not only the attempts to impose law and order but many other relationships to the government have been unsettling to the Dakota. The Pine Ridge Indians have been dependents since 1868, when the primitive tribe needed to be fed and protected and guided in its adjustment to civilized society. The government by treaty gives each eighteen-year-old boy or girl farming equipment or household property. The Agency controls the leasing of individually alloted lands; it handles all inheritances; it controls and distributes at its discretion all moneys except wages that come from the government to the Indian; it advises the Indian in a paternalistic manner in many intimate details of his daily life.[7] There has resulted a parent-child, superior-inferior relationship between the government and the individual Indian that extends from the cradle to the grave. Even as late as 1943, the Agency wished to maintain this relationship over many families who had proved their competency to manage their affairs by earning and repaying government loans of money and cattle. The responsibility of many of the Dakota and their ability to succeed in white life have long since been proved, but often they are still treated as more or less irresponsible children. There is no way in which the competent Indian can become a completely independent citizen on the reservation, subject only to the laws and regulations under which his white neighbor lives. The Indian does, in fact, receive some special privileges, but these are little compensation to his feeling of legal inequality and social inferiority.

The fact that the Agency also is the source of food, work, schools, and hospitals—almost every opportunity and service which white men usually earn or provide through taxing themselves—is a source of frustration. One who must always receive and never return is put in a position of obligation that makes him feel overpowered. To people who were so meticulous as the Dakota about repaying gifts, the position of ward is especially galling. This relationship to the government has gone on so long that the Indians now cling to it for security and yet resent it because it does not permit them to be fully responsible citizens. The government has thus become the victim of its own methods for "civilizing" the Indian; it is now responsible for wards who resent wardship, on the one hand, and yet, on the other, are not fully willing to assume greater responsibility for themselves.[8]

The relationship of Indians to the general society of whites both on the reservation and in outside communities has been one of friction, hostility, and insecurity.

It must be remembered that it was the policy of the government, until 1933, for the Indians to merge with the white population. Although forced assimilation is no longer the policy, the white man's educational system, family and social life, religion, and especially his economic system are held up to the Indian as the most desirable forms of living. The white man's type of life has been made the Indian's goal in the past, and toward this goal his society and culture have been moving. Thus when in individual contacts the Indian finds himself ostracized or exploited by white men, he feels threatened and baffled. When he accepts the advice and encouragement of the white man, he often meets with rebuffs from other white men which show him that, as as Indian, he is considered either outside white society or else included only in its lowest stratum. He therefore sees himself as permanently inferior and marginal to the society which exhorts him—and often forces him—to emulate its ways.

EFFECTS OF CONFLICT

The modern social structure, with its poverty, lack of adequate roles and cultural objectives, and social conflicts arising out of lost controls and changing attitudes, is strongly conducive to insecurity for the group and for the individual. As each Dakota man or woman now looks back to the past either from experience or through the stories which have been told him, he senses the self-assurance and the ability of his ancestors to cope with life. They were united and secure in the life they followed, and their institutions gave good reinforcement within the group. By comparison, the modern Indian way of life is one of emptiness, one in which family and community are losing their integration. The contemporary life, as compared with the culture that was functioning in the middle nineteenth century, is only a shadow. Attitudes and values of that culture still strongly affect the behavior patterns of the people, but some of its social institutions are gone or are only vestigial. The realization of cultural loss and being neither Indian nor white in any cultural sense adds to the Indian's insecurity and isolation in the modern world.

This insecurity of the adults, which is now so apparent from the material point of view in their meager incomes and from the psychological point of view in their inconsistent behavior and conflicting attitudes, creates an atmosphere which cannot help having repercussions upon the children as they grow up. The young children can only sense the confusion and the uncertainty of their parents without understanding the causes, and so they themselves feel insecure. This insecurity in the environment is one of the most significant aspects to keep in mind as we turn now to the children's training and social adjustments.

NOTES

1. Scudder Mekeel, *The Economy of a Modern Teton Dakota Community* (New Haven, Conn.: Yale University Press, 1936), p. 5.
2. *My People the Sioux* (Boston: Houghton Mifflin Co., 1928), p. 124.
3. Sioux informants are not in agreement concerning the four chief virtues. J. R. Walker (*The Sun Dance and Other Ceremonies of the Oglala Division of the Teton Dakota* [New York: American Museum of Natural History, 1917], p. 79) reports them as bravery, fortitude, generosity, and fidelity. However, in his translation of a text by an Indian named Tyon, they are listed as bravery, generosity, truthfulness, and begetting children (p. 60).
4. Frances Densmore, *Teton Sioux Music* (U.S. Bureau of American Ethnology Bull. 61 [Washington, 1918]), p. 65.
5. See Jeannette Mirsky, "The Dakota," in *Co-operation and Competition among Primitive Peoples*, ed. Margaret Mead (New York: McGraw-Hill Book Co., 1937), p. 388.
6. This trend is somewhat offset by the fact that many war workers and soldiers have left their families on the reservation with the grandparents or other relatives.
7. One modern translation of the Sioux term for the white man is indeed revealing—*wasicu*, "he who commands."
8. See Erik Homburger Erikson, "Observations on Sioux Education," *Journal of Psychology*, VII (1939), 101-56.

PART II. GROWING UP ON THE RESERVATION

CHAPTER IX

INFANCY

As noted in chapter iv, Dakota concepts of training the child were, and are, in many ways different from those of white society. While many of the objectives of the two systems are similar, the method and timing of training for these objectives differ. Traditionally, the Dakota infant's training in cleanliness, careful handling of possessions, and other forms of behavior that a child has to learn begins later than in white society, and it is not enforced by the strong controls, such as spanking, so common in white child-training. Nor is the Dakota child fed, bathed, and put to sleep by the clock. Today white methods are used increasingly by the more assimilated Indian families, but the stronger discipline characteristic of the training of white children comes chiefly from the schools on the reservation.

The health of the Dakota baby on the reservation today reflects clearly the teaching of Indian Service doctors and nurses, and delivery in the hospital has greatly lowered mortality in childbirth. White concepts of infant care are also followed by some Dakota mothers, and it is indisputable that modern pediatric practices have saved the lives of many infants. Yet, combined with the care of the baby's health learned from white doctors and nurses are training methods based on Dakota concepts.

White ways of child care affect the Dakota child today even before birth. The prenatal clinics, the visits of field nurses to the homes before the birth, and hospital delivery provide the child a better start in life than was likely for the child born in the Indian home before such services were available. Most mothers are now going to the hospital to receive adequate attention and avoid the unsanitary conditions at home.

Some women, however, prefer to have their children in the home because they are afraid of the white man's medicine. Having a child inside the house is in itself a change from the former, and probably more sanitary, practice of being delivered in a clean sand pit outside the tepee, where there was no contact with an unclean bed and the afterbirth was buried. There appears to be little preparation today for many of the births that occur in the homes. Assistance to the mother varies. Women told interviewers in this study that they had their children unattended or, if they had difficulty, called their husbands to assist them. It is the usual practice, however, to have the mother or the mother's sister attend; contrary to the former custom, mothers-in-law also assist. Midwives and medicine men are occasionally called in, but they are becoming afraid to practice as openly as in the old days. If there are accidents, women are quick to condemn the midwife and blame the mother for not securing the services of a modern physician. The only old practices and beliefs connected with births reported in our field study were the occasional burning of the afterbirth and the belief by some mothers that bleeding of the umbilical cord causes the child to be weak.

EARLY CARE AND DEVELOPMENT

Babies are now put in diapers and dresses. When the baby is laid to sleep or carried out of the house, it is wrapped in a square baby blanket, pinned into a tight bundle like the old skin cradle. Erikson comments on the possible frustrations imposed on the child by both the old tight wrapping with its stiff but boardless back and the present tightly pinned blanket,[1] but there is some question as to whether the baby is actually frustrated by such confinement. For the newborn child, the warm wrapping is perhaps comfortable and satisfying. Modern babies are quite frequently unwrapped, often left to play on the bed, or laid in a hammock made of a blanket pinned through two loops of rope hung from the ceiling of the room. Two mothers stated to interviewers in this study that their children did not like being wrapped when carried; hence they always left the arms free. It was noticed that mothers holding their wrapped babies almost constantly rocked them lightly on their knee or passed the child to another woman or girl who rocked the child as long as she kept it.

Most mothers on the reservation today nurse their babies. Where the mother's milk is insufficient or unsuitable for the baby, Indian Service nurses and doctors advise the substitution of canned milk. The scheduled feeding practiced by white mothers is advocated by reservation nurses and doctors, but this advice is infrequently followed, so strong is the Dakota belief that a child should be fed whenever he frets. Resistance to scheduled feeding is also due to the fact that Indian families do not regulate their daily life by the clock.

Reservation doctors and nurses recommend weaning between the ninth and twelfth months, and some women now abruptly wean their babies at this time. But most mothers extend the weaning process over a period of many months, gradually introducing solid foods. The time of weaning reported to interviewers in this study ranged from nine to thirty-six months, with the majority falling in the period of eleven to eighteen months. In the cases of prolonged nursing, as Erikson puts it, the child weans the mother.[2]

Early weaning is probably not so satisfactory as the doctors and nurses anticipate, for the weaned baby is usually given much of the meat and starchy foods served to the rest of the family. Milk is not always available. Furthermore, the special foods given to white babies after weaning (even orange juice) are hard to obtain in the rural communities and may be beyond the means of the poorer families when they are available. One nurse, after three years of clinic work, questions the value of the white feeding and weaning practices on the reservation because many children weaned early are completely deprived of milk, and essential elements provided by the former native foods are no longer consumed.

Our observations indicate little attempt by Sioux babies to get oral gratification by sucking their fingers. This may be due to the prolonged nursing, granted at every request, and the gradual weaning still in practice. Only one child, aged four, was observed with a rubber pacifier, and only two were reported as being given objects to suck on—one a piece of pork and the other a wiener! Erikson believes that the common Dakota habit of snapping the thumbnail against the front teeth is connected with the nursing practices.[3] Both children and adults also constantly pick their teeth with sticks and put all the fingers into the mouth. Frequent playing with the lips is definitely absent. Erikson suggests that these habits are derived from frustrations and discipline that occur when the child bites while nursing at the mother's breast. On the other hand, it seems only logical to assume that many children might learn to suppress the biting of the breast if deprived of food and teethe on a toy or some other object with full satisfaction. From our observations (and also those of Erikson), the teeth-clicking habit occurs predominantly among women and girls. If both boys and girls are subject to the same frustration, the boys appear to find some other release. It is suggested that this is found in the greater aggressive behavior permitted the boys. The possibility that this habit is a form of eroticism has also been advanced.[4]

Full-blood parents place no great importance on the time when a child learns to walk or to talk. In the interviews the mother could usually recall the approximate month in which talking and walking occurred, but she never indicated that she had felt anxiety that a child did not learn soon enough or any special pride that the child showed precocity. The parents assume that children will learn to walk at some time between the ninth and fifteenth month, and they patiently wait for the time with little use of persuasion.

The time of learning to talk also varies greatly; usually talking is begun three to four months after learning to walk. Parents exert no pressure to hasten the child's performance at an early age or to change those who are temporarily satisfied with one word for all objects. The development of the child is watched with amusement and patience. None of the full-blood parents or adults use baby talk, and they usually teach their children Siouan. Many of these children do not speak English readily when they enter school, although they may have a small English vocabulary picked up from older brothers and sisters.

EARLY TRAINING

About the time when the child can understand and communicate with his mother, toilet training commences. Formerly training consisted mainly of putting the little child outside the tepee, but now parents have greater concern about this side of the child's discipline. A few parents continue to put the child outside the door or hold him over a piece of paper on the floor. The majority use an old syrup can, or, if they can afford it, a baby's chamber pot purchased at the trader's. When the children can walk, mothers leave their diapers or underpants off, so that the child can go to the toilet as he pleases. The prevalence of this custom is difficult to estimate because underpants are usually slipped on when visitors, especially whites, are seen approaching the house.

Very few mothers recounted any difficulty in training their children in adequate toilet behavior. They placed the child on the pot after each meal and in a few days the child learned to warn his mother. Much of this training is aided by the example of older brother and sisters who are also using the pot. If there is any great significance in the modern Dakota toilet training, it is that a change has been made from the former mild and gradual methods to pressures hastening sphincter control and excretion in special places. This training, however, is usually neither so intensive nor associated with such strong punishments as is the training usually imposed on white children. Dakota methods are also without the overemphasized concepts of filth concerning bodily functions and the taboos associated with a private place and locked doors. The possible significance of the children's drawings of the outhouse may be questioned. However, in many of these drawings outhouse doors are shown open. This is an observation of a characteristic situation, and it may reflect the children's lack of feeling that such a place should be closed and the interior hidden from view. Another note of unconcern about toilet facilities was observed in households where the children used the toilet chair as an ordinary seat in the house.

As noted in chapter viii, one of the cardinal virtues of the old Dakota society, which is still strong today, was generosity. Gifts of property were made to honor the recipient and the giver alike.

Modern Dakota children are carefully trained in this tradition. Many children are given farm animals when they are only two or three years old, and giving a horse to a child is the traditional way for an uncle or older brother to honor him. Quite aside from the pleasure which any gift brings a young child, receiving an animal has distinct training values on the reservation in developing the interest of the child in rural life. Little boys soon learn to recognize their own animals and are anxious to ride or care for them as soon as possible. Girls' animals are cared for by their older brothers or fathers; even so, the personal interest in watching a pony grow and in learning to ride him have distinct training values. These gifts also have an economic value, for any issue from them is scrupulously regarded as the child's own and is taken over by him as he grows up. If it is sold, the money is used to buy something the child wants or is kept for him. This is the ideal—and indeed the common—practice, but under the pressure of poverty and with the changing attitudes toward property, many exceptions may be noted. Parents are known to have slaughtered or sold the children's animals.

The gifts to children serve to inculcate in them a reciprocal generosity as a means of gaining approval. Children of five, six, and seven give freely and pleasantly to their younger brothers and sisters. Small children learn the more formal type of giving by observing their elders. At one funeral where there was much giving, a small boy of the bereaved family spent his only dime to buy artificial orange powder in order to give a bucket of orangeade ceremonially to the visiting youngsters.

Among the Sioux property does not have the high value associated with it in white society. This carries over into Dakota child-training in ways that are astonishing to white observers. Parents usually put valuable or breakable articles which they wish to preserve out of reach of the young child, and he therefore picks up and handles anything he wishes. However, when valuables are large or not so easily safeguarded, the attitude of indulgence persists. White people will sit outside an Indian home in bewilderment and utter frustration watching children tear a headlight off a car or drag good harness over the ground in play, while the parents sit by undisturbed. To the whites it seems preposterous that people who are so poor should allow children to damage useful objects that have been earned with great difficulty. This is a part of the lack of concern over property that underlies the Dakota virtue of generosity; it is also a way of teaching children not to set a high value on property.

The methods of teaching small children proper behavior are based on encouraging the child to do what is desired by kindness and patience and by example rather than by a long series of "don'ts." To white people Indian child-training appears to consist more of "spoiling" than disciplining, but Indian parents have several means of controlling their children. Warnings and shaming the child are started early by criticizing him for not doing what is proper and approved.

Parents also attempt to divert, rather than prohibit, children from doing undesirable things. Sometimes misbehavior is simply ignored; little children are allowed to scream in rage, which, according to old belief, will make them strong. Spanking is rare, although it seems to be becoming more frequent among mixed-blood families. Full-bloods say that spanking will make a child crazy and are contemptuous of parents who slap or whip.

The punitive controls are the child frighteners, such as the mythical Tchitchi man, Sioko, a crazy man, and a witch who appears as a thistle. These figures are used to keep the child from wandering away from home. Wiwili, a mysterious spirit who frightens or catches children who go near the creeks, is used to keep the children away from the water. Significantly, all threatening or frightening is done through invoking these supernatural figures or humans who are outside the family group. Even more significant is the fact that the human figure used as a child frightener is usually a white man. It can readily be seen that, unless there is some friendly white person in the child's early life, fear may be built up which will condition a child against whites for years, if not for life.

PLAY

Play was a way of learning as well as recreation for the child in the old Dakota society and is so regarded today. Small boys were formerly given little bows and arrows with which to imitate hunters and warriors in their play. They were also given the foot bones of a buffalo, which they used as toy horses and buffalo. Little boys today are encouraged to play with a rope and slingshot and to chase the rooster and smaller animals in the yard, in order to develop aggressiveness. The foot bones, now those of a horse or cow, are called "horses" and "cattle," each being designated by its general form or some facet of the bone as a stallion, mare, mule, bull, cow, or steer. This kind of play intensifies and gives expression to the boy's first interest in animals and the career of a cowboy.

From the time they can walk, little girls have dolls with which they play in imaginary episodes of the activities of older girls and women. This play is frequently centered around dressing and undressing dolls, wrapping them in blankets, and putting them into toy wagons made of boxes. Little girls also have many paper dolls made by cutting pictures out of magazines. These pictures of white people in white clothes have no little significance in determining later standards of feminine dress and appearance. The little girls also play at cooking, washing clothes, and keeping house. It is not long before they are given little chores as part of their play to teach them the household duties of the women.

DRESS

Pine Ridge children dress much like the white children in any midwestern rural community. The only Indian elements in the everyday appearance are the long

WARRIORS FOR A DAY

braids worn by some small full-blood boys, but these are invariably cut by the time the child is ready for school. Doting grandmothers may make a beaded buckskin suit, but it is always thought of as a costume and is worn only at fairs and Indian dances where the child participates beside his costumed elders. Some parents buy wide-brimmed hats and high-heeled boots which enhance little boys' favorite imaginary role of cowboy. Otherwise children in their homes and at school look much like any group of white American boys and girls.

As soon as infant clothing is outgrown, little girls are put into short cotton dresses. As they grow older, they wear the cotton or wool dresses, the sweaters and skirts, and the socks worn by all American schoolgirls. No Pine Ridge girl today wears the ankle-length dress, cloth leggings, and moccasins occasionally seen on the old grandmothers. The shawl, which is still worn by most older women, is not used by the schoolgirl, although she may wear it in her home or at an Indian dance and may adopt it for general wear after she has left school. The schoolgirl's usual outdoor garment is a heavy sweater or cloth coat and the scarf worn over the head by many white girls. It is very rare for an Indian girl or woman to wear a hat. The long pigtails worn by the little girls look much like those in our society. Older girls cut their hair and most of them, like their white counterparts, make some attempt to cultivate a "wave."

Little boys are dressed much like their fathers from the time they discard their baby clothes. Every boy beyond the toddling stage wears the same kind of clothes he will wear all his life—long trousers or dungarees, a shirt, and a felt hat or hunting cap. He may have a suit for dress affairs, as his father has a suit for wear at church or on long trips off the reservation. At school he may wear a sweater. But, by and large, he wears the same costume most of his life.

This habit of dressing children much like adults, without the rompers, the jerseys, and the other articles worn by the young white child, is not without significance. It epitomizes the Dakota philosophy of training, after the early years; the child is hurried toward adulthood.

NOTES

1. Erik Homburger Erikson, "Observations on Sioux Education," *Journal of Psychology*, VII (1939), 138.
2. *Ibid.*
3. *Ibid.*, p. 139.
4. Dorothea Leighton, M.D., U.S.I.S., personal communication.

CHAPTER X

CHILDHOOD

THE years between five and ten are a period of great changes in the behavior of any child, white or Indian. White children show a marked expansiveness and spontaneity in their personalities and a desire to move into social circles outside their families. At about five they are sent to school, to begin their education and to associate with children of their age in the community. By the time they are ready for school, they have been generally trained in the proper relationships to observe toward other people and much of the behavior that they will be expected to exhibit at school.

Dakota children of five or six have also been trained in the proper behavior to observe in their society; but the relationship to adults is less one of obedience to authority, and discipline has been much more in the form of guidance and encouragement to do the right thing than punishment for misbehavior. Hence, by the time he is five or six, the Dakota child has acquired a feeling of security and affection in the family. His training has been far less intensive than the white child's, for it is at about this age that his serious training really begins.

The training for the home duties of men and women, which began in play when the child was younger, is continued now by asking the child to perform many chores. The boys begin to chop wood, carry water, and ride horses to look after the livestock, and the girls wash dishes, clean the house, and take care of smaller children. Horses are substituted for bone toys and real babies for dolls. This work at home increases until, by the time the children are ten, eleven, or twelve, they can do much of the work of fathers and mothers.

Although the avoidance observed between brothers and sisters in the old society has been abandoned, children of five or six begin to imitate the general separation of the sexes in public. Fathers may take young sons into the men's part of the circle at a public feast or into the men's side of the church. The boys also begin to play separately from the girls. The girls feel a greater pressure to avoid boys. They see their mothers and older sisters keep to themselves and show fear of men. The little girls are also taught to be modest and are criticized for striking back at aggressive brothers or other boys.

Control over misbehavior is exercised by shaming, which becomes more intense when the child continues to do wrong after he has learned the proper mode of conduct. Shaming is applied not only to misbehaving youngsters but also to the selfish and competitive child, who seeks to gain to the disadvantage of others, an act which brings strong criticism from both parents and other children. It is by this means that children are taught not to disrupt the co-operative aspects of Dakota life.

Observers visiting the Pine Ridge communities in the course of this study frequently noticed older children of the five- to ten-year-old group playing or visiting homes at some distance from their own. This was particularly true of the older boys, who are good riders by this age and can travel into other communities on their horses. Children of eight to ten are taken more frequently on trips to off-reservation towns or to the harvest camps than when they were younger. Both their world of acquaintances and their knowledge of the outside world become broadened. But the most important medium for making new acquaintances is the school, which now becomes the great center of interest in their lives.

Most Dakota children like going to school. They find the school activities of great interest and much more absorbing than the rather monotonous life at home. During summer vacation, many children asked the interviewers when school would begin again. Yet, in spite of their eagerness to attend, problems do arise, particularly over the differences between Indian and white systems of training and the adjustment of the child on entering school. Some of the children faced with new problems of response or adjustment behave in ways which are often baffling to their teachers.

EDUCATION IN THE PINE RIDGE SCHOOLS

The objectives of the reservation schools are to stimulate habits and attitudes desirable for children in the particular circumstances of the Dakota and to build up a body of knowledge to carry on life on the reservation and with white society. The essential work of the day school is teaching the primary tool subjects—reading, writing, arithmetic, and, for many children, the English language—and creating interests in the fundamental economic and social activities of the reservation.

The educational method is based on class projects or activities which are centered around the home, pet animals, and health. Garden projects create an early interest in farming and the production of food—an interest still not highly developed among the older Dakota. Pet animals are kept in the classroom or on the school farm in order that the children may learn affection and consideration for them. In spite of their great traditional interest in horses and dogs, the Sioux are not kind masters, and the children often treat animals cruelly at home. In addition to humanitarian considerations, different attitudes and treatment are necessary if the children are to gain much of their living by handling domestic animals.

The project method is exceptionally well suited for educating the Dakota children because it follows their own method of learning by doing and following the example of others. By bringing the children to participate and to share in the work and the responsibility for completion of a project, this method also reinforces the training for co-operative work already begun in the family.

The project method has a special value for many reservation children who know little or no English when they enter school. Working with bilingual children who can translate for them and help them to build up English vocabularies is a great help to the shy Indian-speaking children. Projects are immensely successful in diverting the timid new child's attention from the strange school situation, which often terrifies him at first, and in getting him to enter into school life. By working or playing with others, he makes new friends and has a good time. Projects are also a basis by which the teacher can establish herself as a friendly and kindly person, interested in the child's welfare and happiness.

The present curriculum at Pine Ridge has been functioning for about seven or eight years—not long enough for an evaluation of its full effect upon children who have finished school. However, it is already evident in the schools that children have become increasingly interested in the rural-life programs and especially in the raising of livestock.

Each day school provides the children with a noon meal, and a lunch is served to the younger students just before dismissal. The hot noon meals have been an important factor in building up the health of the majority of Pine Ridge children, who look upon the quantity and variety of the food as a luxury.

The school program includes the moving pictures and dramatics usually found in white schools and special programs for holidays like Halloween, Thanksgiving, and Christmas. The school games for young children are all white games. The primary grades teach "Tag," "Drop the Handkerchief," "Farmer in the Dell," and other group games in which one child is "it." The majority of children playing unsupervised, however, choose group games of two sides. The boys play "Indian and Whiteman," known as "Indians and Cowboys," in which the preference is to be the cowboy on the pursuing and winning side. Another game, "Beaver," is played by two sides of both boys and girls, one running through the line of the other to reach a point of safety. The small children at the boarding school also make up play about things they see in the weekly school movies. During the winter of 1943 the "game-of-the-week" was likely to be the re-enactment with hobby horses of the rides and fights of "cowboys" or the fights between "sailors" and "pirates" with homemade wooden swords.

The most popular sports are softball and basketball. As few children have either ball or baskets at home, the latter is played almost exclusively in the school gymnasiums. These games have been played for so long that they are now part of the school and community life and are not looked upon as having been learned from the white people.

PROBLEMS OF ADJUSTMENT

For the Dakota child of five or six, entering school is a radical change from the comparatively confined and simple life of his rural neighborhood. The many new children, the teacher, and the competition create strange and often frightening situations to which adjustments must be made.

The child enters a class of many children whom he has never seen. In the larger schools at Kyle and Pine Ridge he may be in a classroom with thirty or forty other children and see a hundred or more older children on the playground. It is difficult for youngsters to feel secure in these large groups, and many refuse to stay in school unless a parent or grandparent remains with them for several days. This is not different from the experience of white children, but Dakota children face many situations for the first time which can be more confusing or frightening. Until they go to school, most children except those living in Pine Ridge town are unaccustomed to travel by car or bus, to large rooms and buildings, to lavatories and flush toilets, and to hallways filled with children.

One of the most important adjustments, and for a short period one of the most difficult for the young child in his new school situation, is with the teacher. The reader will recall that white people have been used as frighteners in many Dakota children's early training. To be placed suddenly under the authority of a white person and to have to depend on her for care can be a very disturbing and frightening experience. Until the teacher can establish herself as a friendly and helpful person, the child may remain highly alarmed.

In some classes this conflict may be reduced if the teacher herself is an Indian. Yet the greater ease of adjustment to an Indian teacher may be offset in part if she uses white school disciplinary methods. Again, the teacher may come from an Indian culture which trains children in a different way. Hence, although she may be sympathetic with her students because she also is an Indian, at the same time she may act in ways to which Dakota children are unaccustomed.

From both the Indian and the white teacher the child must accept direction and authority which are imposed more sharply and severely than in the child's home. He must move with groups, march in line, accept instructions, and refrain from following his own fancy to the degree to which he has been accustomed. Another great difficulty for many children from non-English-speaking homes is inability to understand the teacher's simplest directions and, indeed, much of what is going on in the classroom.

Observers in this study noted that in the early grades there were many systems for competition among the children and many ways of rewarding individual behavior. Little children were asked to perform before the class. Drawings were compared to select the best. The work of one individual was held up before the others as an outstanding example. Charts with the names of the class, showing individual records or gold stars for perfect work, were hung on the walls as devices to reward competitive effort and to stimulate those on the bottom to do better.

It is only natural for a white teacher, or an Indian teacher who has been trained in the white school system, to introduce competitive activities into classwork, but the younger Dakota children find them difficult to understand. Some, it is true, particularly the mixed-bloods, accept competitive work readily, and others soon learn to compete; but many refuse to enter into competition, withdraw from activities, and sometimes become unwilling to make any response.

Part of this behavior is due to the lack of preparation for competitive activity. The ideal of Dakota life in the old days was co-operation, and, although competition was permitted adults in limited fields of activity,[1] it was not taught the young child. Such competition as existed was to maintain position and good performance relative or equal to others in the band. There were no "stars" and no laggards. Severe criticism was exerted on the child who sought to "shine" in unapproved ways or before he was old enough. The great sensitivity to shame, built up from his earliest years, also kept down any desire to excel to the disadvantage of others. And so it is today; competition is discouraged by sharp criticism and provoked embarrassment. To be asked to compete in class goes against the grain with the Dakota child, and he criticizes the competitive ones among his fellows.

BEHAVIOR IN SCHOOL

It should be reiterated that most of the children enjoy school after the first difficulties are overcome, but certain conflicts have been described above because they stem from fundamental differences between white and Indian cultures. Other typical behavior problems are embarrassment, refusal to participate or talk, and running away. The stimuli for this behavior are apparent in the school situation already discussed; i.e., fear of the teacher as a white person, inability to speak English, and the demand for individual performance and competition. The conditioning factors of early Indian child-training cause not only the conflict but also the resultant type of behavior.

To "freeze up" or suppress all response is a human reaction, and one which

FOUR SIOUX BOYS

the Dakota children see their elders exhibit on numerous occasions. It is the Sioux pattern not to give one's self away or show any emotion which would lower one's self-respect or pride before outsiders.

Running away from a difficult or overwhelming situation is also learned by the Dakota child. As a little child he is taught to run away at the appearance of whites. He sees his parents quit work or move from a community when they do not like or cannot face a situation. According to the Dakota pattern, it is quite acceptable to escape personal conflict by running away, and no stigma is attached to such action. Hence it is to be expected that children who do not adjust easily to school will run away. Moreover, the child is not punished when he runs home.

The problem of embarrassment or being ashamed is more difficult because it is such a common reaction among Dakota children and is evoked for no reason perceptible to the teacher. The reader is already aware how strong a social pressure is exerted by ridicule and criticism. Perhaps examples of how this is taught the child and the emphasis laid upon conforming and keeping up with the group will explain why the Dakota child is so sensitive to shame.

Young boys used to make a little camp outside the camp circle. In imitation of their warrior fathers they would try to slip into their homes and steal food. Those who returned to the boys' camp without food had marks painted on their faces as a sign of disgrace.[2]

This attitude still appears in the children's games, in spite of their adoption of white competitive sports. Not so long ago, a school track team was reluctant to run because they knew they could not win, and a basketball team did not want their parents and neighbors to come to an interschool game for fear they would laugh at their mistakes or failure to win.

Thus the white man's desire to excel is turned by the Dakota into a fear of becoming ridiculous through losing. It is this attitude that makes children withdraw and become highly embarrassed when they are asked to recite in broken English or to perform before others in things they are only learning to do.

Behavior between boys and girls is also a problem to the teacher new to the Indian schools. The younger boys and girls voluntarily divide into sex groups when they come into the classroom and sit at different tables. Teachers often attempt to change this habit, not realizing that it is deeply intrenched in many of their students. This custom usually breaks down easily in group games, but in spite of classroom influence the children maintain strong sex divisions throughout their day-school years.

Aggressive behavior on the part of the boys[3] and the girls' fear of them, which are deeply ingrained in Dakota culture, also tend to maintain sex divisions in school. Observers in this study noticed that children passing in the school halls and playing in the yard showed an amount of aggression not characteristic in white schools. Boys were constantly hitting or pushing the girls, who sometimes retaliated by fighting back or ganging up on a single offensive boy. Teachers received many complaints about the boys' behavior, and parents occasionally came to school to register their complaints about the treatment of their daughters at the hands of the boys.

Before passing to the description of older children's behavior, it is important to note that problems which are so apparent among the adolescents and adults at Pine Ridge begin very early in the individual's life. The day school, by the way in which it treats the child when he enters school and helps him to adjust, to find security and happiness, can reduce much of the conflict and prepare the child for a more stable adjustment in later life.

NOTES

1. Winning war honors, giving away property, and adhering to womanly virtues.
2. Black Elk, *Black Elk Speaks* (New York: W. W. Morrow & Co., 1932), p. 59.
3. For a discussion of Sioux aggression see chap. xii and Appendix II.

CHAPTER XI

ADOLESCENCE

This chapter covers roughly the years from eleven to seventeen in the life of the Dakota child, including the last years a child spends at home before going to boarding school, the boarding-school years, and entrance into adult life. Physiologically this period covers both late childhood and adolescence; but, because the Sioux child's life centers on the boarding school, the material of this chapter has been organized around it.

The age at which students enter boarding school depends on the number of grades in the day school in their home community. Some children begin boarding school as early as the seventh grade. Most of the reservation children, like those of Wanblee and Kyle, enter at the ninth or tenth grade. Age at entrance ranges from fourteen to eighteen.[1]

LATE CHILDHOOD IN THE COMMUNITY

By the time the child has reached his twelfth or thirteenth birthday, his home is still the only place of any security. Within his Indian society, there are no other groups and few activities in which he can participate and form any bonds of close relationship. At home, his family relations appear on the surface to be happy and pleasant, but many of the boys show restlessness under the direction and discipline of their mothers. Although the fathers undertake some direction of their sons' behavior and work at home, this authority often appears very ineffective. There are, however, some marked exceptions, like Charlie Charging Bull's father, who is described in the next chapter.

The strong traditional bonds between Dakota brothers are also evident at this age when boys do not stay so much in their homes and begin to rove about the district in groups. As a rule, boys are kind and loyal to their sisters and act immediately in their defense. However, life-histories and school reports reveal an increase in fighting between boys of this age group in both the home and the school. Perhaps this is due in part to the type of behavior allowed and encouraged in boys when they are younger, but the strong resistance at this age to parental control and the development of quarreling with age mates are forms of over-aggressive and rebellious behavior which reveal anxiety as well as signs of growing up.

At home the boys now accept responsibility for doing household and farm chores and, by the time they are fourteen or fifteen, many accompany their families or go alone to work in the harvest fields of white farmers. For those who go with a gang of men or married brothers and their families, this is an opportunity to break away from the confinement of parental control. Boys at this age leave also because of their desire to travel and to see the towns outside the reservation with their rodeos and movies.

Girls of twelve and thirteen show behavior almost opposite to that of the boys. They become more identified with the family as they become old enough to take an adult role with their mothers in the household work. They continue to look after younger brothers and sisters. In fact, if there are many children in the family, the older sister carries much of the responsibility of feeding and bathing the small children. The sketches of Mickey and of Priscilla in the next chapter show examples of the role and important function of the older sisters in the family.

The twelve- and thirteen-year-old girls, now approaching physical maturity, are kept at home more than the boys for protection. The girls appear afraid of boys and men, and they always travel with older girls or elders in their family. This is in keeping with the old Dakota custom; for, even though the girls now have many opportunities to travel alone—going to school, to the store, or to social affairs—they do not seem to wish to go by themselves. Observers in this study noticed that very few girls of this age ride horseback, although many girls a few years younger ride around the communities in the summertime. Formerly girls and women rode when the family traveled, but they gave up riding thirty or forty years ago when missionaries and teachers made them feel it was immodest.[2] Older girls and women today travel in their communities either on foot or in a wagon.

The older girls rarely play with boys of their age; the separation of the sexes in play, started at an earlier age, now becomes complete. This is due in part, of course, to the fact that the boys spend many of their out-of-school hours on horseback, while girls do not. Outside the school, girls' association with people at any distance from home and their attendance at church meetings, young people's groups, and community dances are always under the chaperonage of their families or older women. On a few occasions our observers saw young full-blood girls going to a community dance in company with older brothers, a situation that would never have occurred when the brother-sister taboo was in force.

The girls like to go to the outlying towns and to the harvest fields with their families or relatives, for these occasions provide almost the only opportunity for

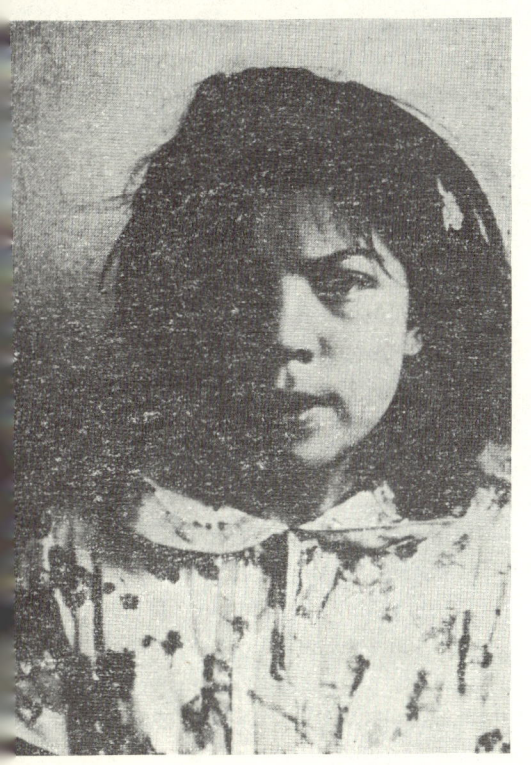

FOUR SIOUX GIRLS

them to see the world outside the reservation. The motion-picture theaters are the greatest attraction. During the winter months the children in the rural areas see movies at school, but these are shown infrequently; in the school year of 1942-43 the school at Kyle had none at all.

GOING AWAY TO SCHOOL

The education of Dakota children at the Oglala Community High School at Pine Ridge town follows the objectives and methods of the earlier grades.[3] A graduate must have credits in English, history, mathematics, the social and physical sciences, and vocational training, but much of the education in these fields is acquired through integrated project work. The high-school projects are centered around the school herd and farm, the girls' practice cottage and home economics workrooms, and the arts and crafts shop. The major objective is to teach the fundamental knowledge required by people who are going to live by cattle and the land in a small rural home and in reservation society.[4]

Boys learn by doing all types of work necessary for the successful running of beef herds. One of the most important activities in the practical training is a junior livestock association, through which boys can earn cattle by work at school and, on graduation, take them home as a foundation herd. Simple carpentry and machine repair needed to service the farm home and equipment are also part of the boys' training.

Girls are taught the essentials of home management, including nutrition. They may also learn at school a number of crafts which will bring additional income into the home, and many become skilled weavers and potters.

Allied with the vocational training in some respects is the performance of school maintenance work by the students. Such work as the care and milking of the school dairy herd, repair work, and the construction of new buildings like a rammed earth barn can readily be made valuable training in farm life. Helping in the school kitchen and dining-room may also be useful to girls. But operating the school laundry machines, cleaning the campus and classrooms, and similar chores fall into the category of institutional labor, whatever training value may be connected with them. Owing to the limitation of appropriations for Indian schools, such work is necessary; but its educational value is slight, and much of it is still carried on as a traditional part of the former school system where the aim of the superintendent was to make the school self-sufficient, regardless of the educational value of the work involved.

In the field of social studies the main emphasis is on reservation organization. Study of the structure and function of the local agency, the constitution and tribal government of the Pine Ridge Indians, and the history of the Indian Service and its policies are all designed to give the students knowledge of how their society functions. The general subjects in the field of civics are also included.[5]

Equally important to the education of Dakota youth is experience in self-government. The student body has its own council for directing the school social activities and advising faculty committees on student problems. The girls have a councilor system in their dormitory, and the boys have a dormitory government of mayor and officers modeled after the famous Boys' Town in Omaha. These self-government institutions serve both as training in democratic methods and as practice in the exercise of group controls and responsibility to the group which are sorely needed in the adult reservation society.

The boarding school has a fully developed recreational life which follows the pattern of athletics, entertainments, dances, and parties in the average American high school. The Oglala football, baseball, basketball, and track teams compete with other high schools in the regional and state tournaments. Classes present plays and exhibitions. The dormitory groups entertain one another at evening parties of dancing, games, and refreshments, and about once a month a class or the student council holds a school dance in the gymnasium. The three motion-picture shows each week in the school auditorium, one being free to all students, are major recreational events.

Except for an occasional week end at home and a short Christmas vacation, the boy or girl attending boarding school is separated from the life of his community for nine months of the year and is brought into a society organized in a white pattern with many differences from his home life. For one thing, his whole day at school is regulated by time, from six in the morning, when he arises to the power-plant whistle, to nine-thirty in the evening, when he is ordered to put out his lights. Classes, chores, athletics, study hall, and meals all take place according to the clock. The Dakota child has had some experience with a regular schedule in the day school, but life completely run by the clock calls for considerable adjustment on the part of many Indian children who, as noted in the preceding chapters, have little acquaintance with white concepts of punctuality.

Eating and sleeping are also different. The three large and regular meals to which the child sits down each day in the dining-hall and the regular eight hours of sleep are not usual in the Indian home.

Cleanliness and neat personal appearance become much more important than in the day school. This is strongly impressed upon the child when on entering school he is examined for head lice and skin sores and, if necessary, treated by the advisers or school nurse. He is sent at once to the showers and given clean clothes, and much pressure is brought to bear upon him to keep clean. Each child must keep his bed and personal property in orderly condition and help to clean his dormitory room and building.

In the boarding school the child has many more teachers than in the elementary school. His home-room teacher organizes his project work as well as teaching the academic studies. There are also music and vocational instructors, athletic coaches, directors of social activities and maintenance work, and dormitory advisers. The child's association and informal relationships with many white and Indian teachers are a very important factor in the development of his personality and attitudes at this time. He comes to these persons for help and decisions which he would normally expect from his parents. Through personal relationships that occur outside of class, the teacher learns more of the student's character and has the opportunity to advise and direct in his development.

In addition to the advice and guidance which the teachers offer in both formal and informal contacts, their way of life has a very strong, though indirect, influence upon the attitudes of the children. In comparison with the rural homes of Indians and most whites on the reservation, the teachers' homes seem luxurious. Their clothes, their cars, and their trips off the reservation are a sharp contrast to the colorless and, on the whole, empty life of most adult Dakota. These things have obviously come to the teachers through salaried positions, and the inference to the children is that salaries make possible the good life. Hence, many children come to look upon Indian Service or other salaried employment as preferable to farming or ranching. Thus the objectives of the school—teaching children the values and satisfactions of life on the land—are partially negated by the values and satisfactions of life as an employee which are always apparent to them. This paradox is, of course, unavoidable and, to some extent, it exists in many teaching situations elsewhere. It does, however, create doubt and conflict in the minds of children in the reservation schools.

The social relationships between boys and girls in the boarding school are based on the modern white principles of "normal" associations of young people in the classroom and on the campus. The Indian boys and girls "date," walk and sit together, and meet in the town as do students in any small-town high school. Restraint and self-consciousness are common among Indian children when they enter boarding school because this type of behavior is not sanctioned in the home communities. However, movies, magazine stories, the visits to white high schools, and the example of older boys and girls soon overcome the traditional pattern of avoiding the opposite sex in public. In general, boys and girls are well behaved and friendly toward each other; the hitting and slapping so common between the young boys and girls decreases among those of fifteen and sixteen. Occasionally, the love affairs in school lead to couples' running away.

Up to about 1930, student behavior was controlled by the boys' and girls' disciplinarians, who were allowed to employ severe physical punishment. This type of discipline has now been banned, and the milder penalities invoked today take the form of deprivation of privileges and loss of prestige. A more positive control of behavior has been attempted through the organization of student government, but the general effect of the present disciplinary system is lack of consistency. In the classroom the teachers punish misbehavior by scolding, threatening, or frightening the child and depriving him of privileges. In a few classes teachers have organized student government and presented serious problems of offenses against the class, like stealing from the treasury, for group discipline. In the dormitories the advisers reprimand students for minor infractions of the rules but present the major cases to the dormitory council. Punishments meted out by the council vary from doing extra cleaning work in the building to losing social privileges and positions in the student government. In some serious cases, the boys send the offender down the "belt line," which is unofficially sanctioned.

Consistent offenders, children who continually skip classes, run away from school, or become behavior problems to all their teachers, are reported to the faculty guidance committee. However, the action of this committee is frequently indecisive, and the cases are left for further discussion or ultimate solution by the dormitory advisers.

The difficulty in making discipline more effective seems to rise from doubt as to where authority for invoking sanctions lies. Serious cases, such as drunkenness or entering and stealing, are referred to the reservation superintendent of education. In especially difficult cases, school officials occasionally prefer charges in the Tribal Court. This is usually in connection with damage or stealing of property, getting drunk, and sex affairs, types of behavior which are particularly offensive to the white teachers. In the several charges so preferred against boys and girls in 1943, the usual action was to suspend sentence, exact court costs, and place the student on probation to the school. Thus the law was invoked, only to return the case once more to the school. Furthermore, the school is not always consistent in preferring charges. In the case of one boy, who was jailed for stealing and drinking denatured alcohol, charges were withdrawn by the school in a few days because the jail did not seem the "right place" for him and, incidentally, he was needed to play in a basketball game.

In spite of the comparative lightness of sentences imposed by the Tribal Court and the inconsistent attitude of the school, the students manifest a strong fear of the jail—a fear which comes down through the whole historical experience of the tribe on the reservation.[6] The modern school discipline of utilizing the Tribal Court, which is against official policy and regulation, serves to perpetuate a negative attitude rather than to create a useful and positive one. Thus it seems obvious that the invocation of court sanctions in even a very few disciplinary cases creates a heightened emotional reaction against the school and serves to add to the child's frustrations rather than to secure better behavior.

The boarding school is to the great majority of the students an interesting and even exciting environment. The interests of school work, the physical comfort, which is indeed luxury as compared with their own homes, and the associations with schoolmates and teachers often make the high-school years among the pleasantest and most eventful in their lives. Yet the great majority of the students who enter high school do not graduate. The reasons why the school does not hold more students have been the subject of study by the Indian Service and may be indicated only briefly here to show their effect upon the personalities of Dakota adolescents. Some of them lie in the nature of the environment and have little to do with the form or content of the school experience. Others may be attributed either directly or indirectly to the conflicts set up by school life.

Among the reasons which may be said to lie outside the school are the facts that some students are too old on entering to be expected to finish the course and also that many families need the assistance of older children in increasing the family income. Students who are sixteen or seventeen when they are high-school freshmen are likely, by the time they near twenty, to leave for work or marriage. Withdrawal to help the family may well be expected in a poverty-stricken society. At present, most older boys are joining the armed forces.

Another reason for withdrawal seems to lie in the economy. A small number of students leave before finishing high school because the type of education they receive is designed to equip them for a life they believe they cannot live. Many students and their families have no land on which a boy or girl can run cattle and no money to lease land. Furthermore, students do not see in their home communities very good prospects of a happy or profitable life on the land. It takes several years to make money from a herd, and adolescents are likely to become pessimistic at seeing men with more experience than themselves living by rations for a year or two in order to become even moderately self-sufficient. To these students, life off the reservation and the immediate returns from wage work appear far more attractive. Why, they ask, should they go on preparing for something else? This attitude and the expectation of getting wage work after graduation are frequently expressed.

More important than the foregoing reasons to a study of personality are the truancies and drop-outs due to conflicts between the white and Dakota systems of training and treatment of children, especially in discipline. Like many Indian schools, Oglala Community High School has a high proportion of runaways who leave school for a short time or for good. In recent years they have been fewer in number, but they are still frequent enough to show difficulties of adjustment.

The size of the student body—690 day and boarding pupils—and the consequent lack of much personal attention or affection lead to insecurity in children whose family, even if it were broken, has always given them a sense of protection. Hence, they flee from the school to the home of a parent or relative to regain what little security is afforded there. Children brought up by parents who in the Indian fashion rarely reprimand, who patiently wait until a child wishes to carry out a request, and who do not enforce immediate responses with threats of punishment find the disciplinary measures of many white teachers difficult to accept. Being shamed or ridiculed by a teacher before other children on the campus and being threatened with court action cause a number of children to become resentful and run home.

Frequently the conflict arises from having to do things at set times and without choice. For example, during the testing for the present study, one somewhat sullen full-blood boy with considerable artistic ability did not wish to complete the drawing tests, partly because he was suspicious and partly because he did not want to do extra work. He sat through the drawing period and then called his brother and ran home with him. The older boy was allowed to leave home in a day or two to work in the beet fields, and the younger brother remained out of school until the boys' adviser from the school inquired at the home the reason for the prolonged absence.

Conflicts between the full-blood and mixed-blood groups in the reservation society cause some children to leave school. These conflicts, stemming from differences in habits and attitudes of the two groups, are symbolized by the children in terms of color. Since many of the light mixed-bloods are indistinguishable from white children, they are frequently called "white" and "dirty white trash" by the children of predominantly Indian blood. The mixed-bloods sometimes retaliate by calling the darker children "nigger," but usually the term of opprobrium is "dirty" or "lousy Indian."[7] The older mixed-bloods look upon full-bloods as "dumb" and "backward." The full-bloods consider mixed-bloods "tricky," "liars," and (surprisingly to whites) "dirty." Older full-blood girls, who are often neater and more poised in their manner, dislike rooming with mixed-bloods because they are unclean and rowdy. The full-blood girls are especially concerned at having mixed-blood girls see them undressed.

As might be expected from the sex code described in chapter viii, older boys and girls frequently run away for illicit sex affairs. In these cases it is frequently the younger brothers and sisters at school who bear the brunt of the criticism which the Sioux have developed to a fine art. Two boys and two girls ran away from the Pine Ridge school and spent several days and nights in an abandoned cabin, afterward leaving the reservation. The younger sister of one of the girls and another relative, who were also students in the boarding school, were teased about this affair by other students and were accused of being immoral themselves. The two young girls were so shamed by the criticism that they asked to be allowed to go home. When they were refused permission, they ran away. The police were sent for them, and they were put in jail until the mother of one took them home.

These examples show that, when Dakota children under pressure from great conflict can stand the tension no longer, they run away. The high sensitivity to criticism also appears as a related cause for running away. This behavior is the extreme and more explicit overt form of withdrawing internally from situations—the common reaction of Dakota children under stress, as we saw in chapter x.

ENTERING ADULT LIFE

On leaving high school, the Dakota boy or girl must decide whether to return home or leave the reservation to make a living, unless he plans to go to college or vocational school. Deciding what to do and where to go is normally difficult. In 1938 only 36 out of 239 former students of the three high schools on Pine Ridge and the adjoining Rosebud Reservation had left the reservation for more than short periods.[8] This was due in part, of course, to the lack of jobs elsewhere during the depression years and to opportunites for relief employment on the reservation. Since 1940 this trend has been reversed, and in recent years most boys and many girls have left school to join the armed forces or to work in war industries. Neither situation is "normal," but the tendency to remain on the reservation except in boom times is clearly indicated.

Why do Dakota youths prefer to stay on the reservation, where income is low and where life on the whole is dull compared with that in urban centers where they can earn more money? The answer lies in part in the strong sense of family solidarity which is imparted from babyhood to the Dakota child. Perhaps more apparent is the fact that Indians have difficulty in adjusting to life in white communities. Yet the adjustments which the former students must make if he returns to his own home are in many ways more difficult.

When boys and girls go away to high school, their home is the place of greatest security. They return to it after high school, hoping to regain the security and affection they remember from their childhood. But with the need to earn a living and take party in family and community life as young adults, the realities of life at home appear in a stronger light. The idleness of many of the men, the lack of opportunities, the dependence of the people upon the government, the conflicts and instability within families and communities, and the pressure of criticism undermine the young people's faith in themselves and in what education can do for them, as well as their security in their own group.

Life at home is easier and yet harder than at boarding school. On the one hand, the returned student is free from school discipline and routine; on the other hand, he meets the folkways and controls of Indian life. Young unmarried men and women are not allowed to associate as freely in the Indian community as they are in school. They find that life at home is dull in comparison with the activity of classwork, sports, and social life at school. Many young people also find that the limited and rather monotonous meals and the crowded quarters at home are irksome.

Economic adjustments are hard for some youths, particularly the boys. They have been trained at school to live on the land, principally through running beef herds. Some boys have returned home with a few cattle earned through a junior livestock association, which they could use as a foundation for their own herd or pool with their fathers' cattle. But many boys have left school without cattle, or they have had no land on which to run stock or money with which to start operations. Sons of landless families who return home must look for such wage work as they can find on the reservation or go outside with their families for seasonal agricultural labor. As a result, many boys are likely to question the value of their school training.

Nonagricultural wage work on the reservation is largely limited to employment by the Indian Service. Most of the non-civil-service jobs are those of truckdrivers, laborers, janitors, carpenters, and automobile mechanics. Each school has one or more bus-drivers, who also tend the heating and lighting plants, and a housekeeper who cooks the noon lunches and assists the home economics teachers. Wages are low—in 1942 school bus-drivers were receiving $60 a month—but the rent for government quarters and other living costs are also low.

The opportunity for a high-school graduate to obtain one of these jobs is limited, for they are coveted by older people. The young people are likely to try for jobs at the Agency itself to escape the constant requests for assistance from relatives if they live in their home communities.[9]

Each year there are a few young people who go on to college or vocational school to prepare for civil service positions as Indian Service teachers, farm aides, or clerical workers. Almost universally they plan to seek employment on reservations other than their own. Some of them see such work as an escape from pressures for assistance at home. To others it is a way of moving into middle-class white life. Whatever the reason, the fact that these young people wish to work elsewhere is indeed a handicap to their tribe, for it means a loss of potential leaders and intelligent citizens.

For the students who do remain on the reservation, there are strong incentives to participation in community life. Their school training in leadership and their awareness of the poverty and frustration at home lead many of them to say, "I want to do something to help my people," and to try to improve living conditions.

The elders expect the young people who have gone to school to help their own communities. At the same time—not always consciously—the older people expect the youths to adhere to the Dakota custom of remaining silent before their elders and of following the more experienced leaders. This paradoxial attitude is disturbing to young people who feel that, with their greater knowledge of English and white culture, they can and should take some leadership in Pine Ridge affairs.

Leadership is also thwarted in some instances by the attitudes of white administrators. While official policy directs the encouragement of Indian leadership and self-direction, administrators are well aware of the reservation-wide belief that most of the troubles of the Pine Ridge Indians are due to the mistakes of the government. They know also that, since early reservation days, criticizing the agent or other officials in public meetings has been a form of counting coup (striking the enemy to win honor). Hence there is a tendency to treat the young Indian who voices opposition to government programs as a reactionary, an "agitator," or a show-off. The fact that some young Indians have professed a desire to better community life but have remained apathetic in the face of opportunities for leadership does not help relations between the whole group and the Agency. Too often, really thoughtful criticism or constructive suggestions are officially ignored.

The end result of returning home after school is thus dissatisfying for the majority of Pine Ridge young people. Although they find reservation life preferable to the social isolation they experience in white communities, the restraints imposed upon them by their elders and by government and the lack of satisfying community life of any kind frustrate and confuse them. They find few social or economic channels either in their home communities or in government programs by which they can gain stability, economic success, and recognition. Life at home offers no other roles than those of their fathers and mothers. They feel a deep need for new roles and for social status.

This desire for some function and for recognition is readily apparent in the eagerness with which the younger Sioux have volunteered for military service and war industries. Their patriotism is as genuine as that of any other Americans, but they see also an opportunity for activity that circumstances at home have denied to many of them. In the eyes of the older people, and to some extent of the younger, the warrior's is the greatest role of all. To the young men and women it means something to do, a chance to be respected by Indians and whites alike. They gain deep satisfaction from the sense of equality with other young people and from being wanted in the outside world—a satisfaction that these Pine Ridge youths have never felt before.

The exodus of boys and girls from school to jobs outside the reservation is almost a new phenomenon at Pine Ridge. It is said that many Pine Ridge Indians went away to work during World War I, but between that time and 1941 extremely few young people went away to work in industries and to live in cities.

A study of the off-reservation employment of Rosebud Sioux made in 1941,[10] in which many Pine Ridge Indians were encountered, showed that Dakota young people who were taking their first jobs or who had been employed off the reservation for two or three years varied widely in their success in working and living among whites. Some young people had done well in their jobs and, by proving their ability to do skilled work, had advanced in their occupation. More showed instability by moving from job to job or by going back and forth between reservation and town. Social adjustment was not easy for any of them.

Coming to town with little money, they were forced to live in the poorest rooming-houses and sometimes in auto camps. Only when they have achieved some fairly well-paying job could they move to better quarters. Characteristically these young people shared rooms and in general clung together, since their friends were usually other Indians. The 1941 study showed that older Indians moved into good neighborhoods and participated in white society only after years of residence in a large town. Even after ten or fifteen years, their clubs and church guilds were white in pattern but Indian in membership.

The social isolation in a white town which many Dakota young people experience is very discouraging. Young white people coming from the country are also isolated, but they make friends and become accepted more easily and quickly than Indian boys and girls, who do not know the folkways of whites and are not sure enough of their English to associate easily with them. To whites, their speech is odd, and their reserve and timidity make them seem unapproachable or queer. Until they learn how to talk and act like white people, they are excluded from white society. Sensitive to this exclusion, many Sioux are unable to stick it out. They give up the attempt to be accepted by whites and associate only with Indians or leave their jobs to return to the reservation.

A few boys and girls fail to form attachments to either respectable white or Indian society in the towns and yet do not want to return to the reservation. These young people drift to the bottom of the social order. Caught up with the worst element of the white or Indian slums, they live in the shoddiest rooming-houses or Indian camps at the edge of town and frequent the cheapest beer joints, dance halls, and other gathering places of slum-dwellers. Occasionally they are picked up for delinquency or vagrancy. They may have had no work or food for days. Police or social agencies usually return them to their homes. Thereafter they may be classed as delinquents, but beneath their surface behavior may be seen their inability to find any place in either Indian or white society and their confusion at trying to adjust to two conflicting cultures.

It appears that, whether Pine Ridge boys and girls decide to return home or to leave the reservation for work, most of them do so at a price. On the reservation there are few jobs at good pay. In the outside world recreational and social life are limited, at least in the first years of residence. Not all boys and girls fail or follow the same pattern of adjustment within or outside their own groups, but the majority indicate difficulty in fitting into their social environment and a sense of frustration because there is no way to follow and often more ill-will than help from those around them.

Training in the schools is giving Dakota youth a preparation for an economy that will develop in time on Pine Ridge, for intelligent daily living habits, and in many ways for living in any community. But the younger generation appears generally unprepared for their social position either at home or off the reservation and the difficulties they will have to face after their school years. More important than their lack of social preparation is the absence of a well-organized society and well-marked channels to economic rewards and social status. The reorganization which has already begun in some Pine Ridge communities will eventually make opportunities for young people in the cattle programs and business and social councils. In the meantime, boys and girls returning from school will need the planning and active support of their communities and government officials to give them an opportunity and a place at home.

NOTES

1. Most students of Pine Ridge town continue on a day-school basis, and thus boarding-school life does not affect them so intensely as it does those who come from the outlying districts. This study did not include any children who were attending the Holy Rosary Mission or off-reservation boarding schools.
2. Allan Hulsizer, *Region and Culture in the Curriculum of the Navaho and the Dakota* (Federalsburg, Md.: J. W. Stowell Co., 1940), p. 104.
3. The high-school studies at Holy Rosary Mission follow the older type of academic education, but rural vocational work has recently been introduced into the curriculum.
4. Willard W. Beatty, "Training Indians for the Best Use of Their Own Resources," in *The Changing Indian*, ed. Oliver La Farge (Norman, Okla.: University of Oklahoma Press, 1942), pp. 128-38.
5. Office of Indian Affairs, *Students' Handbook, Oglala Community High School, 1942-43* (Chilocco, Okla.: Chilocco School Press, 1942), and "Employees Handbook of Information, 1942-43, Oglala Community High School" (Pine Ridge, 1942) (mimeographed).
6. See chaps. ii and viii.
7. These names are often used by the younger children without knowing the implications. For example, the little mixed-bloods who look like white children will boast, "We're no Indians—we're white trash!"
8. Armin H. Sterner and Gordon Macgregor, "The Pine Ridge Vocational Survey," *Indian Education*, III (1938), 7-8.
9. See chap. viii.
10. John Useem, Gordon Macgregor, and Ruth Useem, "Wartime Employment and Cultural Adjustments of the Rosebud Sioux," *Applied Anthropology*, II (1943), 1-9.

PART III. THE PERSONALITY OF THE DAKOTA CHILD

CHAPTER XII
TEN DAKOTA CHILDREN

TO BEGIN the account of the findings of this study about the personality structure of Dakota children, sketches of ten children are presented. These children vary in amount of Indian blood from full-blood to three-sixteenths, and their ages range from eight to sixteen. They come from the three communities of the study. The personal and social adjustments of these children vary from excellent to very poor. Some of these variations may be partly accounted for by physical conditions or family losses, which may befall the individual in any society; but the influence of their particular cultural position and social climate is apparent in most of these personalities.

It is a premise of this study that a disorganized and threatening social environment causes for a group, as for an individual, great anxiety and feelings of insecurity. People attempt to build defenses against this state of feeling helpless. They try to find safety or to retaliate against the forces that appear to threaten their security. The resulting behavior is derived from a whole complex of circumstances. Therefore, in order to understand the behavior of the children as revealed in the tests which were given them and which are described in the following chapters, we must consider the kind of personality which has developed among the Pine Ridge people as a whole.

The general disorganization of Dakota society today has been discussed in Part I. What have been the effects of this disorganization upon individuals and particularly the effects of the conflicting attitudes described in chapter viii?

The first years of life on the reservation left indelible marks upon the Dakota. With his social institutions deteriorating around him and white institutions and attitudes being forcibly substituted, the individual felt overwhelmed and confused from trying to make some choice. One reaction was to withdraw into himself and to cover up his feelings. This constraint in the face of new situations is a pattern of behavior which has been taught to Indian children for generations. It is the "stoical reserve" which whites have noted as characteristic of the Plains Indians since their first contacts. In the face of continuous changes and repeated frustrations, this reserve has been employed for so long as a means of playing safe that it has kept the individual from giving much release to his impulses or gaining any real satisfaction from life or confidence in himself. The continued retreat inward appears to have contributed to the characteristic apathy which marks the life of each reservation community today. As previously noted, the observer is constantly aware of the slowness and the low degree of social activity of reservation life.[1]

However, a human being cannot continually suppress his emotions and the expressions of his impulse life without compensating in some way, which may become personal maladjustment. For men like the Dakota, who have been trained to be highly aggressive persons with suitable targets for their aggressive drives, continual suppression is bound to result in some violent expression of their frustration.[2] In the increased amount of personal criticism and the splitting of the tribe into progressives and conservatives, New Dealers and Old Dealers, cooperative association members and competitive individualists, sociological full-blood and mixed-blood groups, who hurl at one another such epithets as "dirty Indian" and "poor white trash," some release of their aggression can be observed.

The pattern for this criticism stems from the old culture in which the most common means of social control was ridicule.[3] In the first days of reservation life it was impossible for every man, woman, and child to "freeze up" under the new circumstances. Many began to adapt themselves to the life the Agency held out to them, although retaining their outward calm. These individuals were severely criticized for "joining the enemy" and for not conforming to approved Dakota behavior. As their group grew, they in turn criticized the "long-hairs" or conservatives. Thus application of social controls developed into an increasing amount of criticism and pure release of hostility.[4] Frustrated at almost every turn and in a short time psychologically defeated by the sudden and overwhelming changes, they began to turn upon one another and upon themselves.

Hostility has been expressed in more violent ways than constant criticism. Every so often there occurs some violent personal outbreak in a killing or a rape or the wholesale destruction of property. On one occasion a house was burned around a drunken occupant. Every white person who has lived in the reservation for any length of time can report such incidents, usually ascribed to "native cruelty and barbarity." These are the outbursts, usually released under influence of alcohol, of too-long-pent-up antagonisms against the government employees, all whites, Indian neighbors, and even themselves.

Some of these outbursts take the form of cruel behavior for which there is some precedent in warfare, scalping, and mutilating adulterous women. Now that attack upon enemies has been completely blocked, men have turned increasingly, in times of uncontrolled frenzy, upon women. The restriction placed upon women in the past society made them objects of man's sexual aggression. It is not difficult to understand how men, suddenly blocked in one course of their aggression, should turn in another direction. Since there had been tacit approval of sex aggression in the old society, this became a natural channel for aggressive drive which had been denied other outlet.[5] Thus restrictions in one direction have produced greater activity in another. It is not surprising to find occasional reports of rape or murder and extremes of sexual license.

Another kind of destructive behavior, which is evidence of the restraint which the Dakota have placed upon their inner life, is the self-punishment they exhibit in times of extreme tension. A model for such behavior can be found in the torture features of the Sun Dance, in the ordeals of the vision quest, and in the self-mutilation of mourners at funerals. There was also self-punishment, or institutionalized suicide, in warfare among those who vowed to die rather than retreat.

The forms of self-punishment today are less stylized and harsh than in the old culture, but the practice is still apparent. For example, when one woman heard of the sudden death of her husband, she promised to give away all his household furnishings, horses, and stacks of hay, and her male relatives tore up the husband's garden and destroyed his irrigation dam. On the departure of draftees, mothers attempted to throw themselves under the train. These reactions were in direct response to emotional shock, but now the loss of members of the family group also brings anew the realization of overwhelming personal and group insecurity.

A more common form of self-punishment is anxiety about one's health, welfare, and relationships to other people. Anxiety about personal well-being is not surprising among people who are not only impoverished but also dubious about ever making a living from the resources they possess. Worry about where tomorrow's meals are coming from, about getting money, about being held down, about poor health, and about "what is going to happen" is constantly expressed in daily conversations. This worry develops into a chronic state of apprehension.

The Dakota have found in escape another, but equally unsuccessful, release from their situation and individual constraint. This behavior, too, has precedent in all Dakota practices. A family ashamed of one of its members would leave for another camp; a child ashamed or momentarily insecure in his family could enter for a few days the tepee of a near-by relative, though such an act was damaging to his parents' reputation. Nowadays escape from home, school, reservation, job, and white community has become a common reaction to shame and frustration. Today this running away no longer provides a satisfactory solution, for in each new situation there is still insecurity. Frequent movement from place to place, which has often been ascribed to the Dakota's nomadic background, functions as an unrealistic effort to escape and reflects the great unrest of the people.

The physical and social environment, then, have brought excessive insecurity, anxiety, and confusion to the Dakota since their segregation on the reservation. In an attempt to find some individual security and safety from their apprehension and relief from the problems confronting them, their typical reaction has been to restrain and suppress themselves and to become highly dependent upon the government. Such an adjustment has brought neither personal satisfaction nor personal security. As a result, individuals have become highly aggressive under increased strains, have run away from situation after situation, and have become highly apprehensive about themselves. Frequently, in a sort of emotional exhaustion increased by physical weakening, they become completely apathetic. At times individuals have worked hard to gain economic security, often to be defeated by drought or by the inconsistencies of administrative policy.

The younger adults have not experienced all the woes which have beset the tribe, but they have sensed the despair and frustrations of their elders. They are more willing to work for some security, but they have become anxious through association with the more defeated and unrealistic older people. It is in this social environment and among these attitudes that the present generation of children, to whom we now turn, are growing up and being conditioned.

RED BIRD WOLF

Red Bird is an eight-year-old girl whose degree of Indian blood is reckoned in thirty-seconds, a fractionation which signifies that her ancestors intermixed with whites several generations ago. Since then there has been marriage into the full-blood group. Red Bird now lives with her paternal grandmother and grandfather, Amelia and Frank White Horse. Their home is in a full-blood community composed of the grandfather's extended family group.

Frank White Horse, a man past sixty, is a leader and spokesman in his community. He has married several times, and occasionally his grown-up children by former marriages come to live with him. One son, Charlie Wolf, is Red Bird's father.

Red Bird's grandmother, Amelia White Horse, has been married four times. Three children are recorded from the first marriage, to a man who has since married her sister. By her second husband she had four children and by her third husband, two—a girl of fourteen and a boy of ten, who are now living in the White Horse household.

Mrs. White Horse is an affable and intelligent woman. She is now quite devoted to her husband but a few years ago had a serious quarrel with him. After a heated argument, he left for a relative's home. She not only packed up and left for another part of the reservation but also, with the help of her brothers, carried off her husband's stove and all his furniture to furnish a new home of her own. Despite such temporary disagreements and the history of shifting mates, the

White Horses are now a congenial couple. They maintain a stable home, running cattle, milking cows, and together planting and plowing their cornfield by hand. The new house is a three-room shingled structure, furnished with five beds, a few chairs, a table, and a stove. In spite of the crowded quarters and the number of children and visitors, Mrs. White Horse keeps it neat and well ordered.

The White Horses are among the group of older people who have settled down and taken responsibility for their children and grandchildren. Mrs. White Horse in particular is devoted to them and frequently travels by team in the summer to visit older sons and daughters who are working outside the reservation.

Red Bird and her two little sisters have lived with her grandparents for over three years. In fact, the younger sisters, who came to them as babies, only recently learned that the White Horses are not their own parents. To Red Bird the grandparents are kindly and sometimes overindulgent, allowing her to stay home from school as she pleases and feeding her candy in the trader's store when she should be in her classroom. When Red Bird is strongly disciplined by a teacher, her grandmother will come to her defense regardless of her behavior. Mrs. White Horse was particularly indignant when Red Bird was spanked by her primary teacher, a type of discipline of which the grandparents do not approve. Red Bird maintains a certain amount of control over her grandmother by threatening to leave home and go to her mother if she cannot have her way. She is allowed occasionally to visit her mother, who lives in the home of her parents in a distant community; but visits are not encouraged, as the child usually returns sick and infected with impetigo.

Red Bird's father, Charles Wolf, is divorced from her mother. He is employed off the reservation by the government, and occasionally returns to visit his stepmother and father. He is a good worker and earns high wages as a mechanic, but, like many Indian men of his age group, has few qualms about dissipating his money if his wife and family are not with him to keep him in control. Red Bird's relations with him are not very deep, but she regards him as her father and sometimes threatens to go to live with him.

Of her mother's people—the Howling Buffaloes—Red Bird has a grandmother and step-grandfather. Red Bird's own maternal grandfather, who died about the time she was born, was much older than his wife, to whom he had been married by arrangement with her father. This grandmother had four children, and, when she was widowed, she married her present husband. The family lived for many years off the reservation, the stepfather putting up hay or harvesting potatoes for white farmers in the summer and doing odd jobs in Rapid City during the winter.

Mrs. Howling Buffalo had two children by this marriage who died in infancy.

Her four living children by the first marriage are Red Bird's mother, Cleo; a son who is a well-known rodeo performer; and a son and daughter now in high school.

Red Bird's mother, Cleo, married about ten years after she left school. After her expulsion from school she was put in jail for vagrancy on the streets of a near-by city. She first lived with Charlie Wolf near his home, in a little house that his mother gave them. She was always a shiftless housekeeper. Although her mother-in-law disapproved of her habits, she left it to her son and his wife's mother to reprimand the girl. After Red Bird was born, her parents lived in a tent while the father was employed on C.C.C. projects. She was moved from place to place as the work progressed and was sometimes left with her paternal grandmother, who occasionally took her to kindergarten. In these camps, Red Bird's mother lay in bed mornings, reading pulp magazines, while her husband got up and made breakfast for himself and Red Bird. Her care of the child was very poor indeed. The baby was badly undernourished and nearly died of pneumonia at the age of two.

Six months after Red Bird's youngest sister was born, their father obtained a divorce and married again. Cleo wished to give him the children, but her mother insisted that she keep them. However, the Howling Buffaloes soon went away, leaving Cleo and her three babies to shift for themselves in the family home. It thus became necessary for Cleo to take the children to their paternal grandmother, Mrs. White Horse, for adequate support.

Cleo then ran away with an Indian sailor. In the spring of 1943 she returned home and had a baby in the following winter. Red Bird was well aware of the expected new baby and visited with her mother for a few weeks during the pregnancy. To her the arrival of a new sister was an exciting and absorbing event.

Red Bird is a thin child with dark skin, flashing brown eyes, and a sullen mouth. She is definitely underweight and appears to have been undernourished most of her life. Her general health is poor. At times she appears listless and again irritable.

Toward her indulgent grandparents she shows no very deep affection. She quarrels with her fourteen-year-old Aunt Mary and steals her rouge and lipstick. Her ten-year-old Uncle John is rarely a companion of Red Bird or Mary in the home.

Red Bird's playmates at home are her three- and four-year-old sisters and her eight-year-old aunt, the daughter of Mrs. White Horse's sister. This child lives in a near-by community, where the White Horses live during the summer, and she and her brothers are constantly at Red Bird's house for meals and play.

At school, Red Bird suffers from inability to make any satisfactory adjustment either in her class work or with her teachers and classmates. She entered the second grade with a conditional promotion. Red Bird is blocked and extremely cautious in her approach to new work; but, once she grasps it, she shows some capacity and alertness. Pressed to do well in spelling, for example, she will learn her words and make a perfect score for a few days but then become careless and relapse to a below-average score. She frequently runs away from school for the afternoon. This may be partly due to her inability to master all her work, but probably it is largely the result of her emotional instability. Criticism or imagined failure usually makes her withdraw either mentally or physically from school work, but at times she will become defiant, throwing her papers on the floor and refusing to co-operate for the rest of the period. Like many Dakota children, Red Bird takes more pleasure in drawing than in any other school work. She differs from the other second-grade girls in showing little interest in the dolls and play-house. In the first grade she played with them as often as it was permitted.

With her classmates Red Bird is passive and not very sociable. On arrival at the school she frequently goes into the girls' washroom to remain until classes begin. Red Bird will not play with the boys in her class and frequently slaps them when she meets them in the halls. She likes to talk about boys to her teacher. Red Bird admires older girls, particularly "the pretty ones," as she calls the girls with neat appearance and attractive clothes who return from boarding school. Red Bird apparently imitates them by trying to comb her hair in the latest boarding-school style and by overuse of cosmetics. Her blatant rouge and lipstick, untidily painted fingernails, oddly rolled and cut hair, and excess of pins and jewelry give her, perhaps, a feeling that she looks grown up.

The teacher has had some trouble with Red Bird over stealing articles like scissors from the school, so that she has had to be searched for some weeks to break the habit.

Red Bird's major difficulties are immediately evident in her tests. Her Grace Arthur Performance Test gives her an I.Q. of 86, but her Goodenough Drawing Test gives her an I.Q. of 123. The great discrepancy in these two scores is a key to her problem. As revealed in her spelling lessons, Red Bird is able to do good intellectual work, but she cannot function on a consistently adequate level because she is greatly disturbed emotionally.

Her Rorschach and Thematic Apperception tests show that she fails to respond to her inner promptings and that she has little drive. To the outside world she is passive, and, being strongly blocked, her relations with others are strained. Although she is unstable and withdrawn from others, when they arouse or thwart her, she is likely to respond in a defiant and rebellious way. Such behavior has been exhibited both at home and at school. Red Bird has made and accepted few social controls. This has so hampered her relationships with her age mates that she has only one real school companion, a little girl who is as emotionally disturbed as herself.

Red Bird's tests also indicate that there may be already some sexual disturbance. Her practice of hanging around the girls' washroom before and during school hours, her interest in older girls, and her attention to her appearance also suggest a possible overdevelopment of sexual interest. This may be stimulated by association with her mother.

In the light of Red Bird's family record and her own history, it is not surprising to find that her psychological tests reveal her as a genuinely frightened little girl with definite anxieties. She is handicapped by a poor physical condition and by her inability to utilize her intelligence efficiently. Her short span of life has certainly been sufficiently varied and dramatic to create great emotional unbalance.

Red Bird has become very uncertain of herself from her family situation. Rejection by her mother has been a distinct shock. Although her mother has made clothes for her, visited her in school, and taken her home for a week or two, this brief indulgence without a continued affectionate relationship has been very unsatisfying. Her father once offered her much support, but his departure from the family scene and his responsibility for other little girls have created consternation in Red Bird's mind. Toward her indulgent grandparents, she reveals no deep affection. In one test, she stated that the happiest things she could remember were "when Grandpa and Grandma died" and "when Uncle went to war." This untrue statement about her grandparents shows not only the lack of any close bonds with them but also probably wishful thinking stirred by resentment or anxiety. The best thing that could happen to her, she says, is "go to heaven."[6] This remark epitomizes Red Bird's unhappiness, if not a real wish to be dead. A child with her attitudes and anxiety is indeed in serious difficulty.

Red Bird's personality and history show dramatically how Dakota children are being affected by their surroundings and how their development is being warped by their present cultural disorganization. Her story has been presented at some length to show the disorganization in her parents' and grandparents' lives and its bearing on her development. The shifting of mates and moving of children from home to home by her parents and grandparents are not unusual among their generations.

Red Bird, who has average capacities, and probably had originally normal freedom of action, apparently has had such painful experiences that she is now fearful of expressing herself. Her whole attitude toward life seems to be one of wariness and restraint. She is undoubtedly an extreme case, but she presents a pattern of personality development that is characteristic of many children on the reservation.

WINONA AND ROBERT RUNNING ELK

The Running Elks, a family of pure Indian descent, live in an attractive, painted farmhouse surrounded by small trees and a low fence. The father built this house through a rehabilitation loan from the government. Later he purchased land adjacent to the house for a garden. The house is superior to most full-blood homes on the reservation.

The father died several years ago when Winona and Robert were five and three years old. For many years the father had been an employee of a neighboring white storekeeper, driving the store truck and working in the white man's fields. He spent most of his vacations visiting other reservations to see the Indian fairs and celebrations, particularly the Sun Dances. Winona and Robert remember their father clearly and look upon the summer trips taken with him and the rest of the family as high points in their lives.

The mother remained a widow until recently. A neighboring widower moved into the house to help her with the chores after her oldest boy went into the Marines. After discussing the matter through the mails with her elder son, the mother decided to marry this man. Whether the younger childen were also consulted could not be learned, but doubtless there was some discussion of the event beforehand. The children's relations with him were not reported.

There are now three boys and three girls in the family, all from the mother's first marriage. The first two children born to the parents died. Richard, a crippled son, lives at home. The oldest daughter, Elizabeth, also lives at home, helping with the housework and younger children. She dropped out of school when she felt that she was too old for her class and school work. The next sister, Jane, spent some time in a tuberculosis sanatorium, where she became fluent in English and more like white people in her behavior and attitudes than the rest of her family. She has found much difficulty in adjusting to an Indian home and the sudden freedom thrust upon her. She ran away once and was picked up by Rapid City police for vagrancy.

This full-blood family is related to a line of able Indian leaders. With the exception of the middle sister, Jane, the family appears very stable and cohesive, affording security and affection to each member. Winona, aged ten, and Robert, aged eight, are the youngest children. As the next oldest child is the sister who has been in the sanatorium most of their lives, there has been an age gap between Winona and Robert and their older brothers and sisters at home. The oldest brother is very fond of the youngest children and wrote them constantly from his Marine camp. He took Robert with him for a summer while he worked in the beet fields before he went into military service.

Winona and Robert attend a day school. Their mother forbids them to play with the neighboring white children, and so, since they have no near-by Indian neighbors, they play and ride together.

The mother reared her first children in typically indulgent Indian fashion; but, beginning with Jane, she trained her last three babies by white methods taught her by an aunt, a Chilocco graduate and a trained nurse. Winona's toilet training began when she was only two months old. When she was five months' old, her mother became ill and had to put Winona on a bottle, which was given her according to a regular schedule prescribed by the mother's sister. At fifteen months, Winona pulled the nipple off the bottle and began to drink out of it; so her mother began feeding her by cup. This child training, revolutionary among the full-blood Dakota, caused some stir among the older uneducated relatives. The mother's brother would come to the house and watch the little baby and then shake his finger at the mother and say, "This is no good; this is white man's way." He was particularly shocked that the mother would let the child cry and not feed her when she demanded it. The mother, however, did not carry her white pattern of training to the extreme of early discipline in other forms of behavior and has never spanked Winona. In later years the mother was frequently ill, and much of Winona's and Robert's training fell upon older brothers and sisters, who had been trained in the Indian fashion.

Winona is now a handsome and "typical" young Indian girl in appearance. Her Indian features are accentuated by her big, soft, black eyes and her two long braids of black hair. She has never been ill and now has the appearance of radiant health. She has a great deal of poise and a ready smile but also the reserve characteristic of well-bred Dakota. During this survey, she was usually seen alone, walking to the store for some small purchase or playing about the house. At home she shows the usual Indian child's interest in drawing. She keeps her papers, crayons, and funny papers in paper sacks neatly tucked away in her bureau drawer. Her mother remarked that she is neat about her property and her dress and that she was very careful not to hurt the small trees planted around the house. Winona, like her father, is a Catholic, and attends church fairly regularly. The mother is an Episcopalian, as are Winona's younger and oldest brothers.

In her school work Winona does not show the accomplishments that she could achieve. While eager and diligent in her studies, she shows no special interests. She is slow in reading, possibly owing in part to the fact that the family speaks Siouan at home, although they all can speak good English. Winona's behavior with her classmates is a bit hostile or aggressive at times, possibly as a way of gaining attention. She has been heard to call other children names, and she causes trouble in other ways. She was once sent to Pine Ridge to the boarding school but returned home after one night; her parents did not force her to return. Recently she walked out of her present school when two boys tugged her braids. Her mother returned her to class, demanding that the teacher punish the boys. In general, Winona keeps to herself but would like more associations with children of the same age and interests. Her teacher finds her agreeable to authority and direction and willing to run errands and co-operate. She is quite self-sufficient in managing her daily affairs.

Winona's test scores—an I.Q. of 141 by the Arthur test and 117 by the Goodenough Drawing Test—place her among the most intelligent of the tested group of Dakota children. Although she has good drive toward intellectual achievement, her interests run to practical and commonplace matters, as her school work shows. She is self-contained, but she places no undue restraint on her sense of humor[7] or her ability to act with good understanding and to make decisions. She is, however, outwardly cautious and formal, following the behavior of a well-trained Dakota girl.

She keeps up her contacts with other people but feels little dependence upon them. She also has a tendency to consider relationships and situations for her own benefit. With most adults, and particularly her teachers, Winona is compliant, but with her mother, Winona feels some resentment because she attempts to control Winona's behavior more than she likes. The mother, as a woman frequently ill and upset by the loss of two children and a husband, does not appear to have given Winona the intimate associations that a child needs. The mother's recent marriage and previous ambiguous relationships with a man who has supplanted her beloved father may also cause some of Winona's unfriendliness toward her. The relationship with her mother appears to have directed Winona toward becoming self-contained, and the restrictions which her mother placed upon her have handicapped her in making wider social contacts and developing a better basis for making friends. Otherwise, Winona is an extremely able and well-adjusted young girl who is learning to live in her community without becoming suppressed or losing the best personality qualities of her Indian heritage.

Robert, the youngest child, was born twelve days after the oldest girl in the family died. His mother, ill in the hospital, was overcome with grief. The doctor advised her to put Robert on a bottle immediately. He was allowed to keep it for eighteen months. In explaining this, the mother said, "I guess because he was the last baby we thought he was sort of sickly, so we treated him that way." As in the case of Winona, his feeding was by schedule, and he was allowed to cry rather than be fed at odd hours. His toilet training was also begun very early.

Robert's family life has given him much satisfaction and pleasure. He feels important in it and enjoys good relationships with all its members. His mother he accepts as the controlling person and from her receives much consideration because of his supposed early frailty. However, he is not submissive in accepting her authority. He has the same yearning for his father that Winona shows.

Robert appears now to be a quiet and self-contained boy, who tends to be retiring. He plays with his sister but more frequently plays alone, preferring fishing to competitive games. He has one occasional companion in a boy of his age who rides some distance to Robert's home.

Although he might have attended kindergarten at the age of five, Robert did not begin school until he was seven, because his mother believed that he was not strong. He entered the day school in the spring of 1941 but did not attend regularly then or during the next year. However, he was promoted along with his grade.

Robert shows superior intelligence—an I.Q. of 128 in the Arthur and 144 in the Goodenough test. His intelligence is evident in the manner in which he handles situations that call for thought. He is practical and checks facts against statements, but he is not very systematic in organizing his ideas. His teacher reports that he is an "average" student who is interested but not steady in his work and is likely to dream. His tests also show that his excellent intellectual abilities are handicapped by a habit of daydreaming and a lack of drive and persistence.

Robert has a mature inner life for a boy of his age and prefers his fantasies and solitary life to sociability. The fantasies are used for release from a slight insecurity which he feels with others. Usually he is restrained in the presence of others, but at times he acts impulsively.

Robert is a very pious youngster and accepts a religious control of the world that is not characteristic of many other full-blood Dakota children. He mentions God several times in his tests as the authority and the rewarding and punishing agent of people.

In his personality development Robert appears to be a boy who has been somewhat overprotected at home because, as a small child, he was thought to lack robustness and vigor. This has retarded slightly the development of his social techniques, so that he appears in his social behavior younger than he actually is. However, with his intellectual endowments and continued associations with many other children at school, he should develop rapidly. Like his family, he will probably adapt to white life, but he will also be proud of and content in his Indian heritage.

CHARLIE CHARGING BULL

Charlie is a fourteen-year-old full-blood boy with a round and merry face, who lives in a dilapidated log cabin on the outskirts of a small town. The family consists of father, mother, and older brother and sister. About five years ago Charlie lost a brother a year younger than himself.

The Charging Bulls came to their present home only a few years ago. Before the drought of the 1930's they had a small but well-stocked farm; when crops failed, the father abandoned it to work on reservation relief projects and then as a farm laborer. Thus the family has moved about considerably. In none of the places they have lived have they had close relatives or a neighborhood with which they had blood ties. They now live among miscellaneous Indian families, who remain in the community only as long as there is work or a need to send their children to school. There are also a few resident traders, a hotelkeeper, and white employee families.

Charlie's father is a large, bowlegged man, who associates with very few people in the community. He is usually quiet but is known to have an uncertain temper, threatening to fight or kill when he is sharply crossed or when he thinks any one of his family has been abused. The community fears what he may do. He appears to be a companion to his two boys, frequently riding over the range with them. However, reports of neighbors and the behavior of the children indicate that he is domineering and scolding in the home. He has made his family, especially Charlie, very much afraid of him. He teases Charlie and tells him stories that worry him.

Charlie's mother is a tall, thin, and seemingly carefree woman, who also teases him. She does not directly threaten her children, although she occasionally makes remarks to them such as "If you weren't my son, I'd pound you," or "You sure make me mad." She is more amused than antagonized by Charlie and frequently remarked to interviewers in describing his behavior, "He sure is funny" and "That sure tickled me." She is similarly amused by her young daughter, who is something of a tomboy and a rough playmate of her brothers. When Charlie was little, the mother disciplined him with the traditional Sioux child-frighteners, but this ended when one day he said about a spirit she described as living in the creek, "Mommer, that's your imagination. You ain't got no sense." The mother now attempts to discipline Charlie by keeping him out of school when teachers complain of his behavior, but privately regards many of his pranks as great jokes. Like her husband, she is not loath to rush to the defense of her children and has, on a few occasions, threatened to fight other women. The mother says, however, that disciplining the boys is the father's business and that she has enough to do to look after her daughter.

The father and mother come from different communities; neither has relatives near the present home. The mother went to boarding school, where she had a reputation as a trouble-maker and leader of gangs against unpopular individuals. In her present community she has more friends than does her husband, but she also is considered to be a very slovenly housewife by other Indian women.

Charlie, her second child, was a fat, dark baby. His umbilical cord was not tied well by the midwife and bled for six days. His mother ascribes this as the cause of his occasional fainting when he was a little boy. He remained fat but weak.

When his weight broke his baby "walker," his mother sat him up in a horse collar on the floor. She kept his hair in long braids until he was six. He was weaned at about thirteen months but was given oatmeal and gravy when he was nine months old. At fourteen months he began to walk. He learned his toilet training from watching others, but, until he had achieved this, he used the floor or went out of doors.

Charlie had a speech difficulty during his infancy and early childhood, and he refused to talk like other children until he was about eight years old. Until this time he had a few words of his own making, by which he made known his wants. When he started to talk, speaking only in English, he was already attending play school. About this time his younger brother died. Charlie still lisps a bit and stammers when he becomes overexcited. He usually speaks in English now, even replying in this language when addressed in Siouan by his bilingual parents. He skips many words and is said to do this also when speaking in Siouan.

Charlie now teases his mother in return for her jibes. He says the bacon looks like bad potatoes and, if asked to do something, often says, "If you can't do it, I think I'll just let it go." He does not have any such joking relations with his father. His older brother, Jerry, is his usual companion outside school hours. They support each other when others attack them, and Jerry boasted about Charlie when he competed successfully against him; but they have had several fights and are quite constantly arguing. Yet, when Jerry left for the Navy in 1943, Charlie went along with him and tried to enter also. Charlie plays with his older sister, Lucy, at home; but, as there is some difference in years in their ages, she is not a real companion. Lucy shows a masculine identification by her behavior in her rough-and-tumble family, and, when she speaks Siouan, she uses the masculine endings, as if she were a boy.

At school, Charlie has the reputation of being "bright." He works rapidly but not thoroughly. He was promoted twice in the past year, because he seemed so far ahead of his class and also to keep him busy and thus prevent him from annoying other students. He has been temporarily expelled several times for causing trouble. Charlie has been very annoying to one teacher, whom he can easily force to lose her temper. He picks on little boys and girls and has the reputation of being bullying and mean. One teacher reported he had "a cruel streak." Charlie is usually involved in any fighting or destruction of school property. In spite of this, he gets along well with the one male teacher and works well for him. He has few playmates outside his family and, when he does find one, soon loses him because of fighting or hurting him.

Charlie has an I.Q. of 101 by the Arthur test and 121 by the Goodenough. He is not the brilliant or exceptional student that his school record might imply. He seems to show no real intellectual accomplishment but a quick and artificial display which impresses his teachers and wins their praise. He is unable to organize his work well, and this may keep him from making a better record. He has creativity and originality, but anxiety about himself and his relation to others keeps him from giving any real expression to his inner life. He appears to use it as a retreat and escape, daydreaming and building fantasies that have little relation to reality.

Charlie's personality appears to be built around his fundamental insecurity and anxiety. The quarreling, hitting, destructive behavior he exhibits is reaction to aggression, or fear of aggression, from others. He is afraid to strike back at elders and bigger children but picks on smaller ones. He throws rocks at the school and destroys property to express his antagonisms. This reaction is impulsive and only halfhearted; figuratively, he appears as if he were thrashing his arms about fiercely and crying in fear at the same time. Fundamentally, he would like to be passive, to be treated kindly and affectionately, but the world continues to prick him, and he does not know what to do with himself or how to build up friendly relationships.

His aggressions toward girls are partly based on his impulsively reactive lashing-back at weaker individuals but seem also due to sexual anxiety. He is uncertain of himself in this sphere and unable to be more direct.

Charlie appears to be a young adolescent unsure of his family ties and with no loyal relatives to support him in the community. He tries to build up favor and attention for himself by good performance in school work, but this is only a show that does not win him the satisfaction or security he desires. He appears to be anxious and floating in a social milieu that affords him no moorings.

MELVILLE LE GASSE

Melville Le Gasse is a boy of nine, whose black hair, brown eyes, and light-brown skin mark him with stronger Indian characteristics than is expected of persons of less than one-quarter Indian blood. He has the full physical development expected of a boy his age. Until the fall of 1942, Melville and his family were almost the only mixed-bloods in their full-blood community. They moved here about five years before from a white farming district in a neighboring state, leased several allotments of land, and borrowed money to start a cattle herd. In their former home the family associated with whites and near-whites. Melville had no playmates of his own age in the neighborhood; for one year he attended a kindergarten in the near-by town.

His mother, a very light mixed-blood, grew up off the reservation. The fact that her father was white and a wealthy farmer by local standards gave her a good social standing in the neighborhood. Since they lived in the country, her

SCHOOLBOYS ROPING A WILD HORSE

parents had to send her to a nonreservation boarding school, but she resented the association with an Indian group and the treatment she received from teachers. Marrying a man of Indian blood and moving to the reservation to live among Indians have been embittering social steps downward. She now keeps to herself, devoting her attentions to her children and occasionally bringing some relative, a light mixed-blood like herself, to visit in her home.

The father—a dark mixed-blood with marked French features—also grew up off the reservation. He farmed rather unsuccessfully after he married and looked for greater success when he moved onto his reservation land. He is an unstable person and has not managed his cattle very efficiently, often leaving home to work as an agricultural laborer. He sends back little or none of his earnings and returns penniless. His long periods of idleness and roaming about with other Indians have kept the family poverty-stricken and often without food in the house. In fact, Melville frequently comes to school without breakfast. The habits and irresponsibility of his father have led to family quarrels, to which Melville is usually witness. His mother scolds and browbeats his father.

Melville has three older sisters, who attended a public school and then boarding school, and a brother, Henry, aged sixteen, now away at a nonreservation boarding school. He also had a younger brother and sister, who died, but no information was obtained about Melville's relationship with them. In 1942 one older sister, Mildred, eloped with a young, full-blood man but was brought home by her parents. She now lives at home, a close companion of her mother and a second mother to Melville. She has bought him clothes and most of his Christmas gifts out of her earnings from working in homes in the near-by village. Melville appears to be fond of his older brother, Henry, and writes frequently to him in the letter-writing periods at school.

In his early training, Melville's mother followed the practices of the near-white group of mixed-bloods. She raised him on a bottle with canned milk. She also spanked him, as did his father, a means of discipline which they have decreased but have not yet given up. Having no playmates near by in either his former or his present home, Melville has played by himself around the house. Occasionally he rides with his father to look after cattle and mend fences. His mother does not encourage Melville to play with the full-blood children, saying that he does not understand them, and she has directed his social orientation so that already he regards himself as white. This is her attitude toward her own social position. She dislikes receiving services from the Indian Agency and having her sons in Indian schools.

In his social relationships in the Indian day school in 1942, Melville sought his teacher's protection and gave her his confidence, particularly about his home life and the difficulties of his parents. Melville admired her and her home, which is superior to any of the other homes he has visited. He played with the boys in his class but had difficulty because he demanded to be the center of attention. Occasionally he would pick a fight and then run to his teacher crying or complain later to his mother that he was picked on. He was looked upon as something of a sissy because of his slightly effeminate behavior. This quality was heightened when he accepted the leading feminine part in a class play—a role that no "good" Sioux boy would consider. Occasionally he ran away from school for an afternoon to play with an older boy and a distant relative. Melville showed good interest in his studies, but his teacher felt he was capable of doing better work.

Melville scored an I.Q. of 104 on the Grace Arthur Performance Test and 111 on the Goodenough Drawing Test. His Rorschach and Thematic Appercention tests reveal him as an immature boy with a great sense of insecurity, worried that he may not retain his role of baby in the family and continue to be the subject of constant and protective attention. His anxiety is great, and his confidence in his parents or their affection is slight. This insecurity is reflected in a fantasy where he suffers and dies to cause his parents worry. In one story he pictures himself gone for days on his horse, while his parents search frantically. In another story he is a rugged cowboy who is kicked in the head and finally dies, much to the sorrow and anxiety of his father. Although the boy seems to enjoy the company of his father on the range, actually he makes no hero of him. His mother seems to be a little closer because of the protection she affords him. His brother and sisters, whose actual relationships to him seem to be affectionate and protective, do not appear so in the tests, indicating possibly that they are not the source of support that one would expect. No reference is made to his dead brother or sister, who may have supplanted Melville in the affection of his parents and thus started his great feeling of insecurity. Although he appears desirous of punishing his parents and himself in his dreams, there is no observed evidence that he has been aggressive or harmful. He is more likely to run away from school or feign sickness to stay home with his mother.

Melville's insecurity and anxiety appear to be derived from the precarious economic and social status of his family. His mother is unsatisfied in her social ambitions and anxious over the family's economic position. She disparages his father before Melville. She also indulges and overprotects her son and keeps him from better social development by restricting his play with age mates. Melville, lacking ties with parents or age mates, puts himself in a submissive position to gain their protection.

Melville appears to be trying to solve his emotional problems by removing himself from them and consciously intellectualizing about his situation. At other times he resorts to his imagination and achieves his ambitions in fantasy. When he reacts overtly, he does so rather crudely and impulsively. Caught in a struggle between impulses from within and sensitivity to his environment, Melville ranges in his behavior from compliance to rebellion. His problem in his adjustment to society lies in finding a balance between these forces.

GINNY REYNARD

Ginny is an eight-year-old girl with light-brown complexion, bright dark eyes, and a round, cherubic face. Outside her Indian community she might be easily taken for a little French girl, and not without reason, for she has more French than Indian heritage, with only three-eighths Indian blood. Ginny is an energetic and competent little girl, quite able to look out for herself and her brother Peter, who is a year younger.

They are the youngest of a large family of children, half of whom have already left home. Three older brothers and a married sister now still remain at home with their mother, Ginny, and Peter. Their home is a very small, boxlike frame house, divided into kitchen and bedroom. They have a stove, a table, a few chairs, two beds, and a dresser. As the home cannot accommodate all the family, the older boys sleep either in a tent or in a neighbor's house.

This family has always been extremely poor and has received much help from the government and relatives. The father comes home only on rare occasions, and, although he has recently been well employed, gives very meager and irregular assistance to his family.

The mother is not always able to work. She has just managed to keep her family with the aid of relief and some private charity and by sending some children to boarding school. Attempts by other people to help her have not always been well received. She has become a very cranky and antagonistic woman, filled with complaints against the school and government. In her behavior she shows the resentment and hurt pride that often come from being an object of charity. The mother has also been harassed by the behavior of her older children, who have participated in promiscuity and petty crimes, for which they have been punished in court and severely criticized by neighbors.

At present only Ginny, Peter, and an older brother, Alexander, aged ten, attend school. Alexander is a rather sullen and effeminate young boy who frequently makes complaints about his teachers. This usually brings his mother to his defense or wins him a temporary absence from school. He quarrels with Ginny and his brother. Fighting among the children now at home appears to be a common occurrence. Contrary to Sioux custom, the younger ones are punished by their mother if they start trouble with the older ones.

Ginny was nursed until she was eight months old and then put on a bottle. Her mother was very proud of her for being quick to acquire toilet training.

When she was about two, and again at four, she had pneumonia. At an early age she learned to help with the housework, and by the time she was seven she was able to get meals for a sickly neighbor who had been left home alone. Her mother says that she has trained Ginny by talking to her, but she has also spanked her on several occasions. This usually happens when Ginny runs away from home to play at the store.

Ginny speaks with pride of her father and appears to be treated very kindly by him when he returns home. She states that he has never spanked her. She does not appear to be very intimate with Alexander but looks after Peter in a quite maternal way. At school she is very careful that he does not forget his coat or cap, and has fought with boys in his defense. She also looks after the baby nephew who lives with his mother in the Reynard house.

At school, Ginny is popular with her classmates, according to her teacher. She was enrolled at five in school and by this time greatly enjoys being in class. She is now a leader in the group and takes responsibility in helping the other children. She does good work, has a good imagination, and is rather mature for her age. Both at home and at school she appears self-confident and very responsive to adults.

Ginny's tests show a well-organized, superior intelligence; she scored an I.Q. of 119 on the Arthur test, although only 99 on the Goodenough. She has a wealth of imagination, which she freely and fully reports. This quality is a great help to her as a release and escape from strong depressive and aggressive feelings. These feelings appear to be derived from a deep-rooted insecurity in her brothers and sister and concern about her relation to her mother, who, she feels, has greater affection for the other children. Their quarrelsome and antagonistic behavior increases this uneasiness.

Ginny, however, has not become quarrelsome herself. She has diverted such feelings and energy into a maternal and protecting behavior, which we have seen directed toward her younger brother, nephew, and classmates. In this respect she has become a well-socialized individual and, by protective relationship, has covered her real anxiety about her acceptance by others. Underlying this, however, is a craving for affection.

Ginny is mature in her development and has sufficient inner resources to aid in the stability of her adjustment. She has a tendency to introversion. Her problem of jealously of her brothers and sister and the repression of hostility felt against them should not create any further social problem for her, because of the way in which she has handled it. She tends, however, to organize things to an exceptional degree for an eight-year-old girl. She is overambitious and controlled beyond the reach of the usual emotional ties to other people. In spite of the seeming excellence of her adjustment, any overstrain or increase of tension at home might upset this adjustment, causing her either to withdraw completely or to burst into hostile and antisocial acts.

MICKEY LA FLESCHE

Mickey is nine years old, the youngest of the nine children of a white man and a woman of three-eighths Indian blood. All the children have white skin and features that reveal none of their Indian heritage.

Mickey belongs to the second set of children reared by his parents. They had four children, and then five years elapsed before the five younger ones were born. Two of these older children have gone to Omaha; one has married and now lives on another part of the reservation; the fourth lives in the home. The family lives in a well-built four-room cabin on the edge of a village. Mrs. La Flesche has sisters also married to whites, who are living on a near-by allotment. These families maintain close relations among themselves and have friendly, though not very intimate, social ties with the general Indian group.

Mickey's father is described as an irritable, dominating man in his late sixties. His bad management of a small area of poor land has kept the family poverty-stricken. He has worked unsuccessfully for years, and, in an effort to maintain his family, he has dissipated his children's resources by selling their allotments. His social contacts on the reservation are limited, and his closest associates are his brothers-in-law. The father's place in his family is not very strong. He is quite demanding of them, and no one seems to feel closely attached to him. He works daily in his fields with the oldest of his sons who lives at home. Mickey's association with his father is apparently limited to mealtime.

On Mickey's mother falls most of the responsibility for the support of the family. She is a busy, hard-working woman who spends much time working at a store. She is too busy in her employment and household tasks to give any prolonged attention to Mickey or any other single member of her large family. Although she is fond of all her children, her two eldest girls who have married more successfully to whites are the center of her interest and conversation. Others of her children and relatives are continually visiting in the household. At one time there were eighteen living in and around the home.

The household is normally composed of the parents, Mickey, two older sisters, two older brothers, and one younger brother. Important to Mickey are one older sister, Louise, and his older brother nearest him in age. Louise was mainly responsible for Mickey's training and care, his mother being too involved with the next baby and household duties to give him much attention after he was about a year old. Since then, however, Louise's interests have turned to her youngest brother. The break in this relationship has forced Mickey to seek companionship with his twelve-year-old brother Ralph, but Ralph frequently fights with Mickey over petty things and makes life miserable for him. Mickey brings few playmates to his home but enjoys playing with his little brother.

Mickey does good work in school, fulfilling his assignments willingly and conscientiously, but he is anxious to complete them so that he may play or talk with other children. He is very popular with his teacher and the boys and girls of his age, although the more timid children and their parents complain that he is quarrelsome. Mickey maintains a good disposition on the playground, and his belligerent moods pass as quickly as a cloud blown across the face of the sun. All the teachers of the school and the white people of the town are fond of him for his cheery responsiveness.

Mickey took his tests eagerly and asked to repeat them. His intelligence tests showed he has a superior mentality: I.Q. of 111, Arthur test, and 120, Goodenough. He is capable of better school work than he demonstrates. His Thematic Apperception Test shows that he enjoys greatly the numerous pleasant contacts with other children. However, he is less interested in intensifying these relationships than in developing his inner life.

Some of his responses to the tests show that he has no real love or respect for his father. Instead of the idealized picture that some young children paint of their fathers, Mickey seems to view his father much as he has been described above—an aloof, irritable, unaffectionate old man. Mickey's feelings for his mother and his family reflect the constant come-and-go of people. His concept of a family is one of a friendly yet slightly unstable group of people, rather than a loving and cohesive unit that would help to give him a firmer feeling of security. He feels that his mother is a friendly, though not loving, authority from whom he can obtain very little real affection. His relation to his brother Ralph is not so satisfying as Mickey would like, for Ralph is quite inconsistent in his behavior. He appears to like Mickey, yet at times he becomes quite quarrelsome and domineering. It is possible, although the evidence is scanty, that some of this difficulty arises from Ralph's jealousy over Mickey's greater popularity with all their relatives.

In his contacts outside the home Mickey is universally liked. Quick and anxious to learn, vivacious and friendly with his classmates and teachers, Mickey is a popular and accepted leader. His spontaneous and somewhat uncritical acceptance of anyone who will be friendly keep him busy in all that goes on around him. That he sometimes gets into fights is not surprising in a boy of his exuberance. As was noted in his family relations, Mickey has no real emotional ties to his age mates. Among his relatives and his friends there is no one person with whom he feels genuinely secure and loved. This does not imply that he feels any rejection by others or hostility toward them—for he does not. He shows no anxiety, and it may be that he is too much of an introvert to attract intense affection.

Mickey is a white boy in appearance, attitudes, and behavior. He already appears to regard himself as different from, and even a little superior to, the Indians. This orientation is not surprising when one looks at his family with their white father and their white values and behavior. Their closest relationships in the community are with families of similar composition and standards. Mickey's older brothers and sisters have already moved out of the community, and his family has not made a close integration with the more Indian households. It is probable that Mickey will finish his high-school work and then follow his brother and sisters into the white world outside the reservation. He seems sure to adjust satisfactorily to this world, for his inner poise, his responsiveness, and his friendly, smiling appearance make him particularly popular among his white friends and teachers.

In summary, Mickey is a lively and genial boy, happy and successful in his personal contacts. He has excellent intellectual capacities and sufficient inner security to adjust quickly to a strange environment. The combination of his inner resources and his social adjustment have given him a well-rounded personality. He may, however, find trouble if at some time he feels the need for a deep emotional tie to one person.

PRISCILLA JUDSON

Priscilla is a thin, frail girl of eleven with a dark skin and a sober countenance. She has nine-sixteenths Indian blood. Her birth was normal and her first year of life a healthy one. About the time of her second birthday she began to have convulsions, which appeared occasionally until she was seven. These "spells," as the family called them, frightened and bewildered them. Noticing that when she was made to cry she frequently went into a convulsive state, they treated her with utmost caution and have continued to do so, even though this sickness seems definitely over.

Priscilla lives with her father and mother and fourteen-year-old sister, Della, and sixteen-year-old brother, Don. She also has two older sisters who live and work off the reservation. The family home is a log cabin about a half-mile from the village. In their social position the Judsons belong with the mixed-blood and white families of the village neighborhood, although their nearest neighbors are full-bloods, with whom they are very friendly.

The Judsons follow an almost white pattern of life, but their relations to less-assimilated Indians are strengthened by the fact that the father is three-quarters Indian, descended from several generations of mixed-blood forebears. Through his mixed-blood background and his education, Bill Judson has more training in and acceptance of white ways than the majority of his blood group. Although he speaks Siouan, he has not taught it to his children. He is a lean, tight-lipped man who keeps very much to himself. He treats Priscilla kindly but distantly and has never spanked her. The mother is the controlling person in the family, whom Priscilla accepts as the real authority. She has only three-eighths Indian blood.

On the surface the family appears to be enjoying a pleasant and placid existence. The father and mother are, however, quite restraining and apprehensive in the two youngest girls' outside activities. Priscilla's play has been hampered by her sickness and the great apprehension that her parents have always felt about her being away from the house and participating in vigorous activity. They have forbidden her and her sister to ride for fear of being hurt or to swim for fear of contagion from the water in the creek.

The set of this parental discipline appears to have come from Priscilla's paternal grandmother. She assisted at Priscilla's birth and, until she died three years later, directed the care of the baby. She made a favored child of Priscilla because she was the youngest and sickly. Although this grandmother was of only about one-half Indian blood, she followed the Indian pattern in forbidding that Priscilla be punished physically and in disciplining her by employing the traditional child-frighteners. From the grandmother, Priscilla's father and mother learned to indulge their daughter for fear of harming her, but they also wish to restrain her from moving away from their protection. This has been very confusing to the child.

Priscilla has very little association with her brother Don, who rides every day he can with full-blood friends and visits constantly in their homes. He leans to more Indian behavior and attitudes than any member of the family.

Priscilla is on friendly terms with her older sister Della, who has been her playmate, but the attachment does not seem to be deep. This is also true with her age mates. Della has been made to give way to her sister because of her frailness. Although Della is very considerate, she resents somewhat the demand that she make sacrifices to Priscilla. The youngest of Priscilla's two adult sisters, Elizabeth, nine years her senior, helped to take care of her when she was a baby and is now deeply interested in her development. To this sister, who now lives in another town, Priscilla has formed a closer attachment than to anyone else in her family. She respects Elizabeth's authority and yet competes with her in a joking way. Elizabeth plans to have Priscilla live with her when she finishes grade school, so that she can attend a city high school. Adjustment to the full-blood group is difficult for Elizabeth, and she has refused work on the reservation because of the problems of social obligations that it involves. Adjustment to the full-blood group is becoming a problem to Priscilla also. Recently she inquired of her mother why the Indian children at school called her "Wasicu"—"white girl."

Priscilla is a very intelligent girl, and the limitations placed upon her by illness have led her to develop intellectual, rather than athletic, pastimes. She is one of the few children of her school who make reading their major recreation. Her teacher reports that she is a thorough and ambitious student. She is, in fact, moving through grade school faster than any of her classmates. She is looked upon as a "smarty" by the other children, who regard such behavior as an attempt to win the teacher's favor and to identify one's self with whites. This unpopularity shows up in the school games, in which Priscilla is rarely chosen to play.

She does not play with boys. Although her boy cousins are constantly in her home and she in theirs, she thinks that they are mean. She is seldom seen about the village except in the company of her mother or sister and girl cousin for a quick shopping tour. She is more likely to remain in the village home of a friend of her mother's than to play or talk with the girls around the store and school.

Priscilla's tests show that she has a very superior intelligence (I.Q. 137 on the Arthur test) and is generally quick in her mental approach, with an excellent grasp of ideas and their interrelations.[8] She, no doubt, enjoys this intellectual superiority, for she is making her best adjustment in her intellectual and imaginative life. Her efficiency is somewhat lowered by an overdeveloped habit of daydreaming. She is an impressionable and somewhat immature girl, sensitive to the outer world. She withholds herself from social contacts, which suggests some insecurity. At home this insecurity tends to become confusion over her relationships with parents and adult brothers and sisters. She does not wish to abandon the protection and petting that she is used to, yet she would like to assert her independence and be more mature.

The poor relationships she is making with her age mates also hinder her social maturity. She understands what these relationships should be and how to be direct and definite without undue aggression; but, being unable to "give herself," she remains passive. The fact that she is a spoiled child who expects much and gives little in return may also contribute to her superficial relationships with her age group. She is meeting this problem, which causes her considerable anxiety, by escaping into daydreams. This is a very inadequate adjustment, for in her fantasy she tends to turn toward self-centered heroics or to infantile behavior. Her problem appears to lie in her inability to find security with which she could overcome flights into daydreaming and her wariness and timidity with others.

ANDRÉ DUBOIS

André is a handsome ten-year-old boy of three-eighths Indian blood who attends the fourth grade of the local day school. He lives with his three sisters, his father, and his mother in an outlying town of a predominantly white and mixed-blood population. An older sister is a nurse in a hospital on another reservation. The family have an attractive, small frame house. The parents are both employed, attend church regularly with their children, and are looked upon as good citizens in the community.

The father, whom André resembles, is a mixed-blood in appearance. He is kindly and interested in his children. Although he occasionally takes authority over them into his own hands, he usually leaves their discipline to his wife. His children say that he has never spanked them.

The mother shows none of her Indian blood in her features. Her father is a white man who lives in the same town. Her sister is also white in appearance and has married a white man. André's mother is the dominating and forceful member of the family. She is anxious to have her children become educated and get jobs that will take them further into white society. She wishes to be considered white herself and is a little disturbed by the fact that all her children are dark. She conforms to the behavior standards and ardently upholds the values of whites in the lower salary brackets. Although she likes to have her children play with whites, she also restrains them from associating with children of white parents who are financially better off and stand higher in the local official and social hierarchy.

André's two older sisters go to the Indian boarding school, but their mother plans to send them to a white high school and then to a hospital to train as nurses like the oldest daughter. André seems to be on very pleasant terms with these two sisters. The older looked after him and took him to school when he was little.

André was weaned by his mother at the end of his first year. He had some difficulty with his toilet training, and, as his mother reported, "It seemed as if he were going to wet his pants until he was twenty-one. I was so disgusted I just shook him." The mother looked upon her son with some curiosity and a little apprehension, for she had had no brothers, and André was the first boy in her or her sister's family. She expected that a boy would be "naturally mischievous and misbehaved." When at the age of six he complained of feeling faint and having pains, she put it down to a boyish prank. However, he became seriously ill and had to remain out of school for a year. Later he was allowed to attend irregularly but forbidden to play actively.

André's mother trains him by talking to him about his responsibilities and the right and wrong things to do. As punishment, she takes away the privilege of going to the movies or withholds his spending money. When he was a small boy, she also spanked him.

Neither André nor his sisters cause their parents any serious discipline problems, although both of the parents are away from the home all day. The mother does not, however, neglect the little attentions which make children happy. She always has a cake and presents and occasionally a party for them on their birthdays.

André looks upon his mother as the boss of the family, even asking her permission to go hunting with his father. This, he says, he learned from his good friend, the minister, who is always preaching that women should care for and run their families. André, who always attended church with his parents as a little boy, now goes to Sunday school and in summer attends a Bible school.

André plays with both white and Indian boys in the community. Although there is not much opportunity for it in his neighborhood, he likes to ride horses. His teachers report him to be very popular among his classmates, although a year ago he was rather sullen.

André does very good school work, except in arithmetic. He is not interested in carpentry like his father but spends all his leisure time in drawing. His work is good enough to warrant special instruction. He is not sure that he wants to be an artist and has expressed a desire to become a doctor. His mother discourages this ambition, saying that it is too costly for the parents and implying that it is too much above the family status.

André's intelligence tests gives him an average score: 96 by the Arthur and 113 by the Goodenough. However, his projective tests suggest that his intelligence is better than average, that he has excellent intellectual concepts which he arrives at by seeing the obvious and commonplace and enlarging upon these with a good use of his imagination. He has a power of creativity and a freedom and rhythm which are excellent bases for his artistic interests. His system of control is a somewhat refined intellectual one, with minimum use of either emotional or inner integrative functions. There is not the suppression, however, that characterizes Priscilla and a large proportion of Dakota children.

In his behavioral approach, André is realistic and able to get along fairly well with both age mates and adults. He does show a little insecurity, which appears to stem partly from his earlier separation from other children, necessitated by sickness, and partly from the predominance of women around him. But this insecurity has not affected his adjustment deeply. André has made a good adjustment to his father and mother. He respects his mother as a competent woman and admires his father.

In spite of the insecurity which limits his relations to the outside world, his expression of spontaneity, and the best use of his intellect, André has a well-developed personality and an imagination and balance exceptional among Dakota children. He is both pleasing and interesting to others. He has a good grasp of reality. He has no real problems of adjustment other than the slight feeling of helplessness derived from his period of sickness.

CARMELITA TOWNSEND

Carmelita is a sixteen-year-old girl of three-eighths Sioux blood. She also has French and a little Canadian Indian blood from her father. Although her complexion is dark, she looks more French than Indian.

Until Carmelita attended boarding school, she lived at home and went to a day school in the rural area of the reservation. Her family live in a community of mixed-blood families, who are closely interrelated. They are successful cattle operators, running their herds individually. In social matters, however, they are a very co-operative and closely knit social group. Carmelita's father has an allotment in this community. He was very prosperous during World War I but shortly afterward lost all his holdings through a sudden misfortune and became impoverished. The family were forced to move to another community where the father could get a small job. They struggled for many years and have finally built up a good home and cattle herd in the community where they now live.

The father, troubled by extremely poor eyesight, is helped in his work by a son about twenty years old. The mother, an energetic and very able woman, runs the family. She is one of the most capable housewives in her district and is active in the women's club and community social affairs. Jeanne, her oldest daughter, who lives with her husband, of one-thirty-second Indian blood, on a near-by ranch, is also an energetic and capable woman. When Carmelita was a little girl Jeanne took care of her. Carmelita also has three brothers who have left the reservation to complete their education and obtain employment. Altogether, the family presents a picture of a stable and industrious group, working hard for what it has in material wealth, and ambitious for the young people to move ahead and succeed, whether off the reservation or at home. They are strong Catholics through forebears on both sides of the family and attend the little chapel in their community. Their behavior, morality, and general outlook are those of the more stable whites who farm and run cattle on the reservation. However, the family, as mixed-bloods and of French-Canadian origin, do not feel closely allied with the white residents. When they associate outside their relationship group, it is as leaders among the Indians and to some extent with the school employees.

Carmelita was born about the time of her father's loss of his cattle herd and land. Her mother almost died in childbirth. However, she was soon able to nurse her baby. The child weighed only four and one-half pounds at birth and remained weak during all her childhood. She was undernourished and developed jaundice and rickets which left her frail. The parents were in such straits that they could not provide sufficient food for any of the children. One boy developed tuberculosis. Carmelita showed a positive reaction to tuberculosis but recovered at home. The two oldest children had to leave school to help their father work the garden and cut fence posts for sale. During this period, Carmelita could not attend school regularly and afterward was forced to remain out for a year.

She has worked hard in school, and, although she receives only passing marks, she is well liked by her teachers for her energy. She is co-operative and interested in learning so that she may later go on to college and study to be a home economics teacher. At school she has captained teams, and in the student council she has become a leader. In her general relations with her age mates, Carmelita appears as manager of their activities but remains popular with them all, whether Indian or white. She states that she likes both Indians and whites but feels that the latter treat her better. Alhough she is sixteen, she was not observed to have a boy friend at school.

On the Arthur test, Carmelita received a rating of low average. She apparently recognizes her limitations in this direction and covers up her confusion when confronted by problems she cannot handle by avoiding specific replies or decisions. Her creativity and imagination are in keeping with her mental endowments. She does not give evidence of much fantasy life, nor does she attempt to escape from situations by daydreaming. She accepts the impulses from her inner life but places a strong conscious control on them in adjusting to the world around her. She is sensitive to the reactions of others toward her, but she does not feel much emotional drive toward relationships with them. It may be that the long period of sickness and deprivation in her early childhood gave her the feeling that the outer world is unreliable and untrustworthy, which adds to the insecurity which she feels from her limited intellectual capacity.

This construction of her personality does not seem at first glance to be in keeping with her observed behavior at home and at school. When her activities are examined closely, however, it can be seen that she is really behaving in accordance with her sense of insecurity and her limitations. Aware that she is handicapped in academic work, she puts all her energies into social activities. For this she has learned a routine of behavior, after the pattern of her mother, which gives the appearance of spontaneity and leadership and which wins her praise from family and teachers without straining her beyond her capacities. She manages her schoolmates as the deputy of the teacher and thus has a role of some importance among them which does not require originality on her part and affords a sort of friendly but impersonal relationship with them that satisfies her needs. This type of behavior in a Sioux, and especially a Sioux girl, is unusual enough to merit attention and praise from the teachers, which would compensate to a large extent for her lack of skill in intellectual realms.

Rather than being a genuine leader, she is a conformer, but it so happens that the pattern to which she conforms is one of leadership as seen in her family. She is still very dependent upon the protection of her mother, and to maintain it she adheres to her mother's conventional standards as well as her pattern of managing those about her. Such behavior on the part of a girl does not sit well with the boys, and her relationships with them may in time cause her difficulty.

In summary, it appears that Carmelita has found a way of getting along in the world that is acceptable to the society in which she is likely to remain. It emphasizes her assets and minimizes her liabilities, and it will continue to afford her a considerable measure of satisfaction and security unless she is pushed beyond the limits of her emotional and intellectual capacities.

The reader has now made some acquaintance with ten Dakota children. They were selected not to portray either typical examples of extremes of range of Dakota children's personality types but only to present random cases from each of the age, blood, and community groups of the 166 children studied. It will be noted that the intelligence quotients range from superior to low average, personality development runs from stable to unbalanced, and social adjustments appear satisfactory for some full-bloods and near-whites like the Running Elks and Dubois children but poor for most of the others. André shows that children in families accepting the ways and objectives of white life can develop healthy personalities. Mickey, although in a less congenial white-patterned family, is also developing satisfactorily. Carmelita has gone through many of the more dramatic experiences that are shaping the personalities of Pine Ridge children, but her case demonstrates that biological factors can have the determining influence in personality development. Winona and Robert, although restrained, are Sioux children who have developed without undue feelings of insecurity.

Red Bird, Charlie, Melville, Priscilla, and Ginny, however, are children who feel that they must move with uncertainty and restraint both within and outside their family life. These five children reveal elements in their personality development which are characteristic of many of their generation. They have to one degree or another a sensitivity to disturbances with which they feel powerless to cope. They appear overserious. The bright spontaneity and energy usually associated with children are missing. They have experienced serious sicknesses or known them in their families. Death of a brother or sister is not infrequent. They have felt poverty and the anxiety of having no food in the house and no prospect of obtaining any. Most of their homes are crowded. These things have brought continual worry.

Most of the parents treat their children with much consideration and kindness. Except for the Duboises, who practice definite discipline of their children, parents tolerate more freedom of action and respond to more demands of their children than most whites allow. In spite of this broad tolerance received from their parents, the children do not appear to have close rapport or full faith in them. There is doubt and bewilderment. Many of the fathers and mothers appear too uneasy and harried to give their children real affection.

These characteristics of their lives and personalities will serve for the reader as clues and personal illustrations of the qualities of the group personality of Sioux chidren which is described in the next two chapters.

NOTES

1. It must be pointed out that undernutrition is probably contributing to this apathy. There is evidence of undernutrition among the children tested, and it can fairly be assumed that it exists among persons of all ages. The very low family income and the small amount of food produced at home for the last twenty years support this assumption. See chaps. xiii and xv for further discussion of this point.

2. For definition of "aggression" as used in this study see Appendix II.

3. See chap. viii.

4. As noted in Appendix II, this is a form of aggression. Because the purposes of the aggression shown by Dakota in the old society differ from those of the aggression they show today, the term is qualified when used in this monograph. The form approved by the old culture is termed "self-assertion" or "striving aggression"; the destructive behavior of today is called "hostility" or "hostile aggression."

5. Erik Homburger Erikson, "Observations on Sioux Education," *Journal of Psychology*, VII (1939), 145.

6. This is not a unique response among the sample group of Dakota children.

7. Winona was the only one of these ten children to laugh at things she saw in the Rorschach inkblots.

8. Priscilla did not take the Goodenough Test.

CHAPTER XIII

INTELLIGENCE, EMOTIONS, AND BEHAVIOR

Having glimpsed briefly the personalities of ten Pine Ridge children, we turn now to the personality structure of Dakota children as a group, as shown by the results of the various tests and examinations given to the sample of 166. In the present chapter we seek to give the general personality characteristics of the group, as revealed by intelligence tests and physical examinations, together with what can be learned of their emotional life and moral code in the Emotional Response and Moral Ideology tests.[1] The following chapter shows something of what lies beneath the surface of overt behavior, as disclosed by the projective tests.

It should be noted that the material from these tests gives us a picture of the personality configuration of a *group* of Dakota children. It is not the personality of one child or the personalities of a majority of the children. It could not be said to exist in all its elements in any one child, let alone in a majority. The "Dakota personality," as the term is employed here, means the type which evolves from the sum total of the characteristic responses of our test material.

What is meant by personality, and how does it develop?

Personality, as conceived in this study, develops from the impulses, drives, and motives of the individual; the expression which the individual gives to these impulses, and the control and restraint which he exercises over them; the controls imposed by his culture and the channels it offers to the individual drives; and the opportunities, impacts, and conflicts which the environment sets up. In other words, there are forces within and forces outside the individual which are acting upon him. The way in which he integrates and expresses these forces and resolves conflicts between them, and the way in which the conflicts become ramified into forms of behavior, produce the various qualities and habits which together make up his personality.

In every individual's personality are factors arising from biological endowment, from cultural conditioning in education, and from individual psychological variations. It is now generally believed that the Indian child is not fundamentally different in his biological makeup from any other child. Owing to his particular biological inheritance and subsequent physiological history, each child, be he

Indian, Mexican, Negro, or white American, does vary from every other child in his particular biological organization; but these are normal variations and not differences due to racial inequality or deficiency.

Every child goes through the same developmental stages of babyhood, childhood, and adolescence before reaching adulthood. At each stage of his development, the child has basic needs and goals, such as learning to walk and talk or expressing his sexual drive, which appear at different stages of physical maturation. These needs and goals and developmental stages are biologically determined, but each culture makes different uses of them or imposes different types of training at different times. For this reason we may find Indian children doing different things or behaving differently from children of the same age in other cultures.

Each cultural organization sets up demands and goals which the child must meet if he is to be an acceptable member. The culture may demand that he go to school, be educated in certain concepts and skills, and later become a laborer, a hunter, a priest, etc., and that he do these things at certain times. Each culture offers opportunities for human expression and satisfaction through socially defined routes and procedures. Each culture, through its organization, cares for and trains the young members of the group in its own techniques for obtaining food and clothing, marrying, burying the dead, co-operating in groups, and worshiping or calling upon the aid of the supernatural. These are needs which individuals either have as human beings or learn because of the culture in which they live.

Culture, through its social processes, suppresses some types of behavior and some impulses and permits the full expression of others. In this way, individuals are trained to carry out the objectives of the culture. For example, little Dakota boys were encouraged to express their self-assertion or aggressive tendencies in order that they might develop and exercise the attitudes needed for hunting and fighting. For the most part, in white American culture this plundering type of aggression is suppressed, but aggressive impulses are allowed expression through accepted forms of competing in games or accumulating and displaying possessions.

When a culture no longer provides the necessary outlets and satisfactions for human needs, and new conditions arising from its disorganization interfere with the achievement of previously established and still desired goals, the individual members react in many ways which we term "maladjustment." They may fight for old goals or satisfactions; they may acquiesce, withdraw, or run away from the new situation. On the other hand, they may make new adjustments by redirecting their energies to new goals. These adjustments are compensations which permit the individual to continue as a well-organized personality.

The specific reaction which each individual makes to his culture, or to the disorganization of his culture, differs. Again the individual inheritance factors in his makeup account for some of his behavioral characteristics. The conditions of his home, the status of his family, the organization of his community, and the physical resources by which it lives are also contributory factors to individual differences.

But the psychological basis on which any one individual reacts to external conditions is the same as for every other individual. In other words, all individuals operate on the same psychological principles and have the same physiological and biological mechanisms for experiencing anxieties, fear, love, and other emotions. However, the kinds of emotional reaction and behavior which each individual exhibits differ with different constitutional factors or sets of social or cultural stimuli or conditions. The fact that all individuals function psychologically according to the same principles is one of the most important premises to remember about other racial and cultural groups.

This means that persons coming to Pine Ridge from another culture will find Dakota children behaving differently from the other children they have known because of traditional Dakota training and because of the effects of cultural change. But the psychological processes by which Dakota children have developed their behavior are the same as those of other children.

The type of behavior now exhibited by the majority of Pine Ridge children must be regarded primarily as the result of psychological reactions to disorganized cultural conditions. The behavior is only symptomatic and not the basic problem.

Not all aspects of personality and their interrelations have been studied or become thoroughly understood by students of personality. For example, the exact nature and sources of drives, sometimes called "impulses" or "instincts," are not known, but the behavior based upon them can be observed. It is not completely known whether some personality traits have an inherited biological or physiological basis or are acquired through experience.

In this study no bold attempt to describe exhaustively the total personality or its structure is contemplated. This study attempts only to discover the major aspects of personality by means of tests and observations, in the same way as the medical student starts to study the human body and its functions. The essential aspects of personality studied here include: intelligence, imaginative faculties, inner adjustment of drives, controls, basic emotional attitudes, emotional reaction to surroundings, adequacy of sexual adjustment, and the approach and relationship to families and the social world.

INTELLIGENCE OF DAKOTA CHILDREN

Two tests were used to determine the intelligence of 166 Dakota children: the Grace Arthur Point Performance Scale and the Goodenough Draw-a-Man Test.

In the Arthur test, on which the average I.Q. for white children is 100, the children of Pine Ridge town aged six to fifteen had an average I.Q. of 102.6, and the Kyle children of the same ages had an average I.Q. of 101.1. In the Goodenough Draw-a-Man Test the average I.Q.'s were 102 for Pine Ridge and 113.6 for Kyle.[2] Each group displayed the expected range from subnormal to superior intelligence.

These tests are designed to score intelligence through manual performance rather than through skill in writing English and using arithmetic and other school subjects. A test where responses must be made in English would be a marked handicap to children with as little English as some of the younger Dakota. That the inadequacy of their knowledge and use of English is indeed a handicap in tests, even among older children, is shown by the scores of the Oglala Community High School students in the Kuhlmann-Anderson Test, parts of which are written. In this test, 30 of the 166 children made an average score of 82.3, as compared with their score of 102.8 on the Arthur test.

Several points of interest may be noted from variations within the Pine Ridge and Kyle groups and differences between the two groups. In the Arthur test there were no significant differences between boys and girls or between the community groups. On the Goodenough test, however, the boys in both groups scored significantly higher than the girls. In contrast, the girls in a group of white school children in a midwestern town scored higher than the boys.[3] It is also not without interest that the Kyle children, who are farther removed from white contacts, had considerably higher scores than the Pine Ridge children at the Agency town.

From time to time various persons have doubted the intellectual abilities of Indians and have ascribed to mental deficiency the difficulties which many Indian children experience in school. The I.Q.'s scored by all Indians in tests given as part of the Indian Education Research Project prove that this is far from the truth. Hopi children, for instance, had a remarkably higher average score than the white children on whom the tests were standardized.[4] The Dakota children scored above average, one community group significantly above average in one test. Indeed, nine of eleven groups of Indian children tested in six tribes had average I.Q.'s either above the white average or so little below it as to have no statistical significance.[5]

HEALTH AND PERSONALITY[6]

Nearly all the 166 Dakota children tested were examined by physicians to determine the state of their health. Only one in five was rated as having generally good health, and 40 per cent were classified as being undernourished, as determined by comparing each child's height and weight with the average for his tribal age group. Vitamin deficiency was not noted specifically, but swollen gums, flaring ribs, and enlarged sore tongues probably represent this lack. Evidence of tuberculosis, so often found in poorly nourished children, was noted in about 15 per cent of the Dakota children, but X-ray showed that calcification had developed in most of the cases. Active tuberculosis was very rare. The incidence of the disease varied greatly between communities, but no conclusions regarding its prevalence can be drawn, as X-rays were not taken of all children. About half the children had decayed teeth, and the same proportion had enlarged tonsils. There was no very significant difference between the health of boys and of girls. More girls than boys were classified as having good health, but more of the girls were thought to be undernourished. The health of the older children was better than that of the very young ones. In general, it might be judged that the health status of Dakota children is similar to that of underprivileged whites in rural areas, but no data are available for more exact comparison.

Probably the most significant data from these examinations are those relating to undernutrition, four out of every ten children appearing to be undernourished.[7] It is regrettable that circumstances did not allow the undertaking of a diet study among the Dakota similar to those previously made among the Hopi and the Papago.[8] Such information as was gathered on Pine Ridge shows that average meals of the children are insufficient in caloric and vitamin content. The home breakfast menus for several days reported by a grade-school class in home economics show that no child had milk or fruit and only one had an egg. The typical breakfast included cake purchased at the trader's, fried bread or potatoes or pancakes and syrup, and coffee. A few children had no breakfast before coming to school. During the winter season children have very few green vegetables at home. Families who received rations (and formerly surplus commodities) were given an assortment of food inadequate in vitamins.[9]

It was impossible to compare the day-school children, who eat one meal five days a week at school, with the boarding-school children, who eat at school about nine months of the year, because individuals shift from one status to another so frequently. Boarding-school teachers report, however, that their students lose so much weight during the summer vacation that they do not recover it at school until about Christmas.

The general poor health and undernutrition among the children may affect their personalities, chronic hunger being reflected in temper and behavior. It is, therefore, not surprising to find apathy and some irritability among the Pine Ridge children, as is common among underfed white school children. These characteristics among the Dakota children are not, however, solely attributable to health factors.

GENERAL PATTERNS OF BEHAVIOR, EMOTIONS, AND SOCIAL RELATIONSHIPS

Passing from the child's intelligence and the factors in his health which may influence intelligence and action, we now seek to determine how children behave toward others and how they feel about their behavior. The Emotional Response and Moral Ideology tests present material from which characteristics of the behavior of the children can be ascertained, the emotions surrounding it, and the kinds of relations the child has with the world about him.

In the Emotional Response Test, children are asked to recall occasions when they felt happy, sad, afraid, angry, or ashamed and to say what are the best and worst things that could happen to them. They also tell voluntarily how they behaved on these occasions, and what persons were concerned.

This test employs direct questioning, but the material utilized is offered voluntarily. The child selects actual experiences on those occasions which he recalls because of their emotional impress. Hence, this material presents private experiences not usually obtainable through interviewing methods. For example, a boy states that he was angry when his little sister threw his marbles into the stove. The boy's account of this incident and his reaction to it indicate one type of relationship between brothers and sisters. From the total responses of the boys concerning their relations with their sisters, we have evidence concerning the kinds of behavior between brothers and sisters from the boys' point of view. Similarly, the total responses of the girls concerning brother relationships present data on the brother-sister relationships from the girls' point of view. Organizing this material on the basis of action and response, we can obtain evidence that substantiates and adds to observations of the children's overt behavior.

The Moral Ideology Test seeks to elicit information on what the child thinks are "good things" and "bad things" to do. He is also asked what persons will praise or blame him for doing these good or bad things. The results of this test show an "official" ideology, or what the child has been taught to believe is right and wrong and what the child believes the group thinks. However, in analyzing this material, we find that the child usually recalls some personal experience or behavior about which he feels he acted in an approved or disapproved way. For example, the frequent mention of stealing as a bad thing to do indicates that stealing is probably either one of the worst or one of the most common "sins" among the contemporary Dakota. However, it is not considered equally bad by boys and girls or by different age groups. We can infer from this that some children steal and are punished for it; it therefore is a matter of great concern to them. Other children have less association or concern with it. Thus, by analyzing the behavior reported in the "good and bad things to do" which the children mention, we obtain additional data for our description of the interaction that takes place between the children and others in their society.

When the Emotional Response data are classified into responses about happiness, sadness, etc., a general pattern of children's emotions appears. First, the children are concerned about the behavior of others toward them; and, second, they are very anxious about themselves. The data can then be reclassified on the basis of action initiated by others, action initiated by self, and no personal interaction,[10] to ascertain the direction and nature of behavior, with whom the activity is carried on, whether it is on a friendly or hostile basis, and how the children feel about it. The Moral Ideology Test responses can be classified on the basis of the children's concepts of good and bad behavior and on the basis of individuals or groups who praised or blamed them in such behavior. This test, too, shows kinds of behavior and how the children feel about them in terms of approval and disapproval or satisfaction and anxiety. The data from both tests have been combined to present the behavior of the children in their social groups, the relationships with parents, brothers and sisters, and age groups, and the emotional reaction which the children have in these relationships.

The largest number of responses from the Emotional Response and Moral Ideology tests suggest that the predominant behavior and emotions of the children are reactions to a world that seems to them hostile—a world that is threatening and bearing down upon them, causing them great concern about themselves, and restraining them in their interests and associations with other people. In the social relationships of the children, most action is, or seems to them to be, initiated by others. People are openly aggressive or unfriendly or threaten to become so. The children report many experiences of physical aggression, such as fights, "ganging up," and having toys and property destroyed. They feel that people are also constantly being inconsiderate of them. Disappointments and unfulfilled promises are evident. Restrictions, discipline, and punishment also contribute to the children's feelings that other people suppress or threaten them, but the disciplining restraints are only minor compared with the thoughtless inconsiderateness and antagonisms. Restraint and discipline are part of the process of growing up and learning to adjust to society. However, it is not formal discipline by parents and teachers that really concerns the Dakota child. His sadness, fear, anger, and shame come more from acts of aggression and failures to be kind on the part of other children.

People are not the only menacing beings in the children's world. Animals, which are so abundant in their environment, are also frightening and hostile. It is not surprising that, in a country of rattlesnakes, untrained and abused dogs, and occasionally vicious bulls, the children should experience terrifying encounters. It is surprising, however, to find that horses, which give them so much pleasure and are so much a part of their daily life, also cause Dakota children much fear and anger. Danger from actual experiences with animals and general anxiety about them stimulated half the fear responses of the boys and girls, and the perversity and uncontrollable behavior of animals were the source of the majority of anger responses of the boys. The rough treatment which is meted out to animals doubtless accounts for much of their unmanageability. This treatment may also be an expression of anger and hostility which the Dakota feel against other people but are afraid to show openly.

For a group of children removed by only a few generations from a complete acceptance of primitive beliefs about the supernatural, it is surprising to find that almost none of the dangers of this traditional supernatural world now appear to alarm them. The fear of the *tchi-tchi* man and other child-frighteners is overcome as the children grow older, just as the belief in Santa Claus is outgrown by white children. Only a few children mention the traditional child-frighteners and the owl, an omen of death. Ghosts and such other supernatural figures as now appear to menace them have been taken over from white culture through white playmates and through stories and Halloween parties at school. The more common frightening associations with the supernatural are seeing dead relatives or ghosts and skeletons. Night itself is frightening, but this may be interpreted also as fear of meeting ghosts or alarming objects and fear of being alone.

It should be noted that, although the people and things about them appear predominantly hostile to Dakota children, there are also pleasant and satisfying relationships originated by others. The visits by relatives for family gatherings, the departure and return of family members, and the gifts from brothers and sisters and elder relatives very definitely bring pleasure and enjoyment to the children. The responses concerning these experiences of positive relationships reveal, however, that they occur almost exclusively between relatives. It is society beyond the family or circle of relatives that children feel to be hostile; it seems to dominate their emotional reactions.

The second largest category of responses from these tests reveals the children to be concerned with self-interest in pleasures or anxiety about their own well-being. Little or no direct action with other people is stated or is even inferred. The primary responses of interest are in good times, such as going to the movies, to fairs, and to rodeos. In these activities the children can be with many people and identify themselves with the group in watching some entertainment but avoid intimate personal contacts. The children also enjoy parties like those at Christmas or on birthdays, when they receive gifts. The tests show that the gifts are more important to them than actual participation in such festivities or even being the center of attention. In studying responses by age groups, it appears that it is almost exclusively the youngest children who enjoy the personal relationships at these occasions.

Games are another source of pleasure. This might seem to imply a great deal of interaction with playmates. However, the kinds of play which the children name —riding horseback, throwing a rope, trying to catch horses and cattle, and playing with dolls—indicate a considerable amount of solitary play or play with others in which interest is not centered on co-operation or competition or acting upon one another but on some nonhuman object. For this reason play has been classified with the responses of "no personal interaction." This classification must be qualified strongly, since basketball, baseball, and the group games taught in primary school are also mentioned by the children. It must be remembered, however, that this competitive play is taught by the school and is only occasional in the informal play in the home communities.

The children's concern about their personal welfare may be termed negative and undesirable from the point of view of good mental hygiene and of society. Concern over themselves takes the form primarily of anxiety over being sick, injured, or in pain, which causes them both fear and sadness. The children are also concerned, but to a much less degree, over dying or death as "the worst thing that could happen."[11]

It is not unusual for children to be apprehensive of sickness and painful injuries, and there is much in the environment which directs Dakota children's attention to sickness and death. The extreme cold and storms of winter may cause these children, whose general health and diet are poor, to have more than their share of sickness. Data on the incidence of sickness are lacking. Sick children are generally not well cared for in a Dakota home until symptoms become alarming, and then there is a rush for assistance. Overanxiety about sickness among the children is, therefore, to be expected. Death also might be expected to concern them, for a great many families have lost one or two small children. The ritual days of mourning, the giving-away of property, and the frequently dramatic behavior of the bereaved deeply impress the children.

Self-concern over being sick and dying would not be thought unusual under these circumstances if it were not for the additional high anxiety over the death of others. Worry about the possible death of other people, as measured by the frequency of responses, is exceeded only by that caused by the potential or overt aggression of people and by the behavior of animals. Although the children have strong affection for their relatives, worry about their death or sickness appears to be centered in apprehension about how such catastrophes will affect the children themselves. This preoccupation is thrown into bolder relief by the absence of any responses showing interest in the happiness or activities of other people.

In responses reflecting self-initiated relationships with other people, the children show some interest in visiting relatives and attending family gatherings for recreational or ritual occasions. Such positive interaction is, however, almost as infrequent as the appearance of real interest in the welfare of other people. The self-initiated action with others lies almost exclusively in various forms of aggression—fighting, damaging property, breaking rules, disobedience, disrespect, and stealing. This is in the face of an official code in which stealing and openly aggressive acts within one's own society are the two worst forms of behavior. As a result they feel very sad and ashamed of what they have done.

The evaluation of stealing as the foremost "bad thing to do" among the descendants of a society that praised stealing from the enemy calls for comment. Older generations stole from the government as a form of waging war or retaliating against their conquerors. It was once an admired act which set a pattern in a traditional form for releasing tension. The example of stealing as a means of demonstrating hostility is still set by many adults. In a situation where many people are very poor and often hungry, it is to be expected that for "have-nots" to steal from the "haves" will not be the "worst thing to do." But this behavior has been punished so long and so severely that the children are very conscious of the wrongness of any theft in the official code. In the personal code, stealing within one's own group was and still is "bad" behavior.

Another major characteristic of the children's behavior manifests itself in their failure to make responses in parts of the tests. Many Dakota children withdraw from as much overt activity as possible. One indication of this constraint is the frequency of refusal or apparent inability to answer all the questions of the tests. The second is the high proportion of responses showing anxiety about the hostility of others; and the third is the very low proportion of responses of self-initiated action. The ratio of responses in these three classifications is, respectively, 9, 5, and 1. The children appear to control active behavior and expression of their feelings and to break out into aggressive acts when they can no longer restrain themselves.

AGE AND SEX DIFFERENCES IN BEHAVIOR

The behavior of a child changes as he develops physically and passes from early to late childhood and into adolescence and the post-adolescent period. As he grows older, he moves into the wider circles of his society beyond his immediate family. His behavior changes as he adjusts to, conflicts with, or imitates his fellows or elders. Parental training also changes and influences the behavior of the child at different ages. It is beyond the scope of this study to describe the behavior resulting from changes in physical growth.[12] However, the tests and observations do contain material which shows behavior of boys and girls at different ages as influenced by family, school, church, and community.

The responses to the tests show that, by the time the boys are eight or ten, they have developed strong ties with their families. The majority of responses about happy occasions center in family holiday parties. Presents are a source of great pleasure. Toys and other belongings are very important to the boys, and they become very disturbed if their possessions are damaged or taken away from them.

Although they have not reached the age where formal giving is necessary, they are already conscious of the need to be thoughtful and kind to others.

Pets and riding horses are also a source of pleasure to the boys, but experience has made them afraid of animals. As they become older and can manage animals better, their responses indicate that this fear decreases. They enjoy going to school and to fairs and rodeos, and they are willing to work at home; but these activities are not yet so important to them as they become later.

The family is the center of their social universe and is already regarded as the one source of security. They are still afraid of being left alone, and at this age their concern over the sickness and death of family members is greatest. Little boys are also apprehensive about becoming sick and dying. Apparently they are already aware of the insecurity of the world about them. They also know that to express hostility openly toward others or to steal is bad behavior.

In the next age group, the years from eleven to thirteen, the boys' responses show that they remain less in the home and join groups of playmates and wander around the community with greater assurance. They show more vivacity and more spontaneity than at any other time in their lives. However, the new relationships also bring conflict. The boys get into many fights and quarrels, for which they later feel sad or ashamed. They also begin to steal, to damage property, and to break school rules, and they are ashamed of doing so. These actions reflect in part the aggressiveness encouraged in males at home during their earlier years but no longer channelized by parental training or granted expression by any social institution. It also shows that the boys feels they must fight to get along in hostile surroundings. Boys of this age group have strong feelings of insecurity, and they show more fear of their social environment than the younger age group. This insecurity also appears in increased concern about becoming sick or injured.

The anxiety which they manifest about the aggressive behavior they desire or feel impelled to take seems to stem from the now well-learned attitude that thoughtfulness and kindness are the accepted bases of Dakota behavior within their own group. This principle, learned at home, does not appear to function outside it with consistent success. Generosity is also part of the pattern of thoughtfulness, yet it is not so strongly instilled that the boys eleven to thirteen years old have given up feeling that personal property is of great importance to them.

The responses in the tests do not reveal any types of sex behavior, for there is great restraint about mentioning such matters to outsiders. However, there is evidence of an awareness of developing sexuality and a new consciousness about relationships with girls. The taboo on sex relations is part of the moral code that they hold at this age.

The adolescent and post-adolescent boys, aged fourteen to eighteen, show in their behavior characteristics which were becoming evident in the earlier age group. Relationships to other people are now their major concern. They seem well indoctrinated with the Sioux code of good behavior, which requires thoughtfulness, kindness, generosity, and loyalty to family members. Family solidarity and security are more important to the adolescents than to the middle age group but not so important as to the youngest group.

The older boys show desire for achievement by getting an education. They also want "to be on their own" by getting a job, partly in order to be free of family restrictions. Their recreation is less devoted to playing games and takes on the more adult characteristic of joining crowds to see the sights at fairs and watch rodeos or dances.

There is a marked decline in the vivacity of this age group from the pre-adolescent period. The behavior of adolescents reflects an almost sudden withdrawal, confusion, and inability to find a satisfactory role. Delinquency is more apparent than among the pre-adolescent years. Responses about stealing almost triple as the boys pass from the middle to the older age group, and they reveal great anxiety about it as wrongdoing. The number of these responses about stealing is an index of their delinquent behavior, their lack of opportunity to express aggressive impulses in socially approved ways, and their reaction against the felt hostility of their environment.

Their behavior with girls of their age does not appear in the test material, but they hold sex morality as the least important of their moral concepts. This attitude is in keeping with the training of boys and the traditional attitude of Dakota males. If a sex code is lightly impressed on their consciences, it may be expected that they will feel free to make sexual advances toward the girls of the community. In this behavior, too, they can find release for drives that have been blocked in other directions.

As they grow older, the adolescent boys appear to become frightened, unsure of themselves, and without the interests that will carry them into a life of activity and a career. They may wish to grow up and take their places as men in their society, but their behavior and moral concepts show that they are being defeated by the impact of the social disorganization of their people. Their tests indicate a feeling that reservation authorities, Indian leaders, and even their own communities, where people constantly criticize each other, are all against them. In fact, their fear of the ill-will and unfriendliness of society at this period of their development is higher than ever before. Seeing no niche or role for themselves and a life on the reservation that seems empty, they tend to retreat from life.

The girls follow much the same development as the boys until they reach adolescence, but they appear to reach the various stages a year or two earlier than the boys, as white girls do.

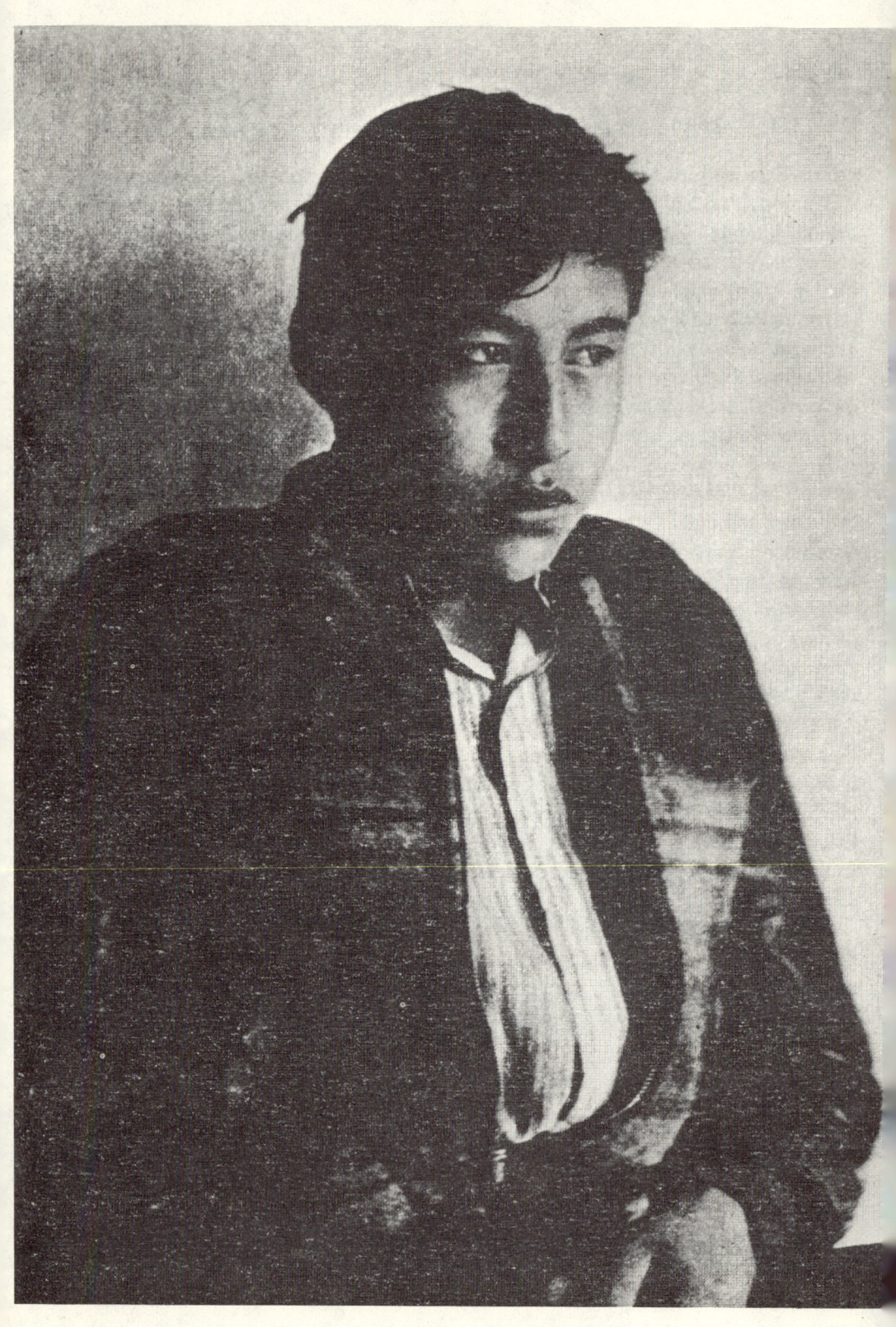

ADOLESCENT BOY

The youngest group of girls, aged eight to ten, feel that the family serves as a great protection to them, as do the boys of the same age group. But the departure of a member from the family circle, or the sickness or death of a relative, upsets the girls' feelings of security in the family even more than it does the young boys'. The girls appear to acquire the pattern of thoughtful and kind behavior and to enjoy the social relationships outside the family at an earlier age than the boys. Their greater enjoyment of going to school and being among the crowd on holiday occasions reflects both a little more maturity and the confinement imposed upon them at home. The little girls do not give as many responses as the boys about being afraid of being left alone, probably because they are kept closer to their mothers. The youngest girls show better social integration because they indicate less concern about themselves and more interest in the welfare of others.

Girls of this age group become involved in fights and quarrels, but they are disturbed about this behavior and the troubles made for them by others. They express also some fear of the opposite sex and show that they are already aware of their sexual role and the conduct expected of them. Fear of the physical environment is also clearly evident from their responses. Even to a greater extent than the eight- to ten-year-old boys, the girls of this age group are afraid of animals and especially snakes. This fear is excessive and may reinforce their general apprehension which develops later.

Girls of eleven to thirteen continue to expand their relationships with social groups outside the family. School creates an excellent opportunity for this, and the pleasure of attending school increases. The family does not decrease in importance but now imposes stronger restrictions on the girls' behavior, obviously because they are approaching or entering adolescence. The consciousness of their sexual role dominates the behavior of the girls themselves. They appear more afraid of the advances of men and boys and the criticism of the community. They are also interested in clothes and personal ornaments.

Because modesty and restrained behavior are expected of girls, fighting makes them feel deeply ashamed. Evidently they try to control such behavior but express some of their aggression in stealing. They show both embarrassment and anger about such behavior, which indicates that they become participants as well as objects of it.

By the time the girls become adolescent or post-adolescent, their behavior changes and in some directions their anxieties increase. They are kept in the home and given a strong position there. Interest in the solidarity and security of the family is maintained. School assumes a more serious aspect as the girls become more interested in getting an education. They continue to have a good time there, and they are now also interested in getting a job, although to a lesser degree than boys of their age. It is in their relationships and attitudes outside the family and formal school life that the girls show the greater change. Life about them appears to cause more apprehension and create more social difficulties than at any earlier age. They are more afraid to be alone, more afraid of the dark, of ghosts, and of what may befall them or their relatives. They are also more anxious now about being sick or dying. The type of responses about sickness and also "getting well" suggests that some of their concern about sickness is associated with menstruation.

The older girls appear to have lost some of their anxiety about direct aggression from others, especially boys. They are now having boy friends without feelings of shame or excessive fear. The rough behavior of boys may arouse their anger rather than fear, and they often strike back. But they feel that this conduct is very bad, worse than stealing. In fact, "stealing" drops out of their replies to the Emotional Response Test, although it appears as bad conduct in their Moral Ideology Test responses.

BEHAVIOR AND ATTITUDES IN RELATION TO THE SOCIAL STRUCTURE

From children's orientation in society it is obvious that the greatest amount of interaction will be with members of the family and with the teacher and age mates at school. This is apparent in responses of the Emotional Response and Moral Ideology tests. From both the types and the frequencies of responses, it appears that the children construct society in the following manner. First is the family, of mother, brothers and sisters, father, and grandparents. Next in importance is the school, made up of playmates and teachers. Great distinction is drawn between playmates of the same age and sex and those who are older or younger or of opposite sex. The rest of society is usually classed as "everybody" or "somebody."

The relationships which the children have with "the family" as a group are emotionally colored with happiness or sadness and with little fear, shame, or anger. They think of "the family" in terms of good times when they are all together, but in terms of sadness when someone leaves, dies, or becomes ill. They also regard "the family" as the most active authority, or praiser and blamer, indicating that all members of the family criticize or punish and also reward them. Examination of the relationship between different members of the family show that intimacies, affection, and conflicts vary greatly, and much of this depends upon whether the child is a boy or girl.

Test responses indicate that the happiest family relationship of the boys is with their brothers, making it evident that the Dakota pattern of solidarity between brothers is continuing. Although boys are also close to their mothers, there is some distance between them because of the mother's function as the family disciplinarian and because of the difference in sex. Since the boys are taught to be reserved before women, they are likely to feel embarrassed in their mother's presence. This embarrassment they feel also before other women, and it is the chief reaction to girl age mates and to their teachers, most of whom are women. The boys' relationship to their sisters appears to be fundamentally an affectionate one, but the responses about their sisters are mainly ones of sadness and some anger. The boys feel sad when their older sisters punish them or do some unkind thing. The boys also feel upset when their sisters leave the family. The shame expected to be shown in associations with their sisters, whom they were traditionally taught to avoid, does not appear in the responses; this indicates that the taboo now rests lightly on the consciences of Dakota boys.

The interaction between fathers and their sons appears much less intense and frequent than between mothers and sons. The boys enjoy a very pleasant relationship with their fathers but do not regard them as real authorities. The role of the father appears less significant among the Sioux than among the Navaho and Hopi[13] or among white children of a midwestern town. It indicates how unimportant the men of the Dakota have become in their families, and how much the boys lack in a well-rounded family life and the necessary training for an adequate and satisfactory man's role.

Grandparents appear to have very slight influence in the lives of the boys, for they make little mention of grandfathers or grandmothers in either test.

The girls' relationships with members of their families differ to some extent from the relationships of the boys. As may be expected from the girls' greater activity in the home, their relationships are closest and deepest with their mothers. The girls appear happiest in their family life, and the mother appears to be the one person with whom they enjoy predominantly happy relationships. Nevertheless, the mothers are also strong disciplinarians to their daughters. The girls do not appear to enjoy an intimate relationship with their fathers, who exercise little authority over them and evoke little respect. In marked contrast to the close ties between brothers, the girls show strong conflict with their sisters. Although the girls appear to enjoy more pleasant experiences with their brothers than their brothers do with them, the girls recall most of their experiences with their brothers with sadness. These were times when brothers were sick or died or went away from the family. They were also times of quarreling with their brothers. As a general mode of behavior, children appear to feel that they wish to get along with their siblings of the other sex, and they recall disputes and conflicts with feelings of sadness rather than anger.

The grandparents appear to have a more significant influence with the girls than they do with the boys. It is usually the girls who are sent to help grandparents in keeping house; so it is not surprising that the girls consider the grandparents as persons of little less authority than fathers. It is probably the grandmothers who direct and criticize the girls most.

We have found that the major reaction of the children to society was one of fear of potential hostile aggression and anger at actual aggression. This reaction is made primarily to people outside the family, classed as "everybody." To the boys the most important groups of people outside the family are their age mates. With other boys there is a great deal of conflict, revealed by the great preponderance of "anger" responses. Although there is much quarreling and censure of one another among the boys, age mates appear in the responses more often as persons who praise than as persons who blame. Hence, we can be sure that age mate relationships are not characteristically unfriendly. The boys look upon other children as important judges of their behavior and as people with whom they wish to get along well, yet the other children cause them much trouble; this creates a serious social problem. The shame that girls cause them indicates that the boys feel tense with the opposite sex. When the boys act aggressively toward girls, the girls fight back by ridiculing and shaming the boys. From all these reactions it is evident that social experience within their own generation during childhood produces insecurity and anxiety among the boys.

In marked contrast, the girls' pleasantest relationships outside the family circle are those with their girl age mates. Indeed, girl friends and teachers appear to be the only individuals except their mothers with whom the girls find truly cordial relationship. The extreme fear and anger which girls feel toward others as a general behavior pattern seem to be most specifically centered upon their boy age mates and the older people in the community. The girls find less pleasure than boys in mixing with the general community. Not only are they frightened and angered in their usual associations outside the family and school but they are also deeply ashamed if anything occurs outside the passive and distant relationships expected in normal daily life.

The type of behavior and relationships in the school present best the social position of the Dakota children. Test responses show that going to school is a very happy experience after the first adjustments are made, and, furthermore, it is looked upon as a moral and social obligation. School, like play, implies a great deal of interaction with age mates and teachers. The test responses indicate, however, that the children's pleasure in school does not come so much from direct participation or intense activity with teachers and other children as from being able to immerse themselves in a crowd that is doing something, where they can be entertained and find something of interest. In this, school is like going to the movies or a fair. Even in doing the definite tasks and attaining the definite objectives each year, the children are performing with a large group. In other words,

INTELLIGENCE, EMOTIONS, AND BEHAVIOR

children are going to school because they like to be with other people. But, fearing the actions others will take, the children keep to themselves as much as possible. In our observations of children at school during this study, we saw this withdrawal in the exclusive little cliques of related children. When they met other individuals, they slapped and hit each other frequently.

Yet, while social satisfaction is the most important part of going to school, test responses show that "getting an education" is also important. This interest in getting an education is one of the few signs of an interest in getting ahead, acquiring some preparation for life, and, in general, desiring to mature. To get a job is also considered in their moral ideology as one of the more important good things to do, but the job itself is rarely defined. Seldom does the child express a desire to be a cowboy, farmer, trader, nurse, or teacher. He only wants to "get a job." The absence of definite career goals from the Dakota children's responses is as significant as their negative attitude toward their environment. The lack of specific roles and objectives or of any organized activity in which they can participate after leaving school seems to frustrate their drives for achievement.

Teachers are the most important adults as guides and disciplinarians in the lives of the boys. The teachers have a more balanced role as praisers and blamers of boys' behavior than do teachers for white children in a midwestern town who were given similar tests. For Dakota boys, however, teachers do not have as significant a role in approving or disapproving of behavior as do the teachers in these white schools. The Indian boys' own age mates appear to be more influential than their teachers and are thus continuing the contemporary Indian behavior pattern. Much of this is attributable to the fact that the teachers, with rare exceptions, do not belong to the Dakota society. It seems also due to the fact that most of the teachers are women with whom Dakota boys feel more embarrassment than do white boys.

In contrast, teachers appear to have more influence on girls than do their fathers or age mates. Since most of the teachers are women, they can carry on intimate relationships with the girls without the embarrassment caused the boys. The girls' greater ease and generally better relationship with their teachers may account in part for the fact that girls like school better than boys. The teacher's position of praiser and blamer, or mother surrogate, is as important to the Indian girls as to white school children in a midwestern town. The Indian girls, however, feel the teacher somewhat less a blamer than do the whites.

Within the general society, elders, ministers, or priests, and the government are specifically designated but seem to have little importance in Dakota children's lives. The trader is mentioned only rarely, nearly always as someone "getting after them" for stealing. The boys look upon government employees and the elders of their community outside the family as more adversely critical than friendly; but, except for the oldest boys, the influence of neither group appears to be strong.[14] The girls are more timid about adults outside the family but rarely mention the government or officials. In fact, they have very little contact with the latter beyond the school staff.

God is the only deity whom the Dakota children mention in their test responses. He is not mentioned in the Emotional Response Test as the source of happiness, fear, or any of the other emotional responses studied, or as the bringer of good things, but he appears in the Moral Ideology Test responses as an authority who praises more than he blames. As a praising authority, especially for girls, he appears to function with greater significance than grandparents or elders and the other people or institutions outside the family and school.

The clergy as authorities apparently have little significance to the government school children. As very few of the school children at the Catholic mission were tested, the position of the priests and nuns cannot be stated. It is probable that they rank more closely with the teachers as people of authority than with the clergy as functionaries in the communities.

The small number of responses which the Dakota children gave regarding themselves as praising or criticizing their own behavior may indicate the slight degree to which their consciences are developed. This situation is in keeping with traditional Dakota organization, where social controls were primarily external. The fact that this system of control by ridicule and criticism or by constant watchfulness on the part of adult society operates today probably accounts for the high percentage of responses in the Moral Ideology Test that people should be punished by going to jail rather than by conscience.

The absence of highly developed consciences among the contemporary Dakota children has, of course, great importance for teachers. These children should not be expected to do something because it is "right" or "wrong" in itself. We can see from their behavior and concepts of authority that Dakota children look to those for whom they have deep affection and respect to set standards of behavior.

Although the responses concerning conscience are far fewer among Indian children than white children of a midwestern town, it is not to be inferred that Dakota children are totally without consciences. Inner controls are being developed more and more from association with whites, especially teachers, although not always from the best perspective. Only through endless patience and friendly interest can the teacher hope to develop in her children inner controls which they need in order to function better in their changing world where external controls are failing.

NOTES

1. For a description of the tests see Appendix I.
2. This is the average for the age group six to eleven, for whom the test was designed. On the Arthur test the Pine Ridge children of this age group had an average I.Q. of 101.1; the Kyle children, 98.9.
3. Average scores for Pine Ridge town were: boys, 107.8; girls, 97.6. For Kyle community the scores were: boys, 116.9; girls, 110.3. White children's scores were: boys, 98.3; girls, 103.4.
4. See Laura Thompson and Alice Joseph, *The Hopi Way* (Chicago: University of Chicago Press, 1944), pp. 100-101.
5. See Robert J. Havighurst and Rhea R. Hilkevitch, "The Intelligence of Indian Children as Measured by a Performance Scale," *Journal of Abnormal and Social Psychology*, XXXIX (1944), 419–33.
6. This section is based upon an analysis by Dorothea C. Leighton, M.D., special physician, U.S. Indian Service, of the records of medical examinations of the children made by several members of the Pine Ridge medical staff. It should be stated here that, because of the variations between examiners and because of the lack of any absolute standards for "good health" or various diseased conditions that can be determined by a single routine examination, the analysis can hardly be considered conclusive.
7. However, medical standards as to what constitutes adequate and inadequate nutrition are so uncertain that this statement should not be accepted with finality. For further discussion of diet as a probable factor in the present condition of the Dakota see chap. xv.
8. See Thompson and Joseph, *op. cit.*; and Alice Joseph, Rosamond Spicer, and Jane Chesky, *The Desert People* (Indian Education Research Project [in preparation]), Part IV.
9. Since July, 1944, the Indian Service has given checks with which to purchase food at stores to Pine Ridge Indians entitled to rations.
10. This classification follows the concept of social interaction, or the reciprocal relationships between an individual and other individuals, animals, objects, or situations, discussed in Eliot D. Chapple and Carleton S. Coon, *Principles of Anthropolgy* (New York: Henry Holt & Co., 1942), pp. 36-41. Social interaction, as described there, consists of an origin of action and a response. In the present study the data of the three categories (action initiated by others, action initiated by self, and no personal interaction) were subdivided into: actions which were of interest to the individual and brought satisfaction to him and actions which were of concern and anxiety and therefore produced dissatisfaction in him.
11. A few children said death was "the best thing that could happen to them." See the case of Red Bird in the preceding chapter.
12. In fact, it is impossible to distinguish satisfactorily the changes due solely to physical growth and those due solely to personal-social development.
13. Comparative data on test responses made by Indian and white school children which are given in this section and the following are from Robert J. Havighurst, "Comparison of Indian Children and White Children by Means of the Moral Ideology Test" (MS).
14. For the boys fourteen to eighteen years old this does not follow (see p. 195).

CHAPTER XIV

LOOKING BENEATH THE SURFACE

THE preceding chapter has described the overt behavior of the children as they have been willing to report it in answer to direct questioning in the Emotional Response and Moral Ideology tests. This behavior reflects the personalities of the group and especially certain dominant personality traits.

Of these traits, the most striking appears to be the anxiety which arises from the lack of personal security among their people and in their physical environment. These children have lost confidence in behaving as their impulses direct, and home training has failed to teach them new channels into which to redirect their energies. In their anxiety from not knowing how to behave they have placed a lid, as it were, on their impulses, and so they act in a very constrained way. Since they do not know how to utilize their impulses, they gain little self-satisfaction; and, because their outward behavior is inconsistent, they also gain little approval from those around them. Rebuffed in their contacts with others and unable to find inner satisfactions, they withdraw further into themselves and lack warm and emotional responsiveness and vigor. Since human beings cannot live under such constant repression of their energy without serious strain upon their personality and so must find release in some way, the Dakota children understandably exhibit varied and seemingly unpredictable behavior and almost conflicting personality traits.

On these unpredictable actions and seeming inconsistencies, the projective tests throw much light by revealing how the individual handles his impulses and emotions. They furnish information about the individual's attitudes and interpersonal relationships as well as about his ideals, disappointments, and fantasies, without the inhibitions he feels when he thinks he is talking about himself.

In the Thematic Apperception Test the child is shown a series of pictures and is asked to tell a story about each of them. The pictures represent familiar situations—a mother and child, two children walking down a road, an old man and a boy. By creating stories about them, the child describes much of his own relationship to other people, his attitude toward his life-situation, and the experiences he would like to have. But he is not conscious of telling anything about himself and so is comparatively free and open.

A similar process takes place when the child is shown the meaningless "ink blots" in the Rorschach Psychodiagnostic Test and is asked what they look like to him. In both tests he gives information about the facts of his real or imaginative life and also his way of approaching problems. One child will tell a story full of detail, the characters will have names, and the narratives will move along to some sort of denouement. Another will describe the situation vaguely, without much attempt to distinguish characters or to resolve the situation. One child will see in an ink blot the whole figure and interpret it in this fashion, while another will spend minutes elaborating on the tiniest detail of form or color. Thus the tests reveal the elements of the child's personality, such as his ability to organize, his compulsive tendencies, his method of control, and, in general, his way of meeting his life-experiences. The results, therefore, show much about the basic personality structure underlying overt behavior.

INSECURITY

From the stories and fantasies given in the Thematic Apperception Test, we learn again that Dakota children conceive of the world as a dangerous and hostile place. Characters in the children's stories often have too little to eat and few of the other material things which make life comfortable. Hence they feel deprived and dissatisfied. In their uncomfortable surroundings they often become tired or sick.

The instability of the children's world is also clearly evident from this test. The characters in the stories, with whom the children identify themselves, are uncertain and suffer many accidents and lose what little security they have.

According to the analysis of the children's stories, the social structure appears equally dissatisfying, for there is not much to do in their environment. The relatively stable family unit provides little enough security or guidance, and no other organization in the Dakota society gives any real direction for the child's energies or rewards for becoming any special type of person. Uncertainty is the feeling which the child senses in the people and groups around him. He sees no worth-while position or function in the future and no attainment of desired objectives. The social world, like the physical world, is a place where there is no definite road to follow, no place to go. This is a terrifying fact for a child to discover and rediscover as he grows older.

A few stable and positive elements in the otherwise emotionally disturbing environment offer some security for the child, arouse his interest, and afford a measure of prestige. The first is the family, which appears in many of the children's stories and responses as a haven and a source of pleasure. The kindly and affectionate relationships with parents and brothers and sisters during early childhood are always recalled with nostalgia. However, as he grows older, the child senses increasingly the anxiety and consternation of his parents and the other adults of his environment. The father particularly appears to fail in affording the expected affection and direction of family affairs; he seems to have little prestige and position in the eyes of the child.

As the stabilizing influence of the family begins to waver, the Thematic Apperception Test shows that the school begins to offer some measure of security and organization to the growing child and some of the continuity lacking in the local society. These contributions to the child's security are basic reasons why associations at school are, in general, pleasant ones.

Another positive factor in the stories told by the boys is their pleasure in riding and in the life of the cowboy. This is the one specific career which appears to appeal to the Sioux boys and to offer them potentially some continuity of occupation and objective in life. The possession of horses appears to be a point of prestige.

The total effect of their environment on the children, however, is the generation of a great deal of insecurity, lack of definiteness and recognized purpose, indecision, and passivity. This is clearly indicated in the details of the stories, in which the characters are not named and in which no clear-cut action or definite outcome occurs. Relationships with people are uncertain, and unrest and conflict are acute. There are few intense and significant social events to give form and content to life. Social continuity is not offered to the children either by white society or by the residue of the old Dakota culture.

ANXIETY AND ITS EFFECTS

The Rorschach Psychodiagnostic Test as well as the Thematic Apperception Test indicates that Dakota children, in fear of what may happen to them, stifle their impulses and energy and their emotional reactions to people and situations around them. We have seen that fear and anxiety are generated in the children by the unpredictability in their parents' behavior and by the frequent or even constant scarcity of food and other necessities in the home. This stifling of themselves is intensified by the controls placed on behavior during early child-training which has been in progress some time before the child reaches six, the youngest age in the sample of tested children. The constraint effected by both processes appears to be accomplished at the cost of the child's vivaciousness and normal development. Refusal to participate in life about them, isolation of themselves from all persons and activities about them, great caution, and a general negativism become the major characteristics of the personality configuration of the group as a whole.

In individuals who cut themselves off or are cut off from others, there usually develops a rich inner life as a compensation. This is characteristic of the "introvert" as the term is popularly used. However, the high degree of emotional tension and inward constraint prevents even this from taking place among the Dakota.

These children can get along through usual situations in spite of the check they place upon themselves, but it deprives them of real spontaneity and imaginal freedom which would give them greater enjoyment of life and people. They become incapable of close or deep emotional attachments to others. Personal interaction is greatly reduced, and their ties to other people are superficial. This behavior has already been observed in the personality sketches. The Emotional Response and Moral Ideology tests revealed a lack of solicitude for others and a desire to be a passive member of a group rather than an active participant.

Occasionally, when impulses and spontaneity from within are blocked and pressures from without cause unbearable anxiety or tensions, the children lose control, flaring momentarily into hostile action. We have seen this behavior take the form of petty and trivial acts of criticism, slapping, or taking other people's possessions. This is their strongest outward resistance to pressure from others, for they are too removed from deep feeling and are too emotionally exhausted to act violently.

Another effect of anxiety stemming from the generally disturbing and unsatisfying character of the Dakota child's world is demonstrated by the "escapism" in their stories of the good life on the plains before the coming of the white man—stories which constantly recur in the responses to the Thematic Apperception Test. Escape through fantasy is common to the disturbed individuals of all societies: one way of adjusting when life become utterly unsatisfactory is to give up trying to deal with objective reality and to spend one's time imagining how nice things used to be or will be. What distinguishes the escape fantasies of the Dakota children is their apparent vividness. Hunting and warfare, living in tepees, wearing the old Indian dress, and dancing the old dances are presented as things that, it is hoped, will come again. They are not recounted as past glories but as satisfactions that may return to make up for the hardships and fears of the present. For children to believe this, to be so trained from childhood, is poor preparation for the actualities of life, to say the least. The conflict of these daydreams with the realities of modern life on the reservation and of white society adds to the insecurity and the resultant anxiety in the child's mind.

AGE AND SEX DIFFERENCES

Data from the Thematic Apperception and the Rorschach tests support the evidence of the other tests that the psychological structure of the children varies as they grow older, come in contact with more of their society, and look forward to adult life. Although in the early years of six to eight uncertainty, repression, and hampered spontaneity are already present, the children appear to be well organized in comparison with later years; their actions show some acceptance of the rules of behavior.

In the next years, from nine to twelve, they appear to lose some of their restraint and show a more active interest and zest for life, with increasing spontaneity. Of the age groups studied, the children of this group appear to be the freest, the most at ease with themselves and the world about them, as their play and open aggressiveness show. This follows the normal development of white children, but, compared to them or even to Navaho children, who are probably more restrained than the white,[1] the Dakota children of nine to twelve lack exuberance and vivacity. They never appear to develop a full inner life and remain unable to resolve emotional tensions.

With the advent of puberty, the children begin to retire more completely within themselves and lose interest in the world around them. There is a decrease in their earlier spontaneity and freedom of behavior. The restraint set up by environmental pressures now appears to take complete control. The personalities of the adolescents seem not to mature; they appear to resign themselves, to become apathetic and passive, and to accept the anxiety the outer world creates. In the face of this empty and unfriendly world, the adolescents and post-adolescents become still more frightened and constricted.

At this age the boys and girls show different adjustments. The boys are more irregular or unbalanced in their control, but they allow a little more expression to their impulses and thoughts. However, this is expressed in increased attention to generalities rather than in practical and efficient thinking. There is also an appearance of ambitiousness in their thinking. This may be expected among a people who once were their own masters and the dominant cultural group in their area. Their ambitiousness now seems only to reflect faintly the self-assertive qualities which did not ripen in the distorted cultural situation. The beginning of a philosophical outlook and ambitiousness are usual in the thinking of young white people of sixteen to eighteen, but among the Dakota boys the first functions as an evasion of coming to grips with reality, and the second as a resort to wishful thinking or a compensation for the futility which they sense in their situation.

The girls as they grow older appear to retain some of the more formal control of earlier years, the result of the modest behavior they have been taught, and they appear to make a more practical adjustment than that of the boys. They continue to be, however, very restrained and careful in their approach to life. As they enter their teens and sense the significance of pubescence, they show extreme agitation when confronted with new or unusual situations; in fright they retire within themselves and seem almost powerless to act. This paralysis lessens as they pass through adolescence.

SUMMARY

The picture of Dakota child personality which emerges from the tests is one of weakness of natural drives and spontaneity resulting from repressive forces set in action early in the child's life. This paucity of impulse and emotion appears to blight the creativity, imagination, and fantasy that are normal in a healthy mental life and to prohibit wholesome relationships with other people. Dakota child personality seems crippled and negative, as if it rejected life. The unfriendly environment, which offers so little opportunity or satisfaction, retards the growth of personality and prevents it from becoming positive, rich, and mature. Life is lived on the defensive.

NOTES

1. Dorothea C. Leighton and Clyde Kluckhohn, *The People and Their Children* (Chicago: University of Chicago Press, forthcoming), Part II.

PART IV. OUTLOOK FOR THE FUTURE

CHAPTER XV
NEW WEAPONS FOR SECURITY

IF LEFT at this point, the picture that has been drawn of the Pine Ridge adults and children might seem gloomy indeed. It is necessary to recall, however, that this is a group picture. Not all the parents and grandparents nor all the children are frustrated beyond achieving a normal or successful life. Children such as Robert, Winona, and André have made good personal adjustments and will probably lead satisfactory lives. In an improved and enriched environment their achievements and satisfactions can increase. The children have the level and range of intelligence we may expect from an average group of school children anywhere in America. They show ambitiousness, although it is usually of the daydream variety. These are potentialities of personality which will flower in a more favorable environment.

Looking back across their history, we can see significant events which contributed particularly to the present condition of the Pine Ridge Dakota. From their effect on the people we can gain insights for possible approaches to their regeneration. The extermination of the buffalo has often been pointed out as the basic reason for the present disorganization of the Plains Indians. Certainly the loss of the buffalo was the deathblow to Plains Indian culture, but the present predicament of the Pine Ridge Dakota is not a direct result of this episode. They achieved during the first decade and a half of this century a new, if less complex and rewarding, way of life, centered in a cattle economy. The loss of this economy, in the cattle sales of 1916 and 1917 and the subsequent land sales, appears as the most significant single catastrophe in the history of Pine Ridge people.

The occupation of the men, who had been the keystone of the Dakota cultural structure, abruptly vanished. The cowboy life to which they had so easily adapted themselves was now without purpose. A well-organized family life had continued up to this time. The band-derived communities had survived without severe dislocations. The churches were becoming strengthening factors in the social and religious life. But, soon after the loss of the herds, demoralization of the people spread to all their social institutions. By 1924 the government became as alarmed over the Pine Ridge Indians' failing will to live as over their lack of sufficient food and increasing sickness.

This appearance of starvation in the middle of the 1920's is significant in the light of the apathy which has become so general. Most of the Sioux of North and South Dakota were showing signs of undernutrition about this time, and all had been losing their cattle, although not always by such drastic methods as occurred on Pine Ridge. This meant that they were losing their supply of meat—their staple food for centuries. Even during the time between the disappearance of the buffalo and the building of large cattle herds, the Sioux had been supported by government rations. The years after 1916, when beef was no longer included in their rations, were their first experience in living without meat for a long period of time. The loss of the beef and the cattle was an ecological change which has continued for nearly thirty years. This change might, and probably did, cause modifications in the physiology of the Sioux. Health conditions and observations of diet among them substantiate the assumption that much of their present behavior may be attributable to physiological causes. The biological factor, although not encompassed in this study, is important to bear in mind as one of the elements of the environment affecting the Sioux.

After their cash from the cattle sales had been dissipated, the Pine Ridge tribe began to accept rations and developed a dependency upon the government which they have never fully overcome. The Civilian Conservation Corps provided work which brought an income to most of the families, but the people remained nearly as dependent as they were at the beginning of the depression or when most of the band moved to the Agency in 1879. The recent war years have brought work and the highest wages which the Dakota have ever earned. But the sources of these wages lie outside the reservation and will probably not continue for many more years. Even the optimum of postwar employment in peacetime industries will not eliminate the fundamental economic and social problems of the reservation. Large-scale nongovernment wage work is improbable in this rural and sparsely settled area.

We have seen that the past social and economic experiences have culminated in serious personal disorganization as well as severe poverty and unemployment. This study has shown that this personal disorganization begins very early in life and is seriously handicapping the children on the reservation today. Although we have no data about personality development of the adults, the behavior observed among them and the insecurity they appear to impart to their children, suggest they have suffered similarly from oppressive environment.

These circumstances lead to the conclusion that the fundamental need of the Pine Ridge Dakota today is a way of life which will give them personal security and an opportunity for creative development. They need a way of working themselves out of the present poverty through a permanent economy based on available resources. They need also greater self-direction to permit the regeneration of society. The development of a reservation-wide cattle economy and community councils for local self-government offer logical approaches to these goals.

The local government program has already promoted the revival of the cattle economy to increase income and improve living conditions and of a democratic political organization to give the Indians greater direction in their community and tribal affairs. The condition of the Pine Ridge people requires that emphasis be placed upon the human objective and especially upon the objective of relieving the psychological distress which now prevails. The government programs—economic, social, educational, and political—have as their ultimate objective the welfare of the Indians; but, in the effort to achieve this objective, the focus has rested too frequently on the more concrete goals of material improvements and methods of promoting their attainment. Awareness of the long distance which many Pine Ridge Indians must travel to gain self-confidence and freedom from fear can aid in orienting programs of rehabilitation toward producing the personality development and inner security basic to their success.

In one community, Red Shirt Table, the Agency has already worked intensively in the sponsorship of a program of integrated activities for greater economic and social welfare. It has stimulated, organized, and guided but has carefully refrained from any form of domination. The community's response in renewed activity and personal happiness is already apparent. The people have formed a cattle association with a business committee of Indian men and a community council for directing local affairs. Old and young gather regularly at the new school for work groups and recreational affairs. Men come to repair their farm equipment at the shop; women bring their garden produce to can at the kitchen. The school curriculum is centered around these activities. Although the Agency started the program for able-bodied and interested families, through Indian insistence it now includes all the community. The aged and the disabled who cannot actively participate and the uninterested and skeptical also have the opportunity to share in the cattle herd and all the community affairs. As the program succeeds, personal stability and security are spreading through the community.

The primary values which this program appears to have for the men are the restoration of cowboy life as an occupation around which sentiments and prestige have already been built (including the renewed importance of the horse, which is also a point of prestige) and the development of leadership and responsibility. The importance which the men play in this program is in keeping with Dakota tradition. The men were the keystone in the former social structure, and the culture was organized around their careers and achievements. The

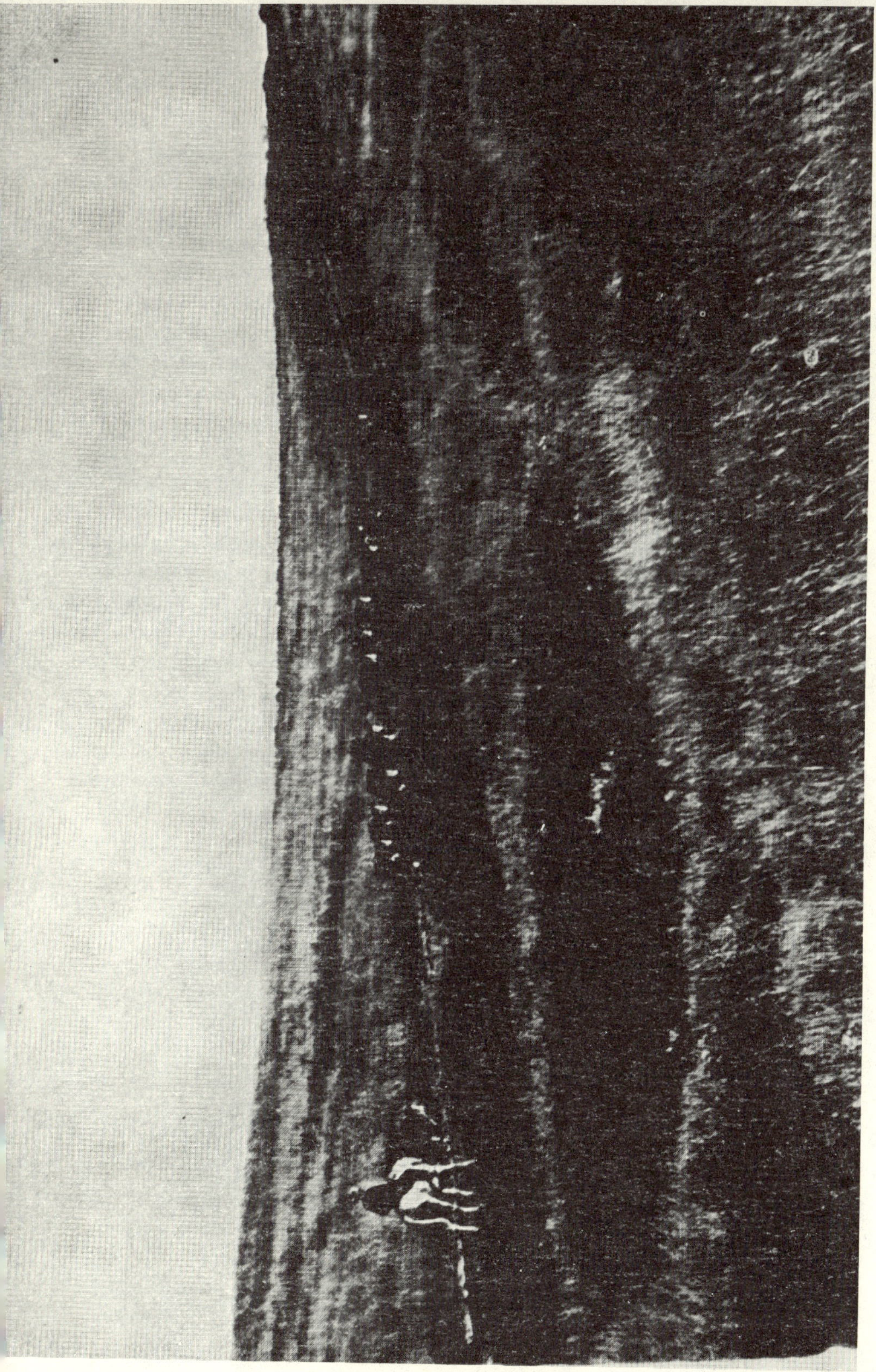

restoration of an occupation which the Sioux already regard as manly and desirable will prove invaluable to their morale. With a permanent occupation they can provide for their families and gain their respect. Through business committees and community councils, the men can again acquire status and leadership. Not the least important is the promise that, through their new social position and self-respect, the men will become more significant as fathers to their children.

The values of the program are not limited to the men. The women and girls can also increase the activity and significance of their lives. In the present society the women have increased their importance in family life and have already emancipated themselves from their former supplementary role. Through organized clubs and guilds, the parent-teacher association, and the community and tribal council, they have accepted active community leadership.

In the school program the children may gain security and confidence by orienting their lives to objectives which they see are attainable in the daily activities developing around their homes. As the schools attune their program more closely to positive, functioning elements of Dakota child-training and society, the children may become freer in expressing their feelings and desires. Increased emphasis upon group activities with less individual competition, a stable system of discipline with the student groups giving rewards and imposing punishments, and social studies centered upon Dakota acculturation appear to be aspects of school experience which may help immeasurably in aiding personality development.

Children and adults sure of themselves and their objectives will be equipped to strengthen economic and social techniques toward achieving an organized and personally satisfying society and to attain a healthy adjustment to their environment.

APPENDIX I

TECHNIQUES USED IN THE STUDY

The techniques used in the study were drawn from social anthropology, psychology, psychiatry, and medicine, but the great bulk of the data on which the study is based was obtained from interviews and psychological tests conducted under the supervision of the writer by members of the field staff drawn from the education and health divisions of Pine Ridge Indian Agency and by an anthropologist who was also a Rorschach specialist. Some of the field staff received preliminary training in interviewing and conducting tests from members of the University of Chicago Committee of the Indian Education Research Project. Training, discussion, and evaluation of material were carried on by the supervisor and the staff in the Kyle area for the first few months of the study.

INTERVIEW TECHNIQUES

The method of interviewing followed the techniques developed by W. Lloyd Warner and others in the study of Yankee City[1] and F. J. Roethlisberger and W. J. Dickson in the Western Electric Company study.[2] The staff made several visits to the parents and relatives of each of the 166 children tested. Indian leaders, councilmen, government employees, missionaries, cattlemen, and traders were also interviewed regarding the institutions, functions, and group relationships of the community. Although occasional direct questioning about some subjects was unavoidable, the ethnologist's usual method of questioning informants through interpreters was not followed.

RECORDS AND PHYSICAL EXAMINATIONS

Information regarding each child's school work and behavior in the classroom was supplied by teachers on a school record prepared by the research staff. This information was amplified by observations in the classrooms and among the play groups. The medical examinations were made by the Agency staff of doctors and nurses according to an outline prepared by physicians on the research staff.

PSYCHOLOGICAL TESTS

The psychological tests used in the studies of the five tribes made by the Indian Education Research Project were selected from many types after consideration of their suitability to non-English-speaking children, their freedom from cultural bias and handicaps, and the variety of data they would yield. The basic objectives of the tests were to supply information about intelligence, personal behavior, emotional development, moral ideas and attitudes, and the structure of personality. Some of these tests elicited not only emotional reactions and attitudes toward other people but also voluntary reports of personal behavior and experiences. Other tests were employed to find what lay at the bases of the overt behavior; what effect surroundings had upon the basic impulses, emotions, and mental processes; and the expression, controls, or defenses which the individual made to these reactions. The tests were selected to obtain information at different levels of psychological behavior. A brief description of the various types of test follows.

The Grace Arthur Point Performance Scale (short form)[3] was used to score intelligence by a set of nonverbal tests. This performance scale consists of six parts which have been selected for their relative freedom from cultural elements and need for English reading, writing, and arithmetic or other subjects learned in school. The total test includes the Knox Cubes, Seguin

Form Board, Mare-and-Foal Test, Healy Picture-Completion Test, Porteus Mazes, and Kohs Blocks. The Healy Test was eliminated from the computation of the scores because experience showed that it required familiarity with white life beyond what the Indian children possessed. The Arthur test measures ability to solve situations, speed of reaction time, and willingness to conform, as well as other aspects of intelligence. It is adequate to measure the I.Q. for children up to the age of fifteen.

The Goodenough Draw-a-Man Test[4] was also used for scoring intelligence of children up to eleven years of age. In this test the child is asked to draw a picture of a man to the best of his ability. The scoring is made on the proportions of the figure and the details of anatomy and clothing which the child includes. The I.Q. is calculated from the results.

The Kuhlmann-Anderson Test[5] was given to some of the sample group of Dakota children in the Pine Ridge school, but it was not part of the test battery designed for the Project. This test, like the well-known Binet-Simon, requires understanding of English and reading ability, and hence it gave some comparative check on the use of the relatively culture-free intelligence tests among the children. The Kuhlmann-Anderson Test also includes performance tests.

Stewart's Emotional Response Test (revised)[6] asks the child to recount occasions when he felt happy, sad, angry, afraid, or ashamed and what are the best and the worst things that could happen to him. It thus obtains experiences associated with certain emotions. The responses present emotional relationships and attitudes toward different persons, objects, and situations on the overt level. These relationships can be classified into types of behavior which give some cultural expectancies. In chapter x of this book are described the bases on which the responses of the Dakota children were classified for the kind of behavior toward people of different roles in the society and analyzed for the type and nature of relationships which the child experienced with other people and institutions. The responses of this test were combined with those of the Bavelas Test of Moral Ideology.

The Bavelas Test of Moral Ideology asks the child what he thinks are "good" and "bad" things to do and thus obtains the official or public moral standards learned by the child. These questions aim to find out what the child thinks he should or should not do, not what he actually would do in a given situation. In asking who would praise or blame him for doing good and bad things, respectively, the questions are intended to discover the child's attitudes toward persons in his society who are rewarding or punishing agents. Thus the test gives the major fields of moral behavior and the people concerned with such behavior.

Murray's Thematic Apperception Test (revised)[8] employs a series of pictures of people in various groupings and indefinite circumstances about which many interpretations might be made. Pictures on cards are presented in sequence to the child, who is asked to tell a story about each. For the Indian children, some of Murray's pictures were redrawn by an Indian artist and the people put in Indian clothing. For the Dakota, some of the pictures used in the Southwest studies were again redrawn to change the appearance of people and scenes to familiar forms. After some experimentation, eight of the twenty pictures were presented to all the Dakota children tested. Each child was allowed to select two pictures of the remaining twelve. Many of the children acted very constrained in telling stories. By deviating from the prescribed method and allowing the children to select two pictures, it was hoped that they would have more to say about pictures which they had selected.

It is assumed that the child, in telling stories about these pictures, will project unconsciously his own experiences, the bases of his relationships with other people, his reactions to his environment, and the nature of his imagination. An analyst can determine from the stories the intellectual and emotional configurations, the nature of social relationships, and the kind of expression permitted to the impulse life of the individual child.

The Rorschach Psychodiagnostic Test[9] is another projective device for estimating the structure of the child's personality. This test employs a series of ten cards, each containing a standarized meaningless "ink blot." The child is asked to tell what each blot looks like to him. In his approach to and description of the things he sees, the child shows his intellectual and emotional characteristics and his fundamental reactions. Analysis of the material gives a picture of the structure of the personality—its expressed and controlled drives and interests, its conflicts and defense mechanisms, and the nature of adjustments made to itself and to others.

Not all the children took every test or examination, but enough took each so that deductions might be fairly drawn. The types and numbers of tests made in the study are shown in Table A.

ANALYSIS AND INTERPRETATION

The interview material, focused on family and community life, child-training, ways of making a living, and social and religious institutions, was analyzed by the writer and used as the basis for Parts I and II of this book. This material was supplemented by government records and by literary sources which give the history and former culture of the Dakota.

Dorothea Leighton, M.D., special physician of the United States Indian Service, summarized the data on the health of the children contained in the medical examinations.

TABLE A

		COMMUNITIES		
Tests	Total	Kyle	Wanblee	Pine Ridge
Total children tested	166	90	30	46
Intelligence tests:				
Grace Arthur Point Performance	146	83	26	37
Goodenough Draw-a-Man	136	86	10	40
Kuhlmann-Anderson*	34	8	0	26
Physical examinations	151	81	30	40
Stewart and Bavelas tests	158	86	29	43
Projective tests:				
Murray's Thematic Appreciation	130	63	30	37
Rorschach Psychodiagnostic	154	81	30	43

* Given at one school to 34 children of the sample group: not a part of project techniques.

Each set of psychological test results was analyzed at the University of Chicago. Dr. Robert Havighurst and his associates prepared the statistical data on the Arthur, Goodenough, and Kuhlmann-Anderson intelligence tests and the Stewart and Bavelas tests, all of which lend themselves to statistical analysis. Results of these tests were compared with those from all the tribes studied and with results from some of the same tests administered to a group of white children in a midwestern town where the Committee on Human Development of the University of Chicago has made a study utilizing many of the tests employed in the Indian Education Research Project. Results of the Thematic Apperception and Rorschach tests were interpreted independently for each tribe. In chapters xiii and xiv of the present book, conclusions about the intelligence, physical condition, overt behavior, and underlying organization of the group personality of Dakota children are presented in this order.

Since few of these tests had been employed with Indian children previous to this Project,[10] it was necessary to check the validity of each test for Indian children. This was done by comparison of tests results of white children, where possible, and by comparison of the results of one test with those of the others, as far as data permitted. Test results were also compared with the material obtained by observation and interview.

The average I.Q.'s for the Indian tribes were compared with one another and with white standards. The Indian groups scored averages similar to, above, and below the white standards and, by not being consistently above or below the standard, indicated that they were not at an advantage or a disadvantage in taking these tests. The results of the Emotional Response and Moral Ideology tests showed significant variations among the tribes and differences from the results of the white children in a midwestern town. These differences were expected because of the different cultural backgrounds and were explainable on a cultural basis by the anthropologists for each tribe.

An experiment was then made to check the correlation of the comparable data of each test and the life-histories obtained by means of interviews. This was done first with data of a few individuals from each tribe. Each test and the life-history material were analyzed and interpreted without reference to the other data, the subjects of these experimental cases being unknown to the analysts. A report of each child's tests and life-history was then given to all the analysts, who were asked to match them on the basis of the interpretations. For example, the Thematic Apperception analyst was asked to select from the reports on the life-history and the Emotional Response, Moral Ideology, and Rorschach tests those which belonged with one of his Thematic Apperception reports.

The reports about each child were then compared and the existing discrepancies discussed. A high correlation among the findings appeared. In order to facilitate comparison, data from each test describing phases of the personality were organized according to the following outline, prepared by William E. Henry, of the University of Chicago.

OUTLINE FOR INDIVIDUAL CASE ANALYSIS

Designed from an analysis of areas of personal dynamics to be discerned from study of the Thematic Apperception Test: to be used as an outline for analysis of individual case protocols of Thematic Apperception and Rorschach tests and other techniques and for the intra-case comparison of data derived from each of these techniques.

I. Mental Approach
   A. Level of intellectual capacities
   B. Adequacy and efficiency of intellectual functioning
   C. Organization and logic of intellectual approach
   D. Intellectual approach to new problems

II. Creativity: Extent and Nature
   (Includes Imagination, Originality, Fantasy)

III. Behavioral Approach
   A. General overt pattern (descriptive summary of overt pattern as observed in action)
   B. Peer relationships (all subadults) (includes comments on relation to male and female peers, general acceptance of and by peers, nature of relationship to them)
   C. Adult relationships (acceptance/rejection of adult authority, nature of relationship to them)
   D. School adjustment (to teacher and to work)
   E. Specific problems of Area III

IV. Family Dynamics
   A. Relationship to mother, father, siblings, and of each to child (overt and covert aspects)
   B. Resolution of primary ties to parents
   C. Summary of family emotional atmosphere
   D. Specific problems of Area IV

V. Inner Adjustment and Defense Mechanisms
   A. Basic emotional attitude (strength of drive toward solution of emotional problems)
   B. Attitude toward inner impulse life, acceptance/rejection
   C. Anxiety, insecurity, general and specific
   D. Nature of ego defenses (relate Area V to Area III)
   E. Control, system of (inner, conscious, outer, and constricted)
   F. Approach to interpersonal dynamics, nature of emotional ties to other people
   G. Maturity

VI. Emotional Reactivity
   A. Drive toward outer world
   B. Spontaneity and personal freedom of action

VII. Sexual Adjustment
   A. Adequacy
   B. Anxiety
   C. Specific problems (includes differentiation of aim and object)
VIII. Descriptive and Interpretative Summary
      Patterning and organization of items in Areas I through VII including statement of nature of adjustment in two areas: self and social
IX. Prognosis
X. Descriptive Summary of Data

Note.—This is essentially an outline for delineation of present adjustment and does not stress etiology. Comments on etiology would be included in Area VIII.

Ten Dakota children were then analyzed by the same method. These children were selected because of differences in age and degree of Indian blood from the cases of boys and girls who had taken all types of tests and had an adequate amount of life-history data. The personality sketches integrating data from all these reports, which appear in chapter xii of this book, were written by the author with the assistance of William E. Henry and Dorothea Leighton, M.D. These sketches attempt to describe the personality of the child as it appears from his daily behavior, his personal history, and the background of his family and community. Data from his tests are then presented to show his capacities, the underlying personality configuration, and aspects which account in part for his observed behavior and adjustments.

NOTES

1. W. Lloyd Warner and Paul S. Lunt, *The Social Life of a Modern Community* (New Haven: Yale University Press, 1941), I, 49-53.
2. F. J. Roethlisberger and William J. Dickson, *Management and the Worker* (Cambridge: Harvard University Press, 1939), pp. 272 ff.
3. Mary Grace Arthur, *A Point Scale of Performance Tests* (New York: Commonwealth Fund, 1933).
4. F. L. Goodenough, *Measurements of Intelligence by Drawings* (New York: World Book Co., 1926).
5. F. Kuhlmann, "The Kuhlmann-Anderson Intelligence Tests Compared with Seven Others," *Journal of Applied Psychology*, XII (1928), 545-94.
6. Kilton Stewart, "Test of Emotional Response" (MS).
7. A. Bavelas, "A Method for Investigating Individual and Group Ideologies," *Sociometry*, V (1942), 371-77.
8. Henry A. Murray, *Thematic Apperception Test Manual* (Cambridge, Mass.: Harvard University Press, 1943).
9. Bruno Klopfer and Douglas McG. Kelley, *The Rorschach Technique* (New York: World Book Co., 1942).
10. Grace Arthur gave her Performance Scale to a group of Indian children from various tribes who were students at Haskell Institute. About 250 Rorschach protocols had been collected from four Indian tribes (A. Irving Hallowell, "The Rorschach Method as an Aid in the Study of Personalities in Primitive Societies," *Character and Personality*, IX [1941], 237). Stewart's Emotional Response Test had been used extensively by the originator among non-European peoples, but the findings have never been published.

APPENDIX II

AGGRESSION IN PERSONALITY

"Aggressive" is a term often applied to the Sioux character and even to the culture itself. For this reason, and because the word is used with widely varying connotations in psychological and sociological literature, it is necessary to explain its use in this monograph.

Aggression as used here, following Kardiner,[1] is the attitude, emotional reaction, and behavior directed toward a person or object that causes pain or interferes with the gratification of some need or desire. Types of aggression may be differentiated according to its stimulus which sets the drive in action, the specific behavior which takes place, and the goal. The somatic sources of the drive have not yet been identified, but the energy underlying aggression as self-assertion or self-expression appears to be characteristic of all humans. In the face of interference or frustration, this energy is "directed in an active way toward another object in order to establish over it some form of mastery or control; to subject it to ends of utility and pleasure." When this self-assertion achieves mastery, it is well-organized aggression; but, when mastery is blocked before the individual gains satisfaction, aggression becomes disorganized. There is, then, satisfactory and unsatisfactory aggression. Satisfactory aggression is very often socially approved; some self-assertive activities, such as aggressive salesmanship, can achieve success because they are tolerated or encouraged. Other types of aggression are controlled or punished by society.

It is this point of satisfactory and unsatisfactory, approved and unapproved, aggression which needs to be clarified to understand the aggressive behavior of the Dakota. In the account of Dakota child-training and cultural objectives, it was said that Dakota parents encouraged self-assertiveness in their boys for later aggressions against enemy tribes (see chaps. iv and ix). It may be said that the initial cause or interference that provoked Dakota aggressiveness was the threat of other tribes to the Dakota hunting grounds and subsistence and thus to their security. But the secondary social stimuli became the more potent force.

Aggressive behavior was embodied in the warlike conduct expected of Dakota men. The object or goal was the prestige and satisfaction afforded warriors by the men's societies, the positions of leadership, and the esteem of the people.

From the Dakota point of view, the aggression of their men was useful and gratifying and served to master others outside their group. Aggression was thus socially approved. This is the distinction which must be emphasized about the essential nature of Dakota aggression before warfare was barred to them and they were forced to accept reservation life.

It is not difficult to appreciate how a people trained to be aggressive in war and expecting rewards of social success and high status should have difficulty in finding release and satisfaction for all the energy they desired to express when warfare was cut off. They had to find other channels and targets for their highly developed aggressive drive. Added to this major obstacle were all the frustrations of governmental control, pressure to abandon Dakota life for white civilization, and the seeming betrayal by some individuals who gave up Dakota customs. The energy accumulated from cultural stimuli and from reactions to obstacles presented by white domination was directed into destructive activity against members of the tribe and against the officials who represented the government. This behavior, which is now characteristic of much of present-day Dakota activity, takes many direct and obvious, as well as many indirect and obscure, forms which are described in the study. Since it is not socially approved, it brings slight prestige rewards; being disorganized, it brings little real satisfaction to the individual.

APPENDIX

Because the nature and social value of Dakota aggression in the former culture differ so greatly from the aggression so common among them today, the term "aggression" has been qualified when used in this study. The culturally approved aggression of the Dakota is referred to in the text as "self-assertion" or "striving aggression"; the attacking, destructive behavior is referred to as "hostility" or "hostile aggression."

NOTES

1. Abram Kardiner, *The Individual and His Society* (New York: Columbia University Press, 1939), pp. 56-63.

BIBLIOGRAPHY

ARTHUR, MARY GRACE. *A Point Scale of Performance Tests.* 2 vols. New York: Commonwealth Fund, 1933.
BAVELAS, A. "A Method for Investigating Individual and Group Ideologies," *Sociometry,* V (1942), 371-77.
BEATTY, WILLARD W. "Training Indians for the Best Use of Their Own Resources," in *The Changing Indian,* ed. OLIVER LA FARGE. Norman: University of Oklahoma Press, 1942.
BENEDICT, RUTH. *Patterns of Culture.* Boston: Houghton Mifflin Co., 1935.
BLACK ELK. *Black Elk Speaks: Being a Life Story of a Holy Man of the Oglala Sioux as Told to John G. Neihardt.* New York: W. W. Morrow & Co., 1932.
BLAUCH, LLOYD E. *Education Service for Indians.* "Advisory Committee on Education, Staff Study," No. 18. Washington: Government Printing Office, 1939.
CHAPPLE, ELIOT D., and COON, CARLETON S. *Principles of Anthropology.* New York: Henry Holt & Co., 1942.
COLLIER, DONALD. "Plains Camping Groups." (MS).
CREAMER, DANIEL, and SCHWARTZ, CHARLES F. "State Income Payments in 1942," *Survey of Current Business,* XX (1943), 10-22.
DELORIA, E. *Dakota Texts.* "Publications of the American Ethnological Society," Vol. XIV. New York: The Society, 1932.
———. "Sun Dance of the Oglala Sioux," *Journal of American Folk-lore,* Vol. XLII, No. 166 (1929).
DENSMORE, FRANCES. *Teton Sioux Music.* Bureau of American Ethnology, Bull. 61. Washington: Government Prinitng Office, 1918.
EGGAN, FRED. "The Cheyenne and Arapaho Kinship System," in *Social Anthropology of North American Tribes,* ed. FRED EGGAN. Chicago: University of Chicago Press, 1937.
ERIKSON, ERIK HOMBURGER. "Observations on Sioux Education," *Journal of Psychology,* VII (1939), 101-56.
EWERS, JOHN C. "Teton Dakota: Ethnology and History." Rev. ed. Berkeley, Calif.: National Park Service, 1938. (Mimeographed.)
GESSNER, ROBERT. *Massacre: A Survey of Today's American Indian.* New York: Jonathan Cape & Harrison Smith, 1931.
GOLDFRANK, ESTHER S. "Historic Change and Social Character: A Study of the Teton Dakota," *American Anthropologist,* XLV (1943), 67-83.
GOODENOUGH, FLORENCE L. *Measurements of Intelligence by Drawings.* New York: World Book Co., 1926.
HALLOWELL, A. IRVING. "The Rorschach Method as an Aid in the Study of Personalities in Primitive Societies," *Character and Personality,* IX (1941), 235-45.
HASSRICK, ROYAL B. "Teton-Dakota Kinship System." (MS.)
———. "Teton-Dakota Kinship System," *American Anthropologist,* XLVI (1944), 338-47.
———. "Teton-Dakota Religion." (MS.)
HAVIGHURST, ROBERT J. "Comparison of American Indian and White Children by Means of the Emotional Response Test." Indian Education Research Project, Committee on Human Development, University of Chicago. (MS.)
———. "Comparison of Indian Children and White Children by Means of the Moral Ideology Test." Indian Education Research Project, Committee on Human Development, University of Chicago. (MS.)
HAVIGHURST, ROBERT J., and HILKEVITCH, RHEA R. "The Intelligence of Indian Children as

Measured by a Performance Scale," *Journal of Abnormal and Social Psychology*, XXXIX (1944), 419–33.

HAVIGHURST, ROBERT J.; KOROL, MINNA; and PRATT, INEZ. "The Performance of Southwestern and Sioux Indian Children on the Goodenough Draw-a-Man Test." Indian Education Research Project, Committee on Human Development, University of Chicago. (MS.)

HENRY, WILLIAM E. "An Exploration of the Validity and Usefulness of the Thematic Apperception Technique in the Study of Culture-Personality Relations" (MS). Ph.D. Thesis, University of Chicago, 1944.

HULSIZER, ALLAN. *Region and Culture in the Curriculum of the Navaho and the Dakota*. Federalsburg, Md.: J. W. Stowell Co., 1940.

HYDE, GEORGE. *Red Cloud's Folk*. Norman: University of Oklahoma Press, 1937.

JOSEPH, ALICE; SPICER, ROSAMOND; and CHESKY, JANE. *The Desert People*. "Indian Education Research Series," No. 4. (In preparation.)

KARDINER, ABRAM. *The Individual and His Society*. New York: Columbia University Press, 1939.

KLOPFER, BRUNO, and KELLEY, DOUGLAS McG. *The Rorschach Technique*. New York: World Book Co., 1942.

KROEBER, A. L. *Cultural and Natural Areas of Native North America*. Berkeley, Calif.: University of California Press, 1939.

KUHLMANN, F. "The Kuhlmann-Anderson Intelligence Tests Compared with Seven Others," *Journal of Applied Psychology*, XII (1928), 545–94.

LEIGHTON, DOROTHEA C. Personal correspondence.

LEIGHTON, DOROTHEA, and KLUCKHOHN, CLYDE. *The People and Their Children*. Chicago: University of Chicago Press (forthcoming).

LOWIE, ROBERT H. *Primitive Religion*. New York: Boni & Liveright, 1924.

MCGILLYCUDDY, JULIA B. *McGillycuddy—Agent: A Biography of Dr. Valentine T. McGillycuddy*. Standford University: Stanford University Press, 1941.

MEKEEL, SCUDDER. *The Economy of a Modern Teton-Dakota Community*. "Yale University Publications in Anthropology," No. 6. New Haven: Yale University Press, 1936.

———. *A Modern American Indian Community in the Light of Its Past: A Study in Cultural Change*. New Haven: Yale University Press, 1932.

———. "A Short History of the Teton-Dakota," *North Dakota Historical Quarterly*, X (1943), 137–205.

———. Personal correspondence.

MERIAM, LEWIS, et al. *The Problem of Indian Administration*. Institute of Government Research. Baltimore: Johns Hopkins Press, 1928.

MIRSKY, JEANNETTE. "The Dakota," in *Cooperation and Competition among Primitive Peoples*, ed. MARGARET MEAD. New York: McGraw-Hill Book Co., 1937.

MURRAY, HENRY A. *Thematic Apperception Test Manual*. Cambridge: Harvard University Press, 1943.

ORATA, PEDRO T. "Democracy and Indian Education." (MS.)

PROVINSE, JOHN H. "The Underlying Sanctions of Plains Indian Culture," in *Social Anthropology of North American Tribes*, ed. FRED EGGAN. Chicago: University of Chicago Press, 1937.

ROBERTS, W. O. Personal correspondence.

ROETHLISBERGER, F. J., and DICKSON, WILLIAM J. *Management and the Worker*. Cambridge: Harvard University Press, 1939.

STANDING BEAR, LUTHER. *My People the Sioux*. Boston: Houghton Mifflin Co., 1928.

STERNER, ARMIN H., and MACGREGOR, GORDON. "The Pine Ridge Vocational Survey," *Indian Education*, III, Nos. 31 and 32 (1938), 2–8 and 2–7.

STEWART, KILTON. "Test of Emotional Response." (MS.)

STEWART, OMER C. *Washo-Northern Paiute Peyotism*. "University of California Publications in American Archaeology and Ethnology," Vol. XL, No. 3. Berkeley: University of California Press, 1944.

SWANTON, JOHN R. "Siouan Tribes and the Ohio Valley," *American Anthropologist*, XLV (1943), 49–66.
THOMPSON, LAURA, and JOSEPH, ALICE. *The Hopi Way*. "Indian Education Research Series," No. 1. Chicago: University of Chicago Press, 1944.
U.S. DEPARTMENT OF AGRICULTURE, SOIL CONSERVATION SERVICE. "An Economic and Social Survey of Pine Ridge Indian Reservation, South Dakota." Denver: Technical Cooperation, Bureau of Indian Affairs, August, 1939. (Mimeographed.)
U.S. DEPARTMENT OF THE INTERIOR, OFFICE OF INDIAN AFFAIRS. "Circular Letter 2970." Washington, 1934. (Mimeographed.)
———. "Annual Report of the Extension Division, 1942." Pine Ridge Reservation, 1942. (Mimeographed.)
———. "Employees' Handbook of Information, 1942–43. Oglala Community High School." Pine Ridge Reservation, 1942. (Mimeographed.)
———. *Manual of Instructions for Special and Deputy Special Officers and Indian Police*. Chilocco, Okla.: Chilocco School Press, 1943.
———. *Regulations of the Indian Office Effective April 1, 1904*. Washington: Government Printing Office, 1904.
———. "Report of the Commissioner of Indian Affairs," in *Report of the Secretary of the Interior for the Fiscal Year Ending June 30, 1885*. Washington: Government Printing Office, 1885.
———. "Report of the Commissioner, Statistical Supplement," *Individual Income, Resident Population, 1942*. Washington, 1943. (Processed.)
———. "Statement of the Relief and Governmental Employment Provided for Indians, Fiscal Year 1939." (MS.)
———. "Reservation Program, Pine Ridge Indian Reservation." Pine Ridge Reservation, 1944. (Mimeographed.)
———. *Students' Handbook, Oglala Community High School, 1942–43*. Chilocco, Okla.: Chilocco School Press, 1942.
[U.S.] GREAT PLAINS COMMITTEE. *The Future of the Great Plains: Report of the Great Plains Committee*. Washington: Government Printing Office, 1936.
USEEM, JOHN; MACGREGOR, GORDON; and USEEM, RUTH. "Wartime Employment and Cultural Adjustments of the Rosebud Sioux," *Applied Anthropology*, II (1943), 1–9.
WALKER, J. R. *The Sun Dance and Other Ceremonies of the Oglala Division of the Teton Dakota*. "Anthropological Papers of the American Museum of Natural History," Vol. XVI, Part II. New York: The Museum, 1917.
WARNER, W. LLOYD, and LUNT, PAUL S. *The Social Life of a Modern Community*. "Yankee City Series," Vol. I. New Haven: Yale University Press, 1941.
WISSLER, CLARK. *North American Indian of the Plains*. "Handbook Series," No. 1. New York: American Museum of Natural History, 1934.
———. *Societies and Ceremonial Associations of the Oglala Division of the Teton-Dakota*. "Anthropological Papers of the American Museum of Natural History," Vol. XI, Part I. New York: The Museum, 1912.

INDEX

Acculturation, 26–27, 33, 35
Adjustment: in school, 134-35; of students on the reservation, 149; of students off the reservation, 151
Adolescence, 139–52; boys' behavior, 194–95; girls' behavior, 195–98, 208
Age differences, 207
Agencies: Pine Ridge, 32, 53, 72; Red Cloud, 32, 53; Whetstone, 32, 35
Agency controls, 120
Agent; see Superintendents
Aggression, 137–38, 153–83, 190, 194, 197–98, 200, 220–21
Akicita, 116
Allotments, 37, 38, 39–40, 44
American Horse, Chief, 66
Analysis, case outline, 218
Animals: attitudes toward, 190, 194, 197, 206; as gifts, 127; training with, 127, 131
Anxiety, 44, 155; children's, 191, 206–7
Arapaho, 31
Arikara, 31
Arthur, Grace; see Tests
Assimilation; see Acculturation
Assiniboine, 29
Attitudes, 12, 25, 26; of adults, 190–91; toward animals, 190; children's toward school, 132, 146; of oldest generation, 105–9; of parent generation, 109–11; toward property, 127; toward religion, 102; toward reservation, 148–52; toward social structure, 198–202; white, 83, 120–21, 123
Avoidance, 63; breakdown of, in school, 144; brother-sister, 131; see also Relationships

Badlands, 69
Bands, 37, 52, 66
Batesland, South Dakota, 40
Bavelas, A.; see Tests, Moral Ideology
Beatty, Willard W., 152
Behavior, 54; age and sex differences in, 117, 137, 195–98; children's, 153, 184–202, 204–9; Dakota pattern of, 153–56; in relation to social structure, 198–202; in school, 135
Benedict, Ruth, 104
Bennett County, 44
Big Stone Lake, Minnesota, 29
Biology, factors of, in personality, 184

Birth, 123
Black Hills, 22
Blauch, Lloyd E., 78, 84
Blue Earth River, Minnesota, 29
Brothers, 59, 139; in relation to brothers, 139, 198; in relation to sisters, 199
Brulé (subtribe), 21; history of, 29–30, 37, 53

Carlisle Institute, 35, 106, 108
Cattle: early raising of, 35, 37–38; loss of, 27, 39, 110; re-establishment of, 41
Ceremony, 87–91; Buffalo, 94; ear-piercing, 89, 94, 106; give-away, 89, 107, 113–14; keeping of ghost, 94; religious, 87–91; see also Death, Marriage, Peyote cult
Chapple, Eliot D., 203
Cheyenne, 30, 31
Chiefs, 35–37, 53
Children: adolescence, 139–52; ceremonies of, 89; health of, 187–88; infancy, 123–30; peyote and, 101; psychological behavior of, 184–202, 204–9
Christianity; see Religion
Churches, 68, 69, 96–98, 100–102; Catholic 72, 96; Episcopal, 35, 96; Presbyterian, 96
Citizenship, 79
Civilian Conservation Corps, 40–41, 211
Climate, 43–44
Communities: reservation, 66–78, 212; white, 82–83
Competency Commission, 39
Competition, 113, 135
Conflict, 29, 64, 105–21; full-blood–mixed-blood, 147; religious, 93, 109, 113, 121; reservation and school, 134, 146–50
Conscience, 202
Controls: agency, 120; over children, 128, 132, 135, 154; social, 53; by superintendent, 35–36, 115
Coon, Carleton S., 203
Co-operation, 135
Cowboy, attraction to Indian, 108
Crazy Horse, Chief, 31
Creamer, Daniel, 51
Crook, General, 38
Culture, in personality, 184–86; see also Dakota
Custer, General, 21, 31, 33, 38
Custom, suppression of native, 35–36

225

Dakota, 21, 22, 27; effects of reservation life on, 153; history of, 29-36, 41, 53
Death: ceremonies, 94-96; children's concern over, 192
Densmore, Frances, 103-4, 122
Discipline, school, 144-46; *see also* Controls
Disorganization, effects of, 105-21; individual, 153
District, 68, 74-77
Divisions: agency, 79-81; biological, 25; cultural, 25, 29; political, 25; sociological, 25, 26
Dress, children's, 128-30

Economy, 40, 43-45, 149, 211
Education: boarding schools, 142-48; for change, 35, 36, 57; early schools, 35, 37; of girls, 58; methods of, 132-33; objectives of, 132, 142-44, 214; of parents, 109; value of, 200-201
Eggan, Fred, 64
Emotional Response Test; *see* Tests
Emotions, general patterns, 188, 189-202
Employment: children's attitude toward, 201-2; off-reservation, 151
Environment, social, 205, 209
Erikson, Erik H., 14, 26, 122, 130, 183
Escape, 137, 146-48, 153-55, 195, 207
Ewers, John C., 41

Family: biological, 56-60; break-up of, 68, 116-17; child's attitude toward, 192, 193, 198-99, 205-6; conjugal, 62-64; extended, 60-62, 67; as source of security, 194, 197
Father, 57, 109; and son, 139, 199
Fear, girl's, 140
Fort Laramie, Wyoming, 31
Fort Robinson, Nebraska, 32
French, 69
Full-blood communities, 66
Full-bloods, 23-25

Gall, Chief, 32
Games, 133, 143, 191
General Allotment Act, 78
Generation: oldest, 105-9; parent, 109-15
Generosity: of boys, 194; training for, 126-27; *see also* Ceremony, give-away
Gessner, Robert, 42
Ghost Dance, 33
Ghosts, 191
Give-away: *see* Ceremony
Gods, Dakota, 87
Goodenough Draw-a-Man Test; *see* Tests
Government: federal, 78-81; policy of, 117-21; student, 143
Government assistance: federal, 48-49; state, 48
Grandparent, 60, 105-7, 199

Harney, General, 21, 31
Hassrick, Royal B., 8, 13, 64, 103
Havighurst, Robert, 141, 203, 217
Health, 123, 211, 215; concern for, 155, 191-92; of Dakota children, 187; standards of, 203; *see also* Undernutrition
Henry, William E., 8, 13, 218
History, 21-28, 29-41, 210; *see also* Life-histories
Holidays, 133
Hopi, 9, 15
Horses, 39, 45
Hulsizer, Allan, 42, 152
Hyde, George, 41, 64

Impulses, 204, 209
Income, 40, 45, 49-50
Indian Education Research Project, 8-10, 187
Indian Reorganization Act, 44, 50, 71, 81
Individualism, 113
Insecurity, 109, 121, 153, 155-56, 194-95, 205-6
Intelligence: of Dakota children, 186-87; of Hopi and other tribes, 187
Interviews, method of, 215, 217

Joking, between in-laws, 55, 64
Joseph, Alice, 15, 203

Kardiner, Abram, 221
Kinship, 54-55
Klopfer, Bruno, 219
Kluckhohn, Clyde, 15
Kuhlmann, F., 219
Kuhlmann-Anderson Intelligence Test; *see* Tests
Kyle, 10, 67, 68, 70

Land, attitude toward, 112
Laws, governing Indians, 79, 84
Leadership: suppression of native, 35, 68; young people's, 149-50
Leighton, Dorothea, 14, 15, 130, 203, 217
Life-histories, 156-83, 218
Little Wound, Chief, 67
Little Wound School, 75
Lowie, Robert H., 103

McGillicuddy, Julia B., 22, 42
McGillicuddy, Valentine, 33
Marriage, 62-63, 93, 94, 96
Martin, South Dakota, 40, 74
Medicine men, 86, 89, 91
Medicine Root Creek, 70
Medicine Root District, 75
Mekeel, Scudder, 14, 64, 77, 104, 105, 122
Messengers, 53
Method, 9, 11; in child-training, 127-28; used in study, 215-19

INDEX

Mexicans, 68–69
Mille Lacs, Minnesota, 29
Mirsky, Jeanette, 64–65, 122
Missionaries, 37; *see also* Church
Missions, 72, 96–98, 152
Mixed-blood communities, 62–72
Mixed-blood homes, 73
Mixed-bloods, 23, 25
Moral Ideology Test; *see* Tests
Morality, 106–7; sexual, 108; *see* Virtues
Mother, 57–58; and daughter, 140; and son, 139, 198–99
Murray, Henry A., 219; *see also* Tests, Thematic Apperception

Navaho, 9, 15

Office of Indian Affairs, 79
Officers; *see* Chiefs, Tribal council
Oglala (subtribe), 21, 37, 53; history of, 29–30
Oglala Community High School, 72, 142, 152
Ohio Valley, 29
Omaha (tribe), 29
Oregon Trail, 31
Organization, social, of the Dakota, 52–54

Papago, 9, 15
Personality, 184–212; Dakota pattern of, 204; definition of, 184–86; and effect of environment, 211; group, 184; and health, 187; nature of, 11–12
Peyote cult, 100–102
Pine Ridge, 10, 72–73; establishment of reservation at, 32
Platte River, Nebraska, 31
Play: children's, 128; as training, 131
Playmates, 132, 194, 197; girls', 200
Police, agency, 35, 53, 119
Policy, Indian Service, 9, 36, 121, 212
Pregnancy, protection of, 89
Processes, 12

Rabbit Dance, 25
Range, bombing, 70
Rations, 35, 37–39, 48, 106
Red Cloud, Chief, 31, 54
Red Cloud Agency, 32, 53
Red Shirt Table, 212
Relationships: affection, 55; boy-girl, 140; child-parent, 56–58; importance of, 54; respect, 55, 56, 63; *see also* Family, Kinship
Relief, 48–49, 81, 120; *see also* Rations
Religion: Christian, 91–98; Dakota, 85–91, 100; people's, 106; *see also* Churches

Reservation life, 148–52
Reservations: Great Sioux, 21, 31, 37; Pine Ridge, 21, 32
Respect; *see* Relationships
Responses, from tests, 190, 200, 204–9
Rites of passage, 94, 96
Roberts, W. O., 13, 42
Roethlisberger, F. J., 219
Rorschach; *see* Tests

School, attitudes toward, 146; *see also* Education
Schwarz, Charles F., 51
Selective Service Act, 79
Sex: adolescent relations, 147; behavior of boys, 194–95; code, 93, 117–18; differences in child, 207; *see also* Avoidance
Shamans: *see* Medicine men
Shame, 132, 137, 147, 154
Shirt Wearers, 53
Sioux, 9; study of, 10–13, 21; *see also* Dakota
Sioux Benefit Fund, 48, 50
Sisters, 59, 140, 199
Sitting Bull, Chief, 32
Societies: of Oglala, 53; police, 53; in Sun Dance, 89
Spanish, 68–69
Standing Bear, Luther, 42, 106
Stealing, 193
Sterner, Armin H., 152
Stewart, Kilton, 219
Stewart, Omer, 104
Subtribe, 53–54
Sun Dance, 87, 88–91; prohibition of, 32, 52
Superintendents: early, 35, 41; Indian name for, 42
Suppression: as child's behavior, 135–37; results of, 154, 156
Swanton, John R., 41

Talking, child's first, 125–26
Tchi-tchi man, 191
Teachers, 201
Tests, 9, 184–202, 204–9, 215–19; analysis of, 217; Grace Arthur Point Performance Scale, 186–87; Emotional Response, 189–90, 199, 202; Goodenough Draw-a-Man, 186–87; Moral Ideology, 189–90, 199, 202, 203, 207; psychological, 215–16; Rorschach Psychodiagnostic, 205; table of, 217; Thematic Apperception, 204; validity of, 217
Thematic Apperception Test; *see* Tests
Thompson, Laura, 15, 203
Thunder Bull, Chief, 67
Thunder Bull Community, 67–68

Tiyospaye, 52, 53; basis of communities, 66, 116
Toys, 128
Traders, 22, 70, 201
Training of children, 123–30, 131–38, 139–52; with animals, 127; early, 126; in regard to property, 127; toilet, 126
Tribal constitution, 75
Tribal council, 68, 81
Tribal court, 81, 119, 145
Tribe, Teton-Dakota: government of, 53; organization of, 53

Undernutrition, 183, 211
University of Chicago, 9, 10
Useem, John, 50, 152
Useem, Ruth, 50, 152

Values, 105; in child-training, 127, 131, 135; of community program, 213–14; white, 108; *see also* Virtue
Virtue, 89–90
Virtues, Dakota, 106–8

Wage work, 45–47, 49–50; attitude toward, 110–12; school graduates in, 149
Walker, J. R., 88, 103
Walking, children's first, 125
Wanblee, South Dakota, 10, 40, 74
Wardship, 78–79
Warner, W. Lloyd, 14, 219
Wasicu, 116, 122
Weaning, 124–25
White Buffalo Maiden, 65, 87, 108
White Clay, 83
White Clay Creek, 32, 33
White River, 21, 69
Whites, 78–84; attitudes of, 83–84; resident, 81
Wissler, Clark, 42, 64, 104
Withdrawal; *see* Escape
Women, position of, 118–19
Wounded Knee, 33

Yuwipi, 98–99, 102–3

Zuni, 9, 15